D1367483

Character,
Community,
and Politics

Clarke E. Cochran

Character,

Community,

and

Politics

The University of Alabama Press
University, Alabama

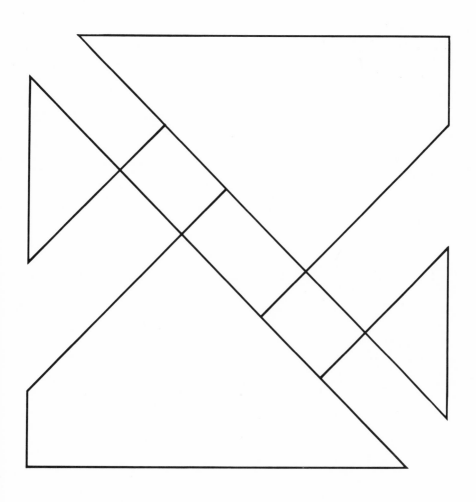

Library of Congress Cataloging in Publication Data

Cochran, Clarke E., 1945–
   Character, community, and politics.

   Bibliography: p.
   Includes index.
   1. Consensus (Social sciences) 2. Community.
3. Character. 4. Authority. 5. Political science.
I. Title.
JC328.2.C62   320'.01'1   81-10303
ISBN 0-8173-0086-4   AACR2

To My Mother and Father

Contents

Preface

The revival of political philosophy has assumed that a theory of human well-being and fulfillment is necessary, but recent work has been preoccupied with questions of epistemology and technical conceptual analysis. Where the nature of the human good has been considered, the paradigm of autonomous individualism has customarily held sway. The present book moves away from prevailing concerns to develop a communal theory of political order.

Character, Community, and Politics revives or redefines a number of fundamental but neglected ideas. Chief among them are commitment, community, responsibility, and character, concepts that I develop through discussion of authority, freedom, pluralism, and the common good. The exposition draws upon a wide variety of fields, such as philosophy, ethics, literature, moral theology, and sociology, borrowing and renewing various concepts in such a way that they come to comprehend a theory of human life and political order that is distinct from liberalism, conservatism, socialism, radicalism, or Marxism.

Political theory must begin with an understanding of human character. Character is structured by solitude, commitment, and responsibility and, to be fully human, requires a disposition toward solitude, defined as a space and time for the "masks," which persons wear in everyday life, to enter into a dialogue with the "center," the essential core of identity. Human character is also ordered by commitment, which relates to an ultimate center of value and so anchors life and integrates action. Without such commitment life is empty and responsible action impossible. Responsible living (commitment and solitude in action) demands accountability to self and others in terms of basic principles.

Community has the double meaning of communion and hospitality. As the former, it is a relation of persons sharing commitments, experience, ritual, and participation. These provide people with a sense of belonging and of union with their fellows. Community is also an encounter of individuals in openness of character, when deep communication may happen; such relations are characterized by tolerance and by attentiveness to the voice of the other.

Community, as communion and as hospitality, calls forth and helps to form solitude, responsibility, and commitment. It provides voices for the silent dialogue, reinforces commitment, and supports responsible action. Hospitality, moreover, has a special healing mission toward wounded character growth.

Although they are extremely important, communion and hospitality are difficult to maintain. They are in constant danger of collapsing into conformity and indifference. Only persons of mature character can form and sustain communities, because they alone are capable of the commitments and the tolerance required. The human person is a social animal, not merely in the broad sense universally acknowledged, but because communal relationships best evoke and express his identity. Only communion and hospitality can fully awaken his highest potential, as we shall see in chapters 2 through 4.

Community understood in this way is the link between individual identity and public order. All communities require authority if they are to last and to contribute to the formation of character. Political order too demands authority. Since authority is essentially related to community, both in public and in private life, it seems that politics can contribute to the development of both character and community.

Such a suggestion will immediately raise in the reader the fear of public interference in private life—that is, fear of the loss of freedom. To combat this alarm it will be necessary to explore the relation between freedom and character and between freedom and political order. I argue that the development of character depends upon a dialectic of restraint and liberty and upon freedom as self-determination. Community contributes to both of these conditions. Chapters 5 and 6 discuss authority and freedom.

It follows that politics may contribute to human development by building communion and hospitality, as the final two chapters demonstrate. Politics can aid communion by supporting social conditions which tie persons together: tradition, authority, common action, responsibility, commitment, participation, and common symbols. Because politics cannot create community directly, it must support communion where it can be found or cultivated. It nurtures the tremendous variety of communities of everyday life. "Political community," then, refers to a community of communities. As we shall see, justice and the common good as comprehensive goals of public policy may be understood in a new way, with reference to policies promoting specific qualities of community and character.

Because the concepts of character, solitude, commitment, responsibility, and community are deeply personal, I have employed the first person singular frequently in the following pages. In those passages where third-person constructions seem necessary, I have generally used the traditional singular terms "man" and "he," since plurals, "he or she" constructions, and other locutions are generally too impersonal to convey the meanings intended. It should go without saying that both men and women are included in all of the concepts and principles developed.

All quotations from Scripture are taken from the New American Bible translation, published by the World Publishing Company, 1970.

Portions of chapter 5 were previously published as "Authority and Community: The Contributions of Carl Friedrich, Yves R. Simon, and Michael Polanyi," *American Political Science Review,* 71 (June 1977), pp. 546–58 (copyright ©1977 by the American Political Science Association), and are used by permission. Earlier versions of portions of chapter 7 are reprinted from "Yves R. Simon and 'The Common Good': A Note on the Concept" by permission of the University of Chicago Press. This article appeared originally in *Ethics*, vol. 88, no. 3, (April 1978), pp. 229–39.

Publication of this book has been made possible by a grant from Earhart Foundation, for which both author and publisher are profoundly grateful.

Many friends, students, and colleagues have read and commented on various drafts of the manuscript. I am especially grateful to Travis Billings, Carolyn Chandler, Terry Davidson, Ned Lynch, Ann McGlynn, Neal Reimer, Carol Sigelman, Lee Sigelman, Rob Sutherland, and Glenn Tinder. Marcia Brubeck's careful reading improved the manuscript in many ways. My gratitude to my teachers, especially John Hallowell, George Morgan, Waldo Beach, and William Poteet, is profound. Their influence appears on each page of the book. Malcolm M. MacDonald, director of The University of Alabama Press, encouraged and supported the project from a very early stage.

A scholar is only as good as his typist lets him be, and I have been blessed by a number of fine secretaries over the span of the manuscript's preparation. Donna Aldridge, Maria Do, Sheila Hatcher, Brenda Hoyle, and Eileen Saunders contributed immeasurably to the final product.

My wife and children have been models of communion and hospitality throughout the research, writing, and revision. Their love, support, and tolerance have taught me more about these realities than I have been able to convey in the following pages.

Character,
Community,
and Politics

The Problem
of Order

That there are colonies
of the violent among us,
devoid of any sense of
communal purpose, best
describes, I think, our
present temporarily
schizoid existence in
two cultures—
vacillating between dead
purposes and deadly devices
to escape boredom.
—Philip Rieff,
The Triumph of the Therapeutic

Political philosophy explores the nature and causes of order and disorder in human living together. It is a commonplace that profound theorizing occurs during times of crisis, arising in response to a thinker's perception of the symptoms of disease in the body politic—war, revolution, corruption, oppression, injustice, or other civic cancers. The political philosopher not only perceives the disorders of his time, as many others do, but senses the basic causes of the malady. Plato tells us that disorder in society reflects disorder in the soul; Aristotle, that it stems from erroneous understandings of justice and equality; Marx, that it proceeds from the contradictions of capitalist production and distribution. Such diagnoses are rooted in a profound encounter of the theorist with a source of order and with the human consequences of disorder. This experience forms the theorist and drives him to articulate it in symbols communicable to others. Plato is formed by a mystical experience of the Good and by the death of Socrates; Augustine, by his sin and his encounter with the grace of God; Hobbes, by the order of the new science and the disorder of the Civil War. Because he experiences both conditions, the philosopher is moved as well to describe the changes necessary for order to begin to prevail over disorder. He prescribes the regimen for alleviation of the sickness of soul and society which troubles him.[1]

In saying this I do not mean to bathe my argument in the reflected glory of the great names of the past. The diagnoses of the past confer no validity on those of the present. Mention of these thinkers, however, anticipates the elements of the theory of political order which I develop through the symbols of responsibility, commitment, solitude, and community. The examples of the past show that it is possible to respond to disorder without becoming an apologist for a particular ideology. My own perception of the illnesses of contemporary life does not differ radically from that of many other observers, so I spend relatively little space on it. I do believe, however, that the prevailing responses and prescriptions offered fail because they do not reach beyond ideology to an order capable of grounding a theoretical response. The principal contemporary responses are more or less easily classified as one or another variety of "ism": liberalism, socialism, conservatism, libertarianism, anarchism. They fail to articulate a theory of human order founded on an experience of existence deeper than the superficial accounts of human nature found in these ideologies. In the course of this book various concepts and symbols will be developed in unfamiliar ways, not from a love of novelty, but from a conviction that only by looking at human experience from new angles can we find any theoretical cure for our social disorders or the will to take the medicine prescribed.[2] In this chapter, then, I shall discuss the failure of the ideologies, particularly the prevailing liberal ideology, to understand or respond to the disorder. I shall introduce as well the ideas that will figure in succeeding chapters.

The forms taken by the sickness in personal and social life are all too well known. Tales of political corruption have become the news media's staple. Rootlessness, geographical mobility, high rates of divorce, abuse of child and spouse, and abortion have made the distressed family a primary subject of dissection, diagnosis, and prescription in popular and academic journals of opinion. Loneliness, alienation, anomic violence, and the daily development of new forms of therapy and self-help testify to the loss of a sense of order.

Politically most symptomatic is the increased manipulation of the agenda and of policymaking by interest groups—not that such dominance is new, but it has become the accepted ideology of public life.[3] We attempt to insure "fairness" in regulatory decisions by insuring that all affected interests have guaranteed access to centers of decision. Nothing seems incongruous about a president's employing staff members whose sole function is liaison with specific groups. The stalemate of conflicting interests prevented the development of a national energy policy for at least five years after the need for it was generally acknowledged. The policy ultimately produced was a complicated nightmare which pleased none and called for no hard sacrifices by any group or by the country as a whole.

Experts and citizens of almost every ideological stripe agree that welfare programs are wasteful, a bureaucratic morass, and an injustice to those who are poor and those who are not. Interest-group infighting, however, prevents significant reform. The situation is identical in health care policy. Likewise, it has been clear for years that fundamental reform of transportation regulation is necessary, but interest-group power has confined such reform to air carriers. In short, acceptance of interest-group domination in terms of the conventional wisdom means that questions of principle, justice, community, common good, and human rights find scant welcome in the political arena.

The rest of this chapter will diagnose the illness signaled by these symptoms. The remaining chapters prescribe the theoretical basis for treatment. But first a word of caution. For me to claim a complete diagnosis would be a symptom of terminal hubris. Surely our ills have many causes, including social and economic conditions, psychological and familial predispositions, and failures of socialization. We cannot, for example, blame the energy crisis simply on government interference, or oil company greed, or God's failure to provide an infinite supply of oil, or on interest-group stalemate. Similarly, anomie may have its roots in modern economic conditions, mental illness, urban living conditions, individual psychological weakness, or other causes. In this book I contend only that ideas have consequences; they do not simply follow history, economics, and social change. How man thinks about himself does affect, in conjunction with other forces, how he behaves. How he views society does influence, in conjunction with other elements, the kind of society in which he will live. The disorders I have mentioned above are not fated but rather result from human choices and pride. My analysis, then, will focus on intellectual causes, not in order to disparage other putative reasons, but to stress what I believe are the important theoretical tendencies which contribute significantly to the totality of the disease.

The Idea of Autonomous Individualism

At the heart of our troubles is autonomous individualism and the ideas of political order which proceed from it. My understanding of this theoretical disorder begins from Tocqueville's diagnosis of democratic individualism:

> Individualism is a mature and calm feeling, which disposes each member of the community to sever himself from the mass of his fellow-creatures; and to draw apart with his family and his friends; so that, after he has thus formed a little circle of his own, he willingly leaves society at large to itself. Egotism originates in blind instinct: individualism proceeds from erroneous judgment more than from depraved feelings; it originates as much in the deficiencies of the mind as in the perversity of the heart.
>
> Egotism blights the germ of all virtue: individualism, at first, only saps the virtues of public life; but, in the long run, it attacks and destroys all others, and is at length absorbed in downright egotism. . . .
>
> Thus not only does democracy make every man forget his ancestors, but it hides his descendants, and separates his contemporaries, from him; it throws him back for ever upon himself alone, and threatens in the end to confine him entirely within the solitude of his own heart.[4]

The solitude of one's own heart (i.e., the loneliness meant by Tocqueville) is the locus of anomie. The heart is lonely because autonomous individualism \ teaches that each person is to make himself, to define himself, and to form and live his own moral and spiritual principles. As such, this idea is originally liberal and continues to be so, but it can be found in other ideologies as well, some of them bitter enemies of liberalism in political practice.[5] Conservatism includes the notion as a principal part of its doctrines, though it is in uneasy tension with the stress on tradition and organicism. Libertarianism, of course, is the political reductio ad absurdum of autonomous individualism. Anarchism, particularly its noncommunitarian variants, holds dear a pristine conception of individuality. Even Marxian and non-Marxian socialism have strains of this idea, though they are not as prominent as in the other ideologies. Socialism attacks the oppression of capitalism, that is, the bourgeois economic institutions which prevent the emergence of the full, individual humanity of persons. Human beings are unable under capitalism to achieve self-development or to enjoy the exercise of their natural capacities.

More generally, this conception of individuality has become widespread in culture as an emphasis on the self. A couple of decades ago Martin Buber remarked that "the I of [the I-It relation], an I that possesses all, makes all, succeeds with all, this I that is unable to say Thou, unable to meet a being essentially, is the lord of the hour." More recently, Tom Wolfe has called the 1970s "The Me Decade," pointing to Jerry Brown and Jimmy Carter and such phenomena as communes, encounter groups, drug usage, and the recent spate of confessional novels, and migration across the land by thousands in trailers. "The new alchemical dream is: changing one's personality—remaking, remodeling, elevating, and polishing one's very self . . . and observing, studying, and doting on it. (Me!)." The evolution of this concept of the self, separate and opposed to social roles, and the notion of authenticity which goes with it, have been treated profoundly by Lionel Trilling.[6] Those who promote authenticity as the aim of life represent, according to Trilling, the disintegration of a self defined in relation to society. Authentic selfhood is believed to lie in rejection of social conventions and in the autonomous definition of one's own laws of being in conjunction with spirit and freedom. The self is assumed to lie hidden under the layers of social custom; to liberate it is to reveal it in all its uniqueness and purity, to break the roles and masks which keep it hidden. The authentic individual is a law unto himself; inauthenticity means giving up one's self-legislating freedom to someone or something outside.

The idea of authentic selfhood is made more plausible by social conditions which sunder the inner life from the outer—impersonal institutions, disintegrated families, rootless living, and fragmented, cynical politics. Since identity is social, the inward focus of the search for authenticity is evidence of social failure as much as of individual pathology. The dominant ideology of autonomous individualism has constructed political and social institutions which do not satisfy the human hunger for identity. The appetite must, then, be sated in unorthodox and unfulfilling ways.

Philip Rieff has perceived a similar notion of selfhood at work in contemporary culture, particularly in the psychoanalytic movement. Modern culture, he argues, reveals the triumph of the therapeutic mode, the triumph of therapies of self. Having rejected traditional faiths and released himself from their restrictions, psychological man (authentic man) goes about seeking self-satisfaction, though he seeks as well some refuge from the doubts and the loneliness such a search produces. "In the age of psychologizing, clarity about oneself supersedes devotion to an ideal as the model of right conduct." Such men seek a "manipulatable sense of well-being." "Religious man is born to be saved; psychological man is born to be pleased." And the psychotherapist becomes a secular, spiritual guide, teaching man how to please himself while remaining on even keel, avoiding anxiety over his loss of faith.[7] Rieff argues that the therapeutic mode has destroyed the possibility of therapies based on faith or commitment. The dilemma is that this mode exalts the "releasing" mechanisms of culture but offers (so far) no ground for reestablishing any "controlling" mechanisms. No previous culture has survived without a balance of these two mechanisms; yet faith can no longer supply the balance, nor does it seem possible for the psychoanalytic mode to create controls from its own resources. Rieff offers an accurate, if pessimistic, diagnosis of the dilemmas raised by the cultural triumph of the idea of autonomous individualism.

Such an idea of self, producing such consequences, is flawed. In chapter 2 I shall suggest an alternative idea in which, *pace* Rieff, commitment can and must play a central part. Here only one critical point may be mentioned. The ideas of authenticity and self-satisfaction are empty: the self they define seeks "self-fulfillment," which is impossible, since it has no natural content. A satisfaction which depends upon subjective experiences of pleasure has no ontological grounding and so misses final or even approximate completion. Such a self can never be at peace because the subjective grounds of pleasure constantly shift, calling to mind the futility inherent in Hobbes's definition of felicity as "a continual progress of the desire, from one object to another; the attaining of the former, being still but the way to the latter."[8] Moreover, because those who promote the ideals of authenticity and autonomy have no coherent idea of the self, they are unable to reconcile the pursuit of individual satisfaction with the requirements of political order. Because there are no grounds for denying the self any desire, there are no grounds for regulation. Because the self may assume a different shape tomorrow, there can be no cohesive political order, which necessarily refers to human constants.[9] The origin of the politics of interest lies in a faulty conception of human nature. Such a vision shatters the links between person and community.

The notion of self just described is not restricted to liberalism, but its original roots are liberal, as is its dominant political manifestation. Thus despite my focus, my critical remarks should be understood to extend to autonomous individualism wherever it is found. Liberalism, like the Snark, is hard to pin down. It cannot be isolated from other ideological movements of the last two hundred years. The features it exhibits at any one time may be obscure at another. Moreover, the resurgence of radicalism in recent years has reminded us that liberals oppose and are opposed by both the Right and the Left. "Liberal" is a term of disparagement, out of fashion with both conservatives and radicals. Yet the liberal norm of individual autonomy is alive, as I argued above, and we can begin to understand our disorders only by focusing directly on this norm itself.

The ideal of individual autonomy originates in the early liberal rejection of revelation and dogma as sources of truth and in confidence in immanent human reason as the source of knowledge.[10] The individual is admonished to stand on his own and to discover for himself the answers to basic questions. While the contemporary affirmation of feeling and emotion as bases of action has weakened the position of reason, it has not thereby lessened the stress upon the autonomous use of rational or affective processes. Liberalism demands that the individual be free from arbitrary restraints on his thoughts, his speech, and his action. Such restrictions of course, are those based on convention rather than on nature. Since conventional reasons may often be given for natural distinctions and since the authority of convention is in principle illegitimate for the autonomous individual, it is not surprising to find liberalism in revolt against tradition and authority themselves as needlessly curbing thought and action.

Certainly, not every tradition or authority has been seen as arbitrary at every time in the history of liberalism. The trend, however, is more and more in this direction. Liberals generally condemn restrictions on individual and group life, as do libertarians, anarchists, and most socialists as well, given the heritage of individualism which they also possess. Thus liberals support more extensive freedoms under the First Amendment, abolition of compulsory school prayer, of laws restricting private sexual practices, and of racial and economic discrimination. The women's liberation movement receives liberal sympathy in its fight to rid society of traditional customs defining the role and place of women and of laws which support these customs. Such laws and traditions are "unreasonable," and hence arbitrary and unjustifiable, constraints on the freedom of individual women to create their own ways of life and to make their own role decisions.[11] It is not to praise or condemn any of these movements that I call them liberal, but only to exemplify liberalism's continuing attack on tradition and authority. Yet as I shall argue in chapter 5, authority and tradition are necessary for individuality. They provide a stable base for personal decision and development.

If the logic of autonomous individualism points toward rejection of tradition and authority, it also signals abandonment of the ideal of community as a union of individuals in affection, trust, sharing, and sacrifice. The liberal tendency is to distrust community because it seems to demand a loyalty and commitment incompatible with personal freedom. Communities seem to mean a submergence rather than a flowering of individuality. Exclusivity and intolerance seem to characterize them. Yet there are societies in which community has been the condition for freedom and in which its decline seems to entail the disappearance of freedom. The liberal attitude toward community is unfortunate, I shall argue, because communal ties are an indispensable condition for the development of individual personality. Moreover, to reject community is to turn away from an important source of social unity and moral development, which play a role in personal maturation that cannot be replaced by wholly rational group affiliations or morality.[12]

The concept of autonomy tends to focus on the unique aspects of each individual and on their protection and development. This emphasis is understandable and even laudable in certain contexts. Yet as a theoretical account of personality it is too narrow. Although it is relatively recent in the history of social thought, this account has become extremely influential. Liberalism sets the self against others, failing to remember how much the personality of each is defined and shaped by human relationships. The individual is unique partly because of his supporting links with particular primary and secondary communities.

So far I have criticized liberalism for its view of individuality in relation to authority and community. I turn now to the main failure of liberalism as a political theory—its inability to articulate a vision of the good society. Just as it fails to articulate a notion of the best character in favor of recommending autonomy as a way of choosing how to be, liberalism does not specify the best social way of life but rather sets out to describe a process for deciding such a question.[13] The process involves peaceful individual and group conflict and compromise in the give and take of political activity.

There is merit in the liberal stress on individual interests and wants. A healthy political realism appreciates that individuals possess conflicting interests. Such realism permeates *The Federalist Papers,* Tocqueville's notion of "interest properly understood," and Reinhold Niebuhr's political theory. Yet each writer had a wider view of politics and society. Politics might constantly display the clash of opposing groups, yet there are standards of justice and common good for the sake of which conflicts must be controlled. Liberalism makes such opposition the only model for political society, which is viewed as the arena where individual and group interests compete for fulfillment. Politics, which exists to satisfy demands, has, therefore, a private, not a public, purpose. The result of this liberal view of individuality is a particular type of theory and practice, familiar in political science as "pluralism," or, to use Theodore Lowi's phrase, "interest-group liberalism."

This is not the place to summarize the by now familiar criticism of pluralism in political science and practice.[14] A few points, however, require emphasis. Pluralism has as its image of social bonding a utilitarian partnership. In a politics of interest competition, alliances and groups can be founded only on mutual advantage. Thus politics makes strange bedfellows. But there is a wide variety of types of human association, some of which may be more appropriate as models for political order. Partnership has its claim, which we have noticed, but the type of association based on affection, trust, and reciprocity does so as well. Liberalism pushes such a model to the background.

Furthermore, liberal pluralism makes any intelligible notion of the common good impossible.[15] Whatever policy emerges out of the interest-group conflict is neither public nor an interest in the ordinary sense of those terms. The product of the clash can be called "in the public interest" only if the process of compromise, bargaining, and power can be said automatically to confer moral and public (common) sanction. Procedures are indeed important, and I do not intend to argue that only certain interests should have access to centers of decision making. Yet procedure is no guarantee of justice or the common good.

Even if interest accommodation could contrive the best policy in certain areas, it could not deal in the best way with matters such as crime, urban slums, pollution, and the cultivation of the arts, which concern primarily the whole society rather than discrete groups within it.[16] Political theory, not to mention political science, must not ignore the substance of policies enacted and the quality of common life in favor of an exclusive concern with means and function. The liberalism which I am criticizing makes the mistake of converting a healthy realism into a normative position.

Liberalism has a number of important strengths, and it has undoubtedly contributed much to improving life. To say that liberalism's essential concern with the freedom and dignity of the individual constitutes a major contribution to man's knowledge of himself and to the daily existence of political societies is not to engage in pious rhetoric. However much needs to be done in extending and protecting freedom and dignity, we must acknowledge the accomplishments of liberalism in securing political and civil freedoms, including that of action, for which economic security is necessary. Liberalism also encourages toleration and diversity as a result of the logic of its commitment to individual liberties in all spheres.

Observe, however, that the strengths of liberalism flow from the very sources of its weakness. The idea of individual freedom leads to the atomization of society as well as to civil liberties. The notion of privacy and security of family leads to the concept of politics first as a supplier of private goods and then as an arena for interest conflict. Perhaps liberalism is waning in the West because of its very success in achieving its goals of political and social liberty, limited government, and due process of law.[17] Yet even if so, this decline suggests its philosophical limitations. The goals have been accomplished, but the ills described above flourish. This means that liberalism's internal dynamics preclude its serving as a comprehensive theory of public order. A theory which would overcome the weaknesses of liberalism today must take its starting place from a premise more fundamental than that of individual autonomy.

The impossibility of building such a framework while retaining individualist assumptions is demonstrated by the work of Henry S. Kariel and Christian Bay, two of the severest critics of liberalism in political science. Both deny being liberals, but both ground their work upon the idea of individual autonomy. In a review of three books on liberalism, Kariel speaks of the failure of politics as "the lack of community."[18] Yet we are not told which requisite elements are lacking. Indeed, adherence to Kariel's idea of politics would bear bitter fruit in the denial of community. For Kariel builds his theory on the ultimate relativity of values and the primacy of the individual over the community—"all we have is ourselves and the ground on which we stand."[19] The goal of politics is self-development; a person creates his own nature and uniqueness through participation.

Bay has attempted to outline a theory of politics rooted in human needs, including the need for community.[20] Yet again we are not told what elements are required. Indeed, the overwhelming emphasis on the individual, and especially on a type of freedom destructive of community, makes it doubtful that community is compatible with the other human needs described by Bay. The liberty Bay would cultivate is explicitly directed against tradition and authority, since the state is seen as a mere instrument for securing optimal individual freedom. Dissatisfaction with accepted values must be cultivated; men must take the stance of "rebels."[21] Politics at its best is a process in which individuals develop themselves through the unhindered expression of their wants, demands, and interests on the public stage. This expression is idiosyncratic and individualistic because it ultimately depends upon impulses; the actor is free when he voices not *the best* in him but *whatever* is in him.

Further evidence for the dominance, and the inadequacy, of autonomous individualism in political thought can be seen in two most influential and controversial recent works: Robert Nozick's *Anarchy, State, and Utopia* and John Rawls's *A Theory of Justice*.[22] Why is it that these two books have caused a far greater stir in the ranks of academic theorists than the works of political philosophers of greater profundity such as

Hannah Arendt, Eric Voegelin, Michael Oakeshott, and Bertrand de Jouvenel? Of course, the writings of this group have not gone unnoticed, but their works did not stimulate a flood of reviews, essays, and books in immediate approval or rebuttal. I believe the reason is that Nozick and Rawls begin from the basic premise of individual autonomy so favored by most theorists today, while Arendt, Voegelin, Oakeshott, and de Jouvenel do not. Thus Nozick and Rawls are working with the most cherished ideas and assumptions of contemporary thinkers. Nozick begins from this premise and draws, through a series of dazzling, if not impeccable, logical moves, a picture of libertarian society that is anathema to liberals, conservatives, socialists, and even anarchists. Rawls, on the other hand, seems to promise a secure defense of cherished liberal social programs and theories; yet he goes too far for conservatives and not far enough for socialists.

Both writers, however, share one fundamental theoretical flaw (I shall mention only one; others I leave to the army of commentators to ferret out). The defect, for a comprehensive theory of political order, is not to examine the idea of autonomous individualism as an assumption. Each writer takes the picture of human nature as given; neither bothers, in very long books, to ground it theoretically. Nowhere does Nozick even attempt to state clearly or to justify his basic assumption that individuals are self-legislating, utility-maximizing creatures who possess certain inalienable rights.[23] Such a proposition has no more philosophical weight than an assumption that men have no rights and exist only to serve gods and kings. Yet the argument is treated as a major theoretical challenge to liberalism. Rawls also fails to ground his suppositions about the individuals who assume the "original position." That they are rationally self-interested persons capable of legislating for themselves is clear. But why it is such an individual who occupies this position rather than, say, Plato's just man, Aristotle's *spoudaios*, or a Christian saint, is never explained. Rawls's work begins without a view of human nature of any substantive content. It is a wholly want-regarding social relativism and thus fails to develop a conception of order based on a definite way of life.[24] Because of this deficiency, neither Nozick nor Rawls, neither Kariel nor Bay, constructs a political theory firmly grounded and capable of speaking to the ills of society—none of them takes the crucial step of addressing the questions of human nature and human interaction directly.

Community Theory

Attempts to build a theory starting with liberal premises cannot recognize the essential role which communal associations play in the fully human life. I propose, therefore, an examination of the concept of community in order to ask whether it can serve as the needed ordering concept in political philosophy. Community is rooted in what is basic and substantial in man, his capacity and need for friendship, mutual support and trust, and sharing. It "brings together persons in their essential being."[25] Thus communities possess greater consequence for human life than do groups based on convenience and utility. To be part of a fellowship, friendship, or family is to share experiences which form the personality for other kinds of relationships. Such communities create and sustain psychic health. When I say this I presuppose an understanding of human character which will be discussed below.

Political science and modern political theory have been slow to recognize the importance of community. Yet religious thinkers, sociologists, and social critics, among others, have recognized its significance for many years. Political theorists could learn much from their example. Community has been a major theme in Christian ethics and theology from the beginning; it has taken on increasingly fundamental importance in the last few decades. The experience of the early Christians is paradigmatic: "Those who believed shared all things in common; they would sell their property and goods, dividing everything on the basis of each one's need" (Acts 2:44–45). In the Christian conception, love is the bond of community between God and man and between man and man. Moreover, it is love which sustains community, with morality centered on its building and maintenance. The church must be an agent of community in the world if it takes seriously the love by which it is created and renewed.[26] Neither Jewish nor Christian social and political thought can be understood apart from the concept of covenant, a union formed by mutual commitment and loyalty.

The idea of community has also been central in sociology from its earliest days as a distinct discipline to the present time. Ferdinand Tönnies in his classic treatment of the ideal types *Gemeinschaft* and *Gesellschaft* firmly established the concept. For Tönnies the Gemeinschaft relation produces a real being with an organic form of life of intimate, private, and exclusive living together. The Gesellschaft relation, which is similar to the partnership of autonomous individuals I have described as the basis of the liberal view, is imaginary and mechanical, based fundamentally upon interest. "Thus, the Gesellschaft can be imagined to be composed of such separate individuals all of whom are busy for the general Gesellschaft inasmuch as they seem to be active in their own interests, and who are working for their own interests while they seem to be working for the Gesellschaft."[27] In the sociological literature, despite variations in usage, "community" frequently denotes social relations characterized by personal intimacy, moral commitment, and common bonds, principles, and actions. The elements of common moral action and the preservation and extension of communal bonds which are central to the Christian concept are also central in the sociological.

The renewed concern for community in contemporary culture is a further indication of its importance for political theory. The emergence of various kinds of communes in recent years heralds a desire by many for intimate relationship. Loneliness in a mobile society is a commonplace in popular thought. Increasing concern with the soundness of the family is also evidence of anxiety about community.

The search can be seen as well in various movements which offer an identity and focus of commitment to individuals adrift. This category includes totalitarian parties and mass political movements, which offer a home and a focus of loyalty. Contemporary religious movements—from the Moonies to the gurus—promise a similar sense of stability and meaning. Looser "movements"—drug, counterculture, sexual liberation, or ecology, for example—also offer features of belonging. Robert A. Nisbet was prophetic when he directed attention to these trends nearly a quarter-century ago.[28] In addition, a great deal of money is made by commercial firms offering a false intimacy to those who cannot find the real thing.

To cite these phenomena is not to approve them. Many are evil and dangerous. Some are harmless, others salutary. I cite them only to show the importance of the concept of community and the strength the quest for it has mustered. If we are to reap only the beneficial effects of the renewed concern with solidarity, we must understand better than we do now the nature of community, communal relations, and human character. I am aware of the ambivalence involved in the quest for community and of the difficulties of finding and maintaining it in modern culture. So inured are we to the phantom pleasures of autonomy that community is feared as well as desired. This is why even in communes, where the search for roots is intense, transience is constant and even admired.[29] The burdens of community are real, so its possibility is problematic in a culture which resists real demands for sacrifice. Carey McWilliams is pessimistic enough to posit "the impossibility of fraternal politics in the conditions of modern times." Modern men, he says, prefer to "move in circles which are 'limited liability communities.' "[30] Nevertheless, community is so central to human life that it must be understood and pursued, even in politics.

Can community be a central concept in a theory of political order? We might recall that it was a major theme in political thought until the sixteenth century and has never wholly disappeared. A number of modern theorists have recognized its importance; Carl J. Friedrich, Yves R. Simon, Bertrand de Jouvenel, Benjamin Barber, Glenn Tinder, and Carey McWilliams have given it sustained attention.[31] I shall argue in the following chapters that the concept of community overcomes the weaknesses of liberalism while retaining its strengths. Let me summarize here the major topics addressed.

There is no necessary opposition between individuality and community. The development of full human character is possible only in the context of one or more sustaining communities. This is not the same as saying that man is a social animal or that his existence requires social support. Man needs, not simply others, but persons related to him in certain special ways. While individual moral autonomy, as long as it is properly understood, is essential for full humanity, we should observe that it is possible for an individual only after he has been educated and nourished by family, friends, teachers, and fellowships within a particular social and cultural context. An autonomous stance may require separation from standards set by others, but it also requires acceptance of responsibility for the consequences of violation of communal norms. Responsibility requires self-esteem and courage, since one cannot hide behind others or behind circumstances in making an autonomous decision. Yet these two necessary qualities cannot be developed by an isolated individual. They are rooted in the respect, affection, and support provided by one's fellows in a community. Autonomy requires self-confidence, tranquillity, and a firmness of character which is only developed in supportive communities where sound decisions are expected and rewarded. We must be careful to make our commitments to groups worthy of them, and we must never absolutize finite groups; but the making of firm commitments to genuine communities is the condition of our ability to know, decide, and act.

Far from stifling individuality, a community provides the ordered background against which character is visible and without which character would quite literally not be possible, because it could not appear to others. Eccentricity is only the most extreme illustration of this point. Integration of an individual into a community is not suffocation of his uniqueness but rather enlargement and enrichment of his personality, for he is allowed to develop hitherto unrealized aspects of his character and to strengthen already realized traits. Membership in a community demands acceptance of certain duties, and it evokes requisite talents and excellences of character. For example, family responsibilities often elicit in parents qualities of devotion, generosity, discipline, and sacrifice which would remain latent outside such a community. The converse of this phenomenon is the disproportionate number of unmarried individuals among those who commit crimes.

In discussing the weaknesses of liberalism, I argued that it is in revolt against tradition and authority. If we must now see the relationship between individuality and community in a different light, we must also look at authority and tradition from a new perspective, because both are necessary, as they supply and preserve the features which distinguish particular communities.

Authority is the cement which holds communities together and is therefore not opposed to freedom, as liberalism supposes. The existence of authority is a precondition of liberty, because it is a prerequisite for community and character. Power-wielders seek regimentation and homogeneity in order to guarantee their effectiveness. Lacking roots in the traditions and beliefs of a group, they must employ external sanctions limiting freedom. Authority, however, finds its root in shared traditions and beliefs. Thus it does not need to restrict freedom from the outside. Rather, it shelters and fertilizes the ground out of which freedom grows. True, it is sometimes necessary for authorities to use power and force. But authority, power, and force are not equivalent. To the extent that coercion is needed to supplement directives, community has not been as fully actualized as possible.

It follows that only from within a theory of political community can a defensible notion of the common good emerge. Since liberal theories of the common good most commonly run aground on the supposed conflict between individual and public goods, only the premise of the fundamental consonance of individual and community can furnish a satisfactory concept of the common good. Similarly, the impasse between liberal and participatory theories of democracy can be overcome only by recourse to a theory of human character which transcends the current level of debate on that topic.

Pluralism must be a part of any theory of political community, for the value of diversity requires the availability of diverse groups and institutions through which heterogeneous interests and needs may be expressed. Yet this cannot be merely another variant of the interest-group pluralism of contemporary political science.[32] Instead, it must be recognized that genuine pluralism concerns different communities and not merely various interest groups. Thus the first issue a theory of political order must confront is the question of how integration and cohesion may be achieved within such a plurality. That is, it must address the problem of how much and what kinds of diversity are compatible with the flourishing of strong group life. Can any one community satisfy the person's need for wholeness? If not, is fragmentation the necessary result? A promising theory, then, must consider how many communities can engage a person's loyalty and what place politics can occupy in a system of multiple loyalties. I shall develop a theory of communal pluralism responsive to these issues.

There is today altogether too much misplaced nostalgia for the good old days. The search for a theory of political community may seem simply another illustration of such nostalgia, but the ideal in question has always been with us. We may have lost certain kinds of communities, but the past was never a golden age of community. Moreover, it is obvious that authority may become oppressive—not inevitably, but it does happen all too frequently. Therefore liberalism, or its lasting aspects, has a positive role to play within the theory of community. The strengths of liberalism are as real as its weaknesses; we are constantly reminded that authority, tradition, and community may fail to achieve their potential, that they may decay and, in the process, stifle rather than support personal development. Therefore the liberal emphasis on individual freedom must constantly promote tolerance, privacy, and diversity, but within the wider context of community.

Our existing conceptions of community derive primarily from small groups, towns, and rural communities and our romantic view of their virtues. The political theorist must take special care not to succumb to such romanticism. Rather, his efforts must be devoted to the exploration of new forms of community appropriate to the contemporary situation. Urbanization, industrial society, mobility, and changed educational, occupational, and social structures must be the context for such new forms. It will not do to idealize the sturdy yeoman, his extended family, and his close-knit farming community, though we may very well learn something from them.

Our theory must also confront the problem of size, which is clearly connected with the problem of new forms. The concept of community seems appropriate to small groups, families, and towns. Can it really be applicable to large political units, such as cities and nations? The concluding chapters argue that an answer lies in the direction of a community of communities, that is, in the direction of the new pluralism suggested above. Here the warm, personal relations which characterize the paradigmatic vision of the small group become attenuated. Yet common support for the subsidiary communities constituting the larger political entity may make up for the loss of intimacy.

Benjamin R. Barber has said of Anglo-American liberal constitutionalism: "If the parochialism of our political thought issues from the potency of our political experience rather than the insularity of the philosophical traditions that inform that experience, what is required to counteract its influence is an alternative experience, not an alternative philosophy."[33] I hope that the following pages reflect both philosophy and personal experience. It is all too common for theoretical arguments to leave experience far behind. Yet in the end it is the argument's truth to experience which confers validity.

Human Character

The study of man must start with an appreciation of man in the act of making responsible decisions.
—Michael Polanyi, *The Study of Man*

I begin far from politics. Ordinary political discussion and commentary largely do without the concepts of commitment, solitude, responsibility, attentiveness, risk, honesty, and love. Political activity, on the surface at least, avoids such concerns. Nor are they often the subject of graduate seminars in departments of political science. Insofar as they do find their way into ordinary politics, as honesty does in questions of corruption or faith and love in Jimmy Carter's first campaign for the presidency, they do so in a specific context which blocks their appeal to the heart of the ordinary citizen. We expect or hope that our politicians will be honest; that is, we will be upset if we catch them stealing. We do not expect politics to make us honest with ourselves and others or responsible toward the truth.

I believe, however, that our inquiry into political order must begin from such concepts as faith, responsibility, and solitude, because a theory of politics must be grounded on an understanding of the human condition. The reason is perhaps axiomatic, not deserving explicit attention. But the reader may wonder whether three chapters are necessary before we concentrate on specifically political issues. Discussion at such length is, however, unavoidable if the theory that I shall develop in later chapters is to warrant the reader's assent. As in a mountain hike, the shortest line to a destination is normally not the safest, so in thinking clearly about politics we must take the long way round if we are to avoid the ideological crevices which inevitably imperil such a journey.

The necessity of devoting sustained attention to basic human qualities is particularly compelling in our time. The modern preoccupation with self-examination has made the question of human nature more difficult than ever. Man has always been the creature who is problematic to himself, but today the problem seems to have explicitly touched more persons and stimulated a wider variety of conceptions of man than at any moment in the past. Competing for attention are views of man as the son of God, the rational animal, the maker, the creature of culture, and the erotic animal. Other theories see man as the creature without a nature; that is, as the being who makes himself. Some regard man as the being who enters into relationships of friendship or love with others like himself. Still again, we have seen man characterized merely as complex, determined by the same natural laws of chemistry, physics, biology and, perhaps, psychology as other animals.

To consider all of these ideas and to outline a theory of human nature is well beyond the scope of the present book. I shall not argue for a particular theory of human nature. Rather, I shall concentrate on the more limited area of moral philosophy and develop a theory of character. In doing so, of course, I am making certain implicit assumptions about human nature. I will assume, for example, that men are at least partially rational creatures. Reason is related to all of the basic concepts of character discussed below and provides order for the dialogue of solitude so that it does not degenerate into a meaningless babble. Faith supplies a necessary orientation to reason, while reason keeps faith from becoming blind. Since responsibility requires choices among alternatives, reason is critical in determining how best to meet the requirements of faith and the demands of the particular situation. Character is a moral quality requisite for a fully human life, but it is not the whole of human nature. I shall demonstrate the centrality of moral character, but I shall not attempt to give a complete account of its role.

Character

The expression "human character" requires some explanation. "Character" is out of style; we do not commend a person's character. More in fashion are "self," "identity," and "individuality." These terms could serve my purpose, but "character" is the richer term, conveying more fully what I shall be discussing. All of the designations refer to the distinctive attributes which make a person who he is and not someone else. To that extent the terms are interchangeable, and definitions of one of them often employ the others. Yet "self," "identity," and "individuality" are abstract words, lacking substance and connotative richness. "Self" has chiefly philosophical uses and refers to that in a person which is real and intrinsically he; "selfhood," to the quality by virtue of which one is oneself (my source is the Oxford English Dictionary). Both uses are as recent as the seventeenth and nineteenth centuries and say nothing concrete about a person. "Identity" is similar. The OED notes "sameness of a person or thing at all times and in all circumstances; the condition or fact that a person or thing is itself and not something else; individuality, personality." The entry goes no further except to describe use of the word by a particular author, or authors, in a special sense. "Individuality" is simply the fact of existing separately or the aggregate of properties peculiar to an individual. With this last term, we also find explicit something implicit in the others. "Individual" conveys the sense of a single human being as contrasted with society, one considered in isolation from other persons, a sense precisely at odds with the thesis of this book. Though not all notions of individualism build on the idea of the "isolated" or "abstract" individual, it is at the heart of many theories.[1]

"Character," on the other hand, connotes an aggregate of essential features contained in the other terms and also moral and mental qualities, especially those strikingly displayed by a person.[2] It suggests, moreover, that these qualities constitute a homogeneous whole rather than a mere collection. This notion of wholeness is central to my discussion. The expression "in character" especially conveys this sense of harmony and appropriateness. It might also be noted that the combined senses of harmony and the moral qualities of a person also strongly hint at maturity; a person of "character" is a mature person. Without a qualifying adjective, the term indicates a favorable evaluation. Finally, "character" suggests the social setting of all individual qualities as well as reputation, recognized status, and the part assumed by an actor—in this case, the social roles which persons play.[3] The significance of this last point will be clarified below. The term "person" might serve my purpose, especially since the cognate "personage" has the meaning of an assumed role. The use of these two words, however, would be awkward when "character" nicely combines the senses. Moreover, "personage" is archaic, and "person" can serve well as a neutral synonym for "human being."

As I have indicated, the term "character" has important normative connotations. I shall use the concept it denotes in an explicitly normative way in this book. Specifically, I use it teleologically. Character is not an all-or-nothing matter. Persons may possess it to varying degrees, according to the extent to which they have acquired its elements—solitude, commitment, and responsibility. Thus we may sensibly speak of developed or underdeveloped character, or of maturity of character. The more fully a person has advanced his solitude, commitment, and responsibility, the more full his character and, ceteris paribus, the more fully human he is. The possession of firm qualities of character makes a person better. The virtues expand; the vices contract: we speak of liars and cowards but of honest men and brave men. The vice seems to dominate the person, while the virtue is part of a whole character.

I have suggested that character has at least two elements. First is his distinctive mark, the set of moral qualities which make him who he is. Second is the set of social roles assumed by the person. I shall argue that these two are inseparable, but here I want to show how they constitute two different movements in each life. The second movement, to take them in reverse order, is familiar as the experience of being pulled in many directions, of being required in daily life to respond to situations and persons with socially prescribed sets of behaviors. I attempt to respond to my family according to role models of father and husband. My students expect certain behaviors of me as a teacher. As a "polite customer" I respond, or try to respond, patiently and understandingly to the incompetent waiter. More negatively, my role as an "intelligent, cultured person" requires that I denigrate the vast wasteland of commercial television to demonstrate my superiority to the average American who lives his life in front of the "tube." More negatively still, as a sinner I feel myself to be many persons, lacking even the security of fixed roles, my behavior directed by forces beyond my understanding. This automatic, routine, and fragmented side of life is one element of character. I shall say more about it presently.

The other element is the unity beyond the fragments, the one beyond the many, sensed as an enemy ready to break my tiny pleasures and demand sacrifice and change of heart.[4] It is perceived in moments of purposefulness, creativity, joy, sorrow, and exultation. It is sought as the "I" behind the social masks, and it constitutes a major theme in contemporary literature, philosophy, and psychology. It is the "authentic self," or the "identity" sought or discovered in rebellion against artificial social conventions, the inmost part of personal being submerged by the inauthenticities of society.[5] This way of conceiving the inner core is, I believe, mistaken, but the basic insight is accurate. Reflective thinkers discovered this element of character long before the modern age. We can sense it in the psalmist's experience of God's penetration of his heart:

O Lord, you have probed me and you know me;
you know when I sit and when I stand;
you understand my thoughts from afar.
My journeys and my rest you scrutinize,
with all my ways you are familiar.
Even before a word is on my tongue,
behold, O Lord, you know the whole of it.
. . . .
Truly you have formed my inmost being;
you knit me in my mother's womb.
I give you thanks that I am fearfully,
wonderfully made; wonderful are your works.
My soul also you know full well;
nor was my frame unknown to you
When I was made in secret,
when I was fashioned in the depths of the earth.
[Ps. 139:1–4, 13–15]

Again, we sense awareness of an inner core in Aristotle's suggestion that the end wished for determines a person's character[6] and in the fragment of Heraclitus, "character to man is fate." I shall refer to this core as the "center" of character and to the assumed roles and automatic behaviors as the "masks."

Center and masks must not be conceived in opposition. The contemporary concept of uniqueness is a principal manifestation of such an error, which consists in imagining that there is an entirely individual self in each person and that if it could only be freed from the limitations of convention, everyone would truly be himself, entirely different from anyone else. Quite the contrary, the similarities which bind every individual to his society are not only inevitable but willed. Human beings desire likeness to their fellows. Uniqueness is morally neutral, and complete uniqueness is neither possible nor necessary. A person can have a genuine center and still be an exemplar of his society. Socrates, Jesus, and Lincoln are striking examples. "All good men are in certain ways similar."[7]

Moreover, it is vain to seek to know a center, one's own or another's, apart from the masks. Man remains always a mystery to himself. "We are . . . pursuing a chimera in attempting to grasp the essence of our person, completely divested of all adornments and disguises with which life has clothed it."[8] To endeavor to know myself fully, to see my center without its assumed conventions, is to make of it an object. Could this be done, the center would no longer be central: I would again be fragmented into observing subject and observed object.

I can anticipate the argument of chapter 4 enough to say that the mature person never randomly puts on roles as one might clothes; rather, he selects, modifies, and adjusts them as successive roles and other role players are encountered.[9] When I shop for clothes, I try on only those which have some possibility of expressing me. Similarly, character is in harmony when the center and the masks suit each other. To live from the center of character is not to reject masks but to choose those which are appropriate and to remember that they should express character, not supplant it. There is a way of living character in which the center transforms and infuses all encounters and relationships.

> To become a person, to discover the world of persons, to acquire the sense of the person, to be more interested in people as persons than in their ideas, their party labels, their personage, means a complete revolution, changing the climate of our lives. Once adopted, it is an attitude which rapidly impregnates the whole of our lives.[10]

I describe this way of living as "wholeness,"[11] which is connoted by the very term "character." The value of wholeness is expressed strongly by Plato in his frequent contrasts of the just and the unjust man. The former is like the healthy man whose body is ordered and harmoniously fitted together. The latter is like someone who is sick, whose body is disordered, its parts in conflict with one another. Wholeness refers to the ability of character to be true to itself in all situations. The left hand does know what the right is doing. The person does not work against himself, is not torn apart from within, but is at peace with himself. Wholeness of character is thus related to maturity, to the full development of human capacities, particularly moral capacities.

What I have said so far is quite abstract, but it should indicate how far removed is the idea of character from autonomous individualism and the basic assumptions of most contemporary political thinking. If the notion of a life of wholeness and maturity, a life lived from the center out, through the masks to the world, is to mean anything, I must describe its substance. I believe that wholeness of character comprises a life of solitude, commitment, and responsibility, which form the framework to which all qualities of character must be attached. These are the fundamental necessities; all other aspects of character are subordinate to them.

Solitude

If the center and the masks of character are to be integrated and character as a whole is to develop and grow, dialogue must become part of the inner life. Such is the lesson of the Socratic dialogue, whose inconclusions and paradoxes are designed to awaken a second voice in its characters and its readers. The discourse can thus continue after the last page is turned.[12] Such an exchange occurs only in solitude, which is not simply a place or time apart from others, though it demands that, but a quality of character. This quality is a disposition to discover opportunities for, and to realize the necessity of, quiet, inner space and time, where the meeting of center and masks takes place. Solitude is sensitivity to one's own voices. It is not, however, an individualistic condition. The person who knows himself is able to be aware of others. His inner dialogue readies him for encounter with others. Solitude and hospitality are intimately connected. "Solitude is the flower of life in community."[13]

The aloneness on which solitude depends is not an unqualified blessing; loneliness also develops from it. Because loneliness, solitude, and other concepts are often confused, we must distinguish among them carefully. As we do so, we must avoid trivializing them or wrenching them from their roots in ordinary life by considering them simply as "rights" to privacy or solitude.

Aloneness is a fundamental condition of human life.[14] It is not continuous, but occasions of separation from others punctuate every life.

Indeed, a person can feel alone when he is with many others. It is only when this feeling is combined with the desire to be included in the activities of others and with the sense of being excluded that the pain of loneliness results, either for a brief period or as a relatively permanent state. Such a condition is by no means rare; it defines many lives. Attempts to escape loneliness are only too familiar: alcohol and drugs, superficial friendships, suicide, pornography, singles bars, and defensive walls around one's "privacy."

Human beings cannot escape loneliness, however, but only encounter and confront it, for example, by means of "isolation." Here loneliness is viewed as an inevitable condition of life. Separation from others on a relatively permanent basis is accepted because it is necessary for attaining some goal or for physical, mental, emotional, or moral survival. In this form of encounter, a person withstands the pain of loneliness as a part of life because it is the condition of achieving or maintaining some greater good. Familiar examples are scholars who spend long hours alone in library or laboratory, soldiers stationed far from family and friends, and persons taking positions of substantial responsibility requiring separation from old friends and acquaintances.

Although the two conditions may at first appear no different, solitude opens a new realm of life unknown to isolation.

> Instead of running away from our loneliness and trying to forget or deny it, we have to protect it and turn it into a fruitful solitude. To live a spiritual life we must first find the courage to enter into the desert of our loneliness and to change it by gentle and persistent efforts into a garden of solitude. This requires not only courage but also a strong faith.[15]

Isolation is necessary—those who do not experience it never achieve an important goal. Solitude, however, is far deeper, closer to a person's center. Here achievement and survival give way to the dialogue of the heart in which character blooms and grows. "A man or woman who has developed this solitude of heart is no longer pulled apart by the most divergent stimuli of the surrounding world but is able to perceive and understand this world from a quiet inner center."[16] The divergent stimuli of the world include not only the ordinary demands made by people and by things, but also a person's own masks which he perceives to be out of harmony as he attempts to respond to these demands. More deeply, one may realize in a moment of silence that his masks seem perfectly adjusted, but an ache of emptiness fills the center. Then such a person must go off by himself, to listen to his many voices.

In solitude I am truthful with myself. For this I need faith, that is, trust that in the place apart, truth will be possible and I will really be present to myself. Faith is the second "structural" requirement of character, and more will be said of it shortly. Without faith the struggle to transform loneliness into solitude would be too fearful for success. I am tempted to run from loneliness, from my encounter with myself. I fear to know myself. Faith overcomes the fear.

> You feel you are hedged in; you dream of escape; but beware of mirages. Do not run or fly away in order to get free: rather dig in the narrow place which has been given you; you will find God there and everything. God does not float on your horizon, He sleeps in your substance. Vanity runs, love digs. If you fly away from yourself, your prison will run with you and will close in because of the wind of your flight; if you go deep down into yourself it will disappear in paradise.[17]

This passage draws attention to the fact that others are present in solitude besides the self. Solitude depends on communion with God and with other persons. Moreover, it makes reaching out to others possible.

The preceding paragraph suggests the answer to objections that solitude cannot be an essential feature of character. First, it might be argued that because a person's center can never be completely disclosed, its contribution to the dialogue in solitude will always be distorted. Someone might also assert that the center of character is a nothing, an abyss; only the masks are real. Both objections draw strength from the always mysterious nature of the center, though they move in different directions. Though the center cannot be known as fully as a mask might be, it is knowable. It is not a nothing, because it is formed by faith and commitment. The three features of character cannot be understood in isolation from each other. If character had no faith, it would lack a center. It would be an abyss. There do seem to be persons who have no fundamental commitment, and their lack of a core is revealed in the meaninglessness and incongruity of the masks they wear. With commitment, however, there is a center to hold the whole together.

Faith should not be identified with center. There is an "I" which holds the faith. Otherwise, faith would be impersonal, and the center would be only a system of propositions or dogmas. Because it is personal, discourse with the center is always subject to distortion, just like dialogue between persons. If interpersonal communication is never perfect, should we expect intrapersonal communication to be undistorted? Yet this conclusion is not pessimistic. Despite distortion, an exchange between persons is possible. Because faith anchors the center, despite mystery, the dialogue of solitude makes self-knowledge possible. Moreover, just as in interpersonal dialogue luminous moments of near-perfect understanding now and then burst through, so in solitude self-awareness can flash before us.

Solitude is not a final accomplishment but alternates with loneliness in each person. Thus solitude is a constant encounter with loneliness and isolation, not something put on and off, like a coat. Solitude is a quality of character, a peace and serenity, a constant readiness and receptivity for encounter with loneliness and for dialogue among character's many voices. As Robert M. Pirsig's instructions for putting together a bicycle have it, "Assembly of Japanese bicycle require great peace of mind."[18] Yet tempers often flare in the process. Solitude, serenity, and patience are always qualities to be sought and cultivated, not possessions to enjoy.

I think of Simone Weil's concept of attention, by which she understands a waiting, an openness to penetration by truth.[19] She is referring to a discipline of mind and heart by which the tempting distractions of life are put aside so that the voices of character and others may be truly heard. The author of Lamentations praised such solitude and attentiveness: "Good is the Lord to one who waits for him, to the soul that seeks him. It is good to hope in silence for the saving help of the Lord" (3:25–26). The distractions which plague prayer also beset thinking, reading, and listening to others. Therefore, it seems that each is an activity of the same part of the soul, subject to the temptations and laziness of that part. There is a unity between the inner and outer dialogues; solitude is revealed as a communal state. Solitude, then, is a primary structural requirement of character. Lacking it, the masks of character fly away.

Two other points remain to be made before we turn to faith and commitment. First, often the person who has developed his solitude will feel detached from others, if these others are dominated by their masks and thus by convention alone. Because they have encountered their loneliness, persons of solitude have conquered the desperate needs for belonging, acceptance, and self-esteem. They are thus at peace when they lack relationships with others if the price of such relationships is a violation of the character which has matured in solitude. Such individuals are far removed from the narcissists of our time who desperately crave envy, admiration, attention, and success in competition.[20] The second point is essential for understanding the connections among the structural elements of character. Solitude is the condition for responsibility. In loneliness we give automatic replies to the world. In solitude we can listen receptively and respond honestly. Solitude frustrates self-righteousness and cultivates compassion. One who has lived within his own heart is capable of entering, if only for a little while, someone else's. Reality is obscure unless solitude has produced the conditions for an unsparing view of one's own character and a compassionate awareness of the other.

Finally, a shortcoming of the idea of the dialogue of center and masks must be mentioned. I have argued that it is neither possible nor desirable to transcend completely the roles, or masks, of life. I must, however, acknowledge such a possibility in the instance of mystical experience. Here there is (to use Weil's term) such a "decreation" of self that both center and masks disappear in the encounter with God. The *via negativa* of mysticism is a shedding of attachments to the world, including social roles, not denial of solitude but transformation of it. Mystical experience might be viewed as a dialogue in which all voices save God's gradually become silent.

Faith and Commitment

Without an inclusive faith, the person is fragmented and pulled in as many directions as he sees offering meaning or happiness. If life is to acquire meaning, character wholeness, and solitude peace, then an object of faith outside the self, a transcendent source of order, must become the focus of personal commitment. Ultimately, only being itself will satisfy this necessity and unify character. Just as for Plato the life of philosophy is a life of commitment to the vision of the Agathon, so for each person faith is a life of commitment to that source of value which confers meaning on ordinary things and events. Such commitment may be expressed in religious, philosophical, or ethical belief. Its presence, however, is the mark of a fully human life. Commitment can be associated neither with just any center of value nor with one's own self. Our selves and the many things which appear valuable to us are too limited to fulfill the demands of faith. These apparent goods are feeble, and their very weakness produces an alternation of value centers which undermines commitment. Only commitment to the One beyond the many, through a particular way of approach, will center a life of faith.

Thus commitment is the central element of character. The reference of the term "character" to moral qualities and principles suggests very well the necessity of commitment. Faith in an ultimate source of order creates the orbit in which principles are coherent and the foundation for the constancy of moral quality which allows the designation "character." Commitment is also the heart of intellectual achievement and, indeed, of all skills.

> We must now recognize belief once more as the source of all knowledge. Tacit assent and intellectual passions, the sharing of an idiom and of a cultural heritage, affiliation to a like-minded community: such are the impulses which shape our vision of the nature of things on which we rely for our mastery of things. No intelligence, however critical or original, can operate outside such a fiduciary framework.[21]

Because such commitment is made with universal intent, that is, because it always aspires to completion, faith is not purely subjective. It reaches out beyond the self to reality. Thus the faith at the center of character is not simply faith in or fidelity to oneself. Because the person is always a mystery to himself, faith continually aspires to a secure ground in reality.[22]

Following H. Richard Niebuhr, I will therefore define faith as "the attitude and action of confidence in, and fidelity to, certain realities as the sources of value and the objects of loyalty."[23] From this statement we see that faith has a double aspect. The first is trust in that which gives value to character. Faith is not simply belief but reliance on something. Because man is mysterious to himself, he is utterly dependent upon being, upon an outside source of order that gives meaning to existence and to the realities of mask and center. Faith, then, is the acceptance which character brings to reality, trust that despite evils, sorrows, and puzzles, these experiences and realities are part of an ordered whole. "If we are unfaithful, he will still remain faithful, for he cannot deny himself" (2 Tim. 2:13). Faith is trust of the power by which I am what I am, and it is by such faith that a person lives. Character literally depends on such a center of value. Without this commitment, the center of character seems worthless and the masks empty, which is equivalent to a loss of self. "I am one within myself as I encounter the One in all that acts upon me."[24]

This perspective does not deny that man is a rational animal. It simply asserts that reasoning is always reasoning from within a commitment. In the Old Testament, "man was understood . . . not first of all as a rational animal, but as a promise-making, promise-keeping, promise-breaking being, as man of faith."[25] The fact of promise breaking reminds us that hope is the necessary ally of faith. We know that for many reasons of personal weakness and social condition we shall break our covenants; we shall lose faith and trust. Hope allows us, in full knowledge of our own limitations, to set no conditions on our commitment. We may abandon ourselves in absolute confidence in the object of our commitment, knowing that though we fail, reality will remain what it is. Despite our frailties, Being remains Being. Thus the fruit of hope is security and serenity. Its requirement is patience.[26] And the garden of patience is solitude. I will now reinforce my fundamental contention that faith is the central element of character by discussing the idea of "indwelling." This term is basic to Polanyi's epistemology.[27]

When a person knows something, appreciates or evaluates something, or believes something, he does so intimately, from the inside, not formally, from the outside. To know is to dwell in the tacit particulars of a thing with all one's being. As a person assimilates the tacit particulars to himself, he grasps a picture of the whole of which they are parts. He actively enters into his commitments and dwells in them as a condition of his being able to place particular realities within Reality. As a condition of breaking out of his own subjectivity, a knower must indwell the external world with universal intent, that is, with faith.[28] Thus the most important thing about the knower's commitments is that they are his. He dwells in them, they are the place where he is at home, and they unify and fashion his character. A commitment cannot be rashly made. It comes from, and shapes, the heart.

Such a commitment has no arbitrariness about it. An arbitrary faith is merely an empty space at the center of character. Faith must be responsible because it is made within the context of a calling. This is the deepest source of the link between commitment and responsibility. Faith does not develop from a detached self free to make any of a number of commitments. Rather, faith is a personal response to a situation in which character is deeply involved and for which it is not responsible. That is, man finds himself in a personal situation which requires commitment; yet he is responsible not for the situation but only for his response to it. Thus the situation appears as a calling rather than as a trap, a mistake on his part, or a spectacle for him to watch in enjoyment or in pity and terror. It is his vocation. The human response to this is not to curse fate or God but to respond in commitment. Polanyi puts the matter this way:

> Intellectual commitment is a responsible decision, in submission to the compelling claims of what in good conscience I conceive to be true. It is an act of hope, striving to fulfill an obligation within a personal situation for which I am not responsible and which therefore determines my calling. This hope and this obligation are expressed in the universal intent of personal knowledge.[29]

Nothing so powerfully constitutes the person as those moments in which he senses that he is being called and must respond. Amos would never have found his true character through introspection; God's words were required.[30] Calling, or more precisely the response of commitment, shapes character, because responsibility is determined by faith and because, as shown above, solitude depends upon it.

So far, I have discussed faith as trust in Being. The second aspect of faith is fidelity to the object of commitment. Loyalty is a sign of character, because actions in loyalty to the object of faith reveal both object and character. Faith is the center of character. In loyalty the identification of the person with the object of faith is so strong that the interests of the object are perceived as extensions of the individual's own interests.[31] Moreover, loyalty is a requirement of character for another reason. Faith which does not manifest itself in action loyal to the object of commitment is meaningless.

> My brothers, what good is it to profess faith without practicing it? Such faith has no power to save one, has it? If a brother or sister has nothing to wear

and no food for the day, and you say to them, "Goodbye and good luck? Keep warm and well fed," but do not meet their bodily needs, what good is that? So it is with the faith that does nothing in practice. It is thoroughly lifeless. [James 2:12–17]

Faith is empty without the active, responsible service of loyalty. Responsibility is required in the person's commitment and in its daily living, and such responsibility is the most distinctive element of human character. "It is not man's highest mission to be acute; he is required simply to resolve his life loyally and sincerely."[32] Mother Teresa of Calcutta has said: "God has not called me to be successful. He has called me to be faithful."

One way to see loyalty as a fundamental feature of commitment is to look at love, which is necessarily associated with fidelity to the beloved. Love is primarily a social virtue; I will consider its proper place in chapter 4. Nevertheless, a discussion which draws on faith and hope cannot omit the greatest virtue. A person is as he loves. What I treasure, revere, am loyal to, is what I love. Thus faith always partakes of love, and this is a further reason why it is an indwelling. Love always tries to possess the beloved. For this reason also, faith is a personal investment and not an arbitrary decision. Confidence in the value center means that it is perceived as worthy of love and devotion. A strong love trusts the beloved deeply not only because of the beloved's identity but also because the lover's confidence is reinforced by commitment. Love builds a strong self. Jealousy and loss of confidence arise from doubts about the strength of the lover's own commitment. Faith, trust, and love go together.

Faith, then, is the central element of character. I have just argued that responsibility is fundamentally dependent upon faith. The previous section showed how solitude is impossible without faith. Responsibility is the external manifestation of faith, and solitude its inner assurance. This is not to say, however, that faith does not benefit from responsibility and solitude. I have already argued that the person's commitment must be itself responsible; similarly, faith must be nourished by solitude. Without solitude, life is not only shallow but empty. If faith is not nourished by the dialogue of solitude, it becomes a formulaic faith, a set of dogmas divorced from the experience of encounter with Being. Life then becomes filled with surface activities divorced from the experience of faith which gives them meaning. Religion without prayer is idolatry; philosophy without thinking is sophistry.

Responsibility

I have argued in the previous section that responsibility and commitment are reciprocal. My stress lay on commitment as a response to a calling. Here I will emphasize responsibility, which makes commitment fruitful in action as that element of character which preeminently makes contact with the world. Previously I abstracted the individual from his social setting. I can no longer do so. Though character and society will receive full discussion in chapter 4, I must refer to that relationship now.

Man is, of course, fundamentally social and must respond to others. Responsibility is the most public of the elements of character, for it is the visible sign of solitude and commitment. It is loyalty in action. "To be responsible is to accept obligations that one has by virtue of his commitments, his role in society, his power and authority."[33]

The reciprocity characteristic of the three elements of the soul gives wholeness to character. Responsibility makes solitude and commitment public, but responsibility cannot exist without them. Action is the task of the masks of character, so responsibility has a special relation to them. Yet the masks cannot act, but only react or behave, without the center and the dialogue with it which occurs in solitude. Solitude makes responsible action possible. Analogously, action must refer to faith to be responsible. Action divorced from commitment is a meaningless reflex to various stimuli. Responsibility is thus the product of wholeness of character and acceptance of vocation.

Responsibility depends upon freedom, as we will see in chapter 6. Here it is enough to remark that the idea of responsibility assumes that man is free in the most basic sense; that is, in his daily life each man is able to make and must make choices. Nothing is implied here about the range of his options; these will vary from person to person and from society to society. Each individual, however, in every society is faced with choices, many of which call upon or challenge his basic commitments and hence are moral. Responsibility, then, may be defined as the use of freedom in making choices in such a manner that one is prepared to give an accounting to himself and to others,[34] which can only be made and must be made in terms of the basic commitments of character. Action must be "fitting" in order to be responsible. It must not only answer to the unique circumstances in which it is called forth but also be true to basic principles, to faith.[35]

Thus responsible action recognizes limits set by the situation which demands an answer and by the commitments which order character. In solitude's dialogue, I hold myself accountable for the choices I make. I am accountable to others also, especially to the others involved, since I must be prepared to explain my actions in terms of my understanding of the situation and my commitments. Responsibility, then, distinguishes character from mere existence and automatic or arbitrary behaviors in situations where choice is possible.

The reader will readily see the differences between this idea of responsible character and the current notions of personal growth, refusing any limitations and exalting the energy of impulse over intention linked to commitment. "The ideology of personal growth, superficially optimistic, radiates a profound despair and resignation. It is the faith of those without faith."[36] To whom or to what can growth or the protean self be accountable? Responsibility recognizes, as the notion of the fluid self does not, the limits and the commitment requirements of genuine human life. Polanyi powerfully describes such limits:

> While compulsion by force or by neurotic obsession excludes responsibility, compulsion by universal intent establishes responsibility. The strain of this responsibility is the greater—other things being equal—the wider the range of alternatives left open to choice and the more conscientious the person responsible for the decision. . . . *The freedom of the subjective person to do as he pleases is overruled by the freedom of the responsible person to act as he must.*[37]

Most of us know persons who are afraid to choose and to act because they would have to accept responsibility. They lead pitiable lives, always searching for excuses, forever fearful of having to make a decision. Paul Tournier describes many such persons from his psychiatric practice, patients who live "provisional lives." They are never satisfied, never fully alive; they are always waiting for their real lives to begin. Turgenev describes just such a person in his bittersweet tale of a man who loses his beloved because he is too weak to decide between her and an exciting temptress. Turgenev comments, in an almost detached fashion which heightens the impact of his words, "Weak people never end anything themselves—they always keep waiting for an end." And later: "Weak people, talking to themselves, eagerly use energetic expressions."[38] How often we recognize such instants in our own lives, moments which seem to go on for hours, when we know that we should say or do something, but we seem frozen and able only to wait for the end! And then how we regret our indecision! Prufrock is just such a man, "measuring out my life with coffee spoons." So concerned with his appearance, his masks ("They will say: 'How his hair is growing thin!' "), that he cannot live or interact naturally with others ("Do I dare to eat a peach?"). In his life there will be "time yet for a hundred indecisions, / And for a hundred visions and revisions, / Before the taking of a toast and tea." And how does Prufrock enjoy such a life? "I should have been a pair of ragged claws / Scuttling across the floors of silent seas."[39]

Dostoyevsky also describes such persons: the Church of the Inquisition has constructed a society in which no one except the inquisitors is free, a society in which no one has to bear the fearful burden of freedom. This is why the return of Christ is such a threat to the Inquisitor.[40] More intimately, Dostoyevsky allows us a long look into the heart of a man who is so frightened of responsibility that he is unable to make decisions. The Underground Man attempts to picture his indecision:

> Obviously in order to act, one must be fully satisfied and free of all misgivings beforehand. But take me: How can I ever be sure? Where will I find the primary reason for action, the justification for it? Where am I to look for it? I exercise my power of reasoning, and in my case, every time I think I have found a primary cause I see another cause that seems to be truly primary, and so on and so forth, indefinitely.[41]

An empty, pitiful life, though the Underground Man is also comic. Yet the inhumanity of irresponsibility can also be tragic and dangerous. Milgram's experiments with subjects who believed that they were administering electric shocks demonstrate how inhuman persons can become when they transfer responsibility to another, or more accurately, when they believe they have transferred it.[42] This experiment is usually cited as evidence of the readiness to obey authority, but it seems clear that such blind obedience is possible only if the person believes he is not accountable for his own actions (because he has given—or the "authority" has taken—responsibility). Politics provides the pathetic and dangerous example of Richard Nixon, who still refuses to be charged with the events surrounding the Watergate affair.

Turning to persons who live responsibly presents a more pleasant prospect. Here we find a beautiful, though not painless, fabric of lives in commitment and responsible action. Tournier's theoretical conclusion that "acceptance of one's life has nothing to do with resignation; it does not mean running away fom the struggle. It means accepting it as it comes" is echoed in actual lives.[43] Examples may be found among workers who accept the necessities of their jobs and parents who accept the duties of raising children. Such ordinary people possess the same qualities as the extraordinary men described by Antoine de Saint-Exupéry. He speaks of his comrade Guillaumet, a mail pilot who, after a crash, struggled alone for seven days and six nights against the Andean snow and survived, when it would have been so easy to stop and let the sweet sleep of death take him.

> Guillaumet's courage is in the main the product of his honesty. But even this is not his fundamental quality. His moral greatness consists in his sense of responsibility. He knew that he was responsible for himself, for the mails, for the fulfillment of the hopes of his comrades.

Saint-Exupéry looks also at the core of "ordinary" lives and recalls a gardener's words on his deathbed: " 'And besides, who is going to prune my trees when I am gone?' "[44]

The two greatest Western models of human character, Socrates and Christ, are also distinguished by responsibility to calling. Responsive to his daemon and to his mission to seek wisdom, Socrates refuses to appease the Athenian *dikaesteria.* He remains the speaker of truth to the city when, in order to teach Crito about the requirements of the philo- sophic life, he refuses to escape from prison. Having defined his commit- ment, Socrates accepts the responsibility of acting as a philosopher in the face of death. Christ, too, accepts his calling and the death it requires.[45] His loyalty to the object of his love, his Father, silences his fear: "My Father, if it is possible, let this cup pass me by. Still, let it be as you would have it, not as I." His mission demanded that he respond to his betrayal and sufferings without protest. This he did, trusting in the Father's love. "Father, into your hands I commend my spirit" (Matt. 26:39, Luke 23:46).

Ignazio Silone's novel *Bread and Wine* includes two contrasting studies of responsibility.[46] The old priest, Don Benedetto, is one—a person truth- ful, at peace, in touch with the deepest source of being and with his vocation as a priest to speak Christ's message, whether or not it accords with current government or church policy. Silone's other example, Pietro Spina, is far more complicated. Don Benedetto is at peace throughout the novel; Pietro is growing toward peace. As a revolutionary, he is forced to disguise himself as a priest, Don Paolo. He is then compelled to respond to the needs of the poor villagers among whom he lives, and as he does so he begins to realize the emptiness and the abstraction of his ideology. He must encounter the people at a deeper and more human level. He has not yet found the object of his ultimate commitment, but he has learned to respond rather than react.

The brief portraits above are not meant as proofs of the value of a responsible life and its superiority to an irresponsible one. They are, like Plato's portraits of the just and the unjust, invitations and appeals to the heart and mind. If the people described are familiar, their lives should resonate in ours. The reverberations and each person's reflection on them constitute the empirical ground of my contentions. If the responsible life is, upon reflection, superior to the other, and if my arguments that it depends on solitude and commitment are valid, then responsibility is essential to character. The best proofs of the importance of the elements of character are experiential, not abstract.

I turn now to some other aspects of responsibility awaiting elaboration. First, responsible action involves two moments.[47] The first is the immedi- ate experience, which includes the person's interpretation of an event— someone is angry, the car is out of control, I have a class in fifteen minutes, and so forth. Responsible action is not the rigid application of laws or principles. A person must fully enter into a particular situation (and perhaps its hidden meanings) before a genuine response is possible. Second, reflection before or after the experience, in terms of faith or related principles, attempts to assess whether the action was true to faith or not. Quick action can be responsible because it is open to reflection and because it proceeds from the interiorization and habituation of moral principles.

This last point may well produce the objection that earlier I excluded habitual reaction from responsible action. But I would respond, with Aristotle, that habit is necessary in the moral life, though it alone is not sufficient; reflection, in this case similar to Aristotle's virtue of prudence, is also required.[48] Prior reflection determines that response is fitting in terms of situation and commitment. Subsequent reflection judges the fitness of the habitual response, calling habit to account in order to prevent it from ruling life. Here the interrelatedness of the three elements of character is again clear, for solitude is the place of reflection. Here, too, we see that mere choosing is not what makes life human, but rather what is chosen, just as the object of commitment must not be arbitrary but must be made with universal intent. The inner principles that accompany faith must ground choosing, if it is to be responsible. But a discussion of responsibility is incomplete without consideration of other virtues, including attention or listening, receptivity, honesty, and courage.

Attentiveness requires that a person genuinely listen to the other before responding. Action which genuinely responds to another cannot proceed from an assumption about what the other is saying, doing, or feeling; it must proceed from careful listening, or attention. Too often when a person speaks to us, genuinely seeks our help, we reply with set speeches. We fail to take the time (or to leave behind our own concerns) to heed what is being said. Yet unless we take account of the time, place, and person encountered, responsible action is impossible. The attitude of attention is like listening to music or viewing a drama or a work of art. It is not critical or analytical but appreciative, demanding a quiet self, an intense encounter with the object. Just so, attention demands a quiet, open self and so requires solitude.[49]

Attention is closely connected with patience and receptivity or availability. Genuine responsiveness requires that I not impatiently attempt to cut the other person off or act quickly to end the encounter. Rather, I must listen to what the other is saying, letting it enter and reverberate in the depth of my being. I may disagree with or dislike the other or his words, but I must let them penetrate my solitude and find a response there. That is, I must be ready to give myself to the other. Because we may change in ways unknown to me or him, I must patiently receive what he is or has to give me and just as carefully respond with part of what I am and have to give. If I quickly reply so that I can rid myself of the interruption and resume my own projects, I have failed to receive and so have not answered responsibly. "*Patience*," says Rilke, "is everything."[50] These, then, are the keys to genuine response. It is good to reach out to others with assistance, but if we reach out without letting them come in, without hospitality, we behave as do-gooders, with unconscious condescension, not as responsible and receptive persons. I do not mean, however, that we should be so accommodating as to be afraid to reveal character. The receptive person must be sure of his own commitments.[51] He owes it to the other to listen with his whole self, without hiding behind a convenient mask.

Responsible character demands honesty. Genuine response to a person or a situation demands that I see as clearly as possible. If I deceive myself in my perceptions in order to reply more easily, I have acted irresponsibly. If I lie to myself about my commitments, my loyalty and trust are damaged, and I am unable to fulfill their demands. If dishonesty pervades my relations with others, I keep part of myself hidden, and I fail to be fully available and attentive. The dialogue between center and masks which takes place in solitude is impossible without honesty. Solitude and honest dialogue are essential requirements for responsible action. The extent to which we deceive ourselves is astonishing, but only when we fail to realize the difficulty of the responsible action that honesty intrinsically demands. We often undertake too many projects, for example, because we are afraid to admit to ourselves, and to let others see, that our abilities are limited. Often we are dishonest with others because we do not want to be responsible for the communication that honesty would open. I am, of course, speaking of undistorted communication, not the blunt cruelty which often masquerades as honesty and thereby thinly conceals the desire to hurt. Nor am I speaking of outright lies, most often easy to avoid. The difficulty of honesty most especially involves recognizing, if only partially, the masks which hide us from others and from ourselves.

Responsibility also calls for courage, not exemplary bravery in the face of danger to life, though that is also demanded at times, but a person's willingness to risk the security of his home by opening it in hospitality to another. In tolerating someone else and opening ourselves to him, we act like the host who makes strangers welcome in his house. Perhaps they will make off with the silverware, but hospitality requires that such risks be taken.[52] Responsibility also requires that we confront evil, despite the threat to our security. The courage required is that necessary to act responsibly each day. Saint-Exupéry writes of another of his comrades:

> Pioneering thus, Mermoz had cleared the desert, the mountains, the night, and the sea. He had been forced down more than once in desert, in mountain, in night, and in sea. And each time that he got safely home, it was but to start out again.[53]

We can bear our failures, because in the solitude of our hearts we know that we are limited creatures who, though called to do much, are not asked to be infinitely responsible. Thus we are able to be at peace, knowing that we have attempted to respond but also that our faith does not demand universal responsibility from us. Faith and hope shore up courage.

Conclusion

I have argued that political philosophy must begin from a conception of the essential components of human life. I have attempted to show that human character is constituted by a center and masks and that wholeness of character depends upon their harmony that is in turn the product of solitude and faith and is manifested in responsible action. Solitude, commitment, and responsibility, plus the virtues requisite for their support, form the structure of the fully developed human life, the good life.

In making this argument, I abstracted character as much as possible from social interaction and focused on inner life. Only in speaking of responsibility was it necessary to move substantially into social life, because responsibility is the element of character which bridges inner life and social life. Obviously this abstraction was artificial, though required, I believe, for orderly exposition. The artificiality will continue to be necessary for a time, however, before I bring character and community together, for the next chapter must consider community as a social form. There I shall abstract as much as possible from the elements of character in individual persons.

3

Communion and Hospitality

The Lord God said:
"It is not good for the
man to be alone.
I will make a suitable
partner for him."
Genesis 2:18

"Community" is a term with a long and ambiguous history in social thought, so that without further definition it does not point to any specific kind of human relation. Indeed, in English the term is more obscure than in other languages, since we have one word where German, Italian, and French, for example, use a number to cover general human relations, local communities, and affective unity.[1] Community, in my usage, does not refer to any fixed social relationship or relationships. Community is not a reality like the table on which I am writing. My understanding of the concept avoids reification or any requirement that every specimen be modeled after a particular social or political relationship in the past or present. "Community" is a symbol for relationships in which the experiences of social solidarity, mutual openness of character, and common search for the truth are dominant. All three of these experiences may be present, but more commonly only one or two will be. In combination they will determine the type of community, but the presence of any one will allow us to symbolize the relationship using the concept. The persons who belong develop rituals, symbols, affection, mutual respect, common language, and traditions. They may develop formal institutions and authority structures to maintain and strengthen their bond.

Any attempt to define community confronts the well-known finding of George A. Hillery, Jr., that there are only the most general areas of agreement. Surveying ninety-four definitions, Hillery found that community was often understood to mean a group of people in social interaction having some bonds in common. The most frequently mentioned ties were common life, consciousness of kind, and possession of common ends.[2] Such a consensus, however, is too general and abstract, including too many types of human relationships.

Closer to the mark than Hillery's report is the conclusion of David W. Minar and Scott Greer: "Community is indivisible from human actions, purposes, and values. It expresses our vague yearnings for a commonality of desire, a communion with those around us, an extension of the bonds of kin and friend to all those who share a common fate with us."[3] Robert A. Nisbet approaches more closely the intimacy of community when he proposes that community

> encompasses all forms of relationship which are characterized by a high degree of personal intimacy, emotional depth, moral commitment, social cohesion, and continuity in time. Community is founded on man conceived in his wholeness. . . . It draws its psychological strength from levels of motivation deeper than those of mere volition or interest, and it achieves its fulfillment in a submergence of individual will that is not possible in unions of mere convenience or rational assent. Community is a fusion of feeling and thought, of tradition and commitment, of membership and volition.[4]

The items of importance here are intimacy, commitment, emotional depth, and man in his wholeness. These elements are summarized by D. B. Clark in two essential features of community: a sense of solidarity and a sense of significance.[5] In community persons experience security; feelings of belonging, unity, togetherness, and cohesion are dominant. Community is grounded in the human sentiments which draw persons together—trust, gratitude, and sympathy. Intimacy, emotional depth, and commitment produce solidarity. Community, then, refers to the experience of solidarity in social relations, when men are mutually aware of the common ties that bind them in work, pursuit of the truth, intimate experience, and love. Thus community is likely to be found in many families, athletic teams, church fellowships, and fraternities and between lovers, friends, and colleagues. Of course, such relationships are not invariably communal; they may in fact be filled with strife and hatred. Nevertheless, they are more likely than conversation over cocktails, acquaintanceship, and business partnership to produce a sense of solidarity and intimacy. The experience of belonging and trust can be seen also in the meaning of the New Testament Greek term for community, *koinonia*. It is used in relation to persons who share a reality, that is, Christ, and who thus hold in common life, suffering, and destiny. Hence the experience extends to the sharing of material goods. "The love of God . . . creates a bond of fellowship and solidarity . . . and transforms strangers and sojourners into fellow citizens of the kingdom of God."[6] The sense of significance accompanies solidarity, and although this is more properly the subject of the next chapter, I must point out here that neither solidarity nor significance can stand alone. The sense of significance refers to the experiences of having a place, or station, and an important role to play in society. It refers also to sentiments of achievement, fulfillment, and contribution to the whole of which one is a part.[7]

Solidarity and significance as described above are the most familiar aspects of community when the term is used to refer to the inner experience of a relationship. There is, however, another experience also properly symbolized as community. Persons may be together in a relationship without feeling the solidarity that I have described above yet still having a sense of significance. Such a relationship occurs when two persons meet each other in mutual openness of character. In such an encounter the persons have not yet formed, and may never form, a relatively permanent bond. Their meeting may last for minutes, hours, or days and may be repeated only at intervals or not at all. The essential quality of the relationship is that each participates with an attitude of receptivity to the meanings given by the other. Examples of such relationships are Socratic dialogues, Christ's encounters with repentant sinners, and occasions of mutual respect between adversaries. This form of community, which I shall call hospitality, will be considered later in this chapter. I now turn to consider solidarity more fully.

Solidarity

According to the *Oxford English Dictionary,* the most likely derivation of "community" and its cognates is from the Latin *com* ("together") plus *munis* ("bound, under obligation"). This etymology expresses well the experience of community as solidarity. Members are bound closely together by obligations of service and care. The members of my communities have a claim on me, and I on them. Of course, others have claims on me as well, but of a significantly different sort. My duty to help a drowning man is experienced as an overwhelming rush of direct human sympathy. My contribution to feeding starving persons in another land is normally experienced as a quasi-legal obligation, a particular instance of a general moral law enjoining assistance to my fellow man. What I owe my comrade, friend, or brother, however, is different. It is felt neither as an onrush of primitive sympathy nor as an instance of a general duty; rather, it flows directly from the texture of the relationship, from a web of exchanged love and services. If, as Gouldner argues, a general norm of reciprocity governs all social relations, in community this norm is latent.[8] It seldom occurs to members to total their giving and receiving to see who has come off better and who worse. There are exchanges of costs and benefits, but no one cares to count them. Such exchanges do not interfere with the deep feelings of love, admiration, trust, and belonging which structure the union; indeed, they solidify such feelings.

Viewed from the inside, as is most appropriate, community as solidarity first presents itself as a radical fact of my existence. I do not choose my communities. I seem either to have been dropped into already existing ones or to have been at the center of gradually evolving relationships. This first impression is slightly misleading, as we shall see that choice is always involved in community. Yet the element of choice is in the background, as we see most clearly with a child, who does not choose to be born into this or that family and becomes strongly committed to a community he did not select. His church, his neighborhood, and his friends (or at least the pool of possible friends) are none of his choice. The family is thus the paradigm of community as solidarity. Some other relationships of solidarity are friendship, erotic love, comradeship, collegiality, and common work. Such relations are, of course, not identical. Each has its own characteristics, but in all the sense of belonging, cohesion, and togetherness is dominant.

Despite the tensions and imperfections, all such relationships can be readily distinguished from the relations among acquaintances, business partners (those who are not also friends), buyers and sellers, and competitors. Here the connections are more distant, formal, and impersonal. Inner qualities, feelings, and experiences distinguish community as solidarity from other kinds of relationships. Even though I see and say hello to the checkout clerk at the circulation desk each day I come to the library to write this book, I experience no sense of solidarity with her. Yet I do with persons I have never met or seen whose writings show a concern for the same truths I am trying to explore. So I may rightly call them colleagues, and together we form what Michael Polanyi has called a "convivial order," or a "society of explorers," pursuing the same commitment in our search for truth about reality.[9]

To say that community is distinguished by the experiences of its members is not, I wish to caution, to make the mistake of reducing social realities to psychological ones.[10] There may be a psychological need for belonging, but its mere satisfaction does not constitute community. Solidarity is a *mutual* sense of belonging; moreover, community refers not only to persons' inner feelings and attitudes but also to their actual shared life. Thus if it were possible simultaneously to stimulate electrically the "belonging center" of two persons and to make them mutually aware of the feelings produced, this would not be a community. Actual sharing of sorrows, joys, beliefs, purposes, work, play, symbols, rituals, and obligations is necessary. Otherwise community is not possible. Its importance will be considered further when I treat the bonds of community, but one major difficulty must be confronted before we can turn to that topic.

We know too well that communities showing solidarity may be formed around evil objects. A sense of belonging may be generated among the followers of a person such as Charles Manson. Mass movements and totalitarian societies generate common devotion to beliefs, ideologies, and leaders, successfully stir men to action, and fulfill a need for belonging. To the extent that sharing cements community, any values will do.[11] We know also that many unions, even those centered on worthy objects, are able to survive and grow because they are highly centralized and tightly controlled. They provide belonging and security by sharply limiting the freedom of members to encounter divergent ideas or practices in the outside world. Severe conformity of mind, spirit, and action is often the inner and outer face of community. Do not these evil and coercive features of community disqualify the concept?

It seems to me that this objection may be met and overcome if two essential differences between two types of solidarity are recognized. I shall call "communion" the solidarity which promotes freedom and which displays the traits of belonging, cohesion, trust, and sympathy in connection with good objects. I shall call "uniformity," or "pseudocommunity," solidarity in evil objects, forced conformity to worthy objects, and suppression of individual character. The first essential difference between these two is the type of love which binds each. Uniformity is founded on what C. S. Lewis calls "need-love," which is rooted in insecurity and fear.[12] In itself it is not a "bad" love or a failing, but relationships built entirely on it are weak and perverted. Such love binds men tightly and blindly, because their concern is to flee loneliness or to protect themselves from a fearful external world. Total and exclusive commitment is demanded, and total conformity of belief and behavior is required, because any difference among the members of such a community makes them vulnerable to attack. For example, parents who smother their children with affection and prevent them from growing out of the protective shell of the home are afraid to let them establish characters of their own, because such parents are afraid to live their own lives. They need their children to conform to a certain mold, for they are afraid of life without children as definitions and justifications of their existence. Though such parents give, and constantly, to their children, the gifts originate in a need to keep the children dependent.

Communion, on the other hand, is rooted in gift-love.[13] Members of a communion live a common life not out of fear and insecurity but out of a love of living together and of exchanging mutual gifts. Working together is mutual assistance toward a goal. In such communities, each has something to contribute, and the common life is enriched by the diversity of individual efforts.[14] Members do not fear loneliness, because in addition to the support of their comrades and friends, they have their own resources for encountering it. Need-love, of course, is not absent from communion, which does, as I have argued, satisfy needs. But need is not the prime focus of communion.

The distinction in love between uniformity and communion suggests the second essential difference. In uniformity, even where the object of unity is a worthy one, the members of the community desire to create a single self from all participants. In communion there is a preservation of individual differences. Pseudocommunities tend to demand one function only from their members, who come to resemble parts in a machine. Communions, on the other hand, appreciate many aspects of the individual's character and call upon as many talents as the person possesses. The member may be called upon at different times to lead worship, help with a bake sale, participate in a sports program, or comfort the grief of another. Communion evokes wholeness of character and is a relationship between one character and others. Uniformity is the destruction of distance and difference, so that anxiety may be escaped by submerging oneself in the totality.[15] Even in the successful, tightly-knit utopian communities of the nineteenth century, some space for individual development, for privacy and freedom, was left the members.[16]

It is, of course, true that in communion, need-love is present and some submergence of individuality is required. Yet communion, as I hope to demonstrate, rewards submergence with a deepening of character. As finite creatures, we are always needy, but we may still give and receive with gratitude. A solidarity grounded on uniformity may satisfy the need for belonging, but it does so at the price of a dreadful narrowing and distortion of the human spirit. Uniformity shapes character, but it creates fearful and perverted forms.

Community as solidarity, then, has its dangers, and these must be recognized and avoided or overcome if communion is to serve as a symbol of the good life in common and thus as an ordering concept in political philosophy. The dangers of uniformity are ever present; yet they can be resisted once they have been acknowledged. Because community carries the connotation of uniformity as well as of communion and because what I have called hospitality is an important form of community, I have reserved certain terms for particular uses. Community as solidarity in good objects, and permitting freedom and diversity I shall refer to as "communion." "Pseudocommunity" will designate the uniformity discussed in the preceding pages. "Hospitality" will denote the form of community characterized by mutual receptivity and openness of character. When I wish to refer to communion and hospitality together, I shall say "community." I hope, by adherence to these uses, to avoid confusion among related but distinct phenomena.

The discussion of communion may have left the impression that it can develop only from pleasant encounters such as love, friendship, and shared faith. In fact, it can also emerge from shared confrontation with danger or sorrow. Persons who experience common suffering in times of physical danger or social/moral evil often develop strong bonds of solidarity. They have shared pain or resistance to evil, and such sharing strikes deep into the soul, anchoring bonds of solidarity which frequently extend beyond the end of the suffering or danger. Living through the death of a mutual friend or relative may also serve to bring persons closer into communion. Grief tends to weaken masks, allowing center to encounter center and to form a closer union. The harshness of life, its pain and tragedy, provides as many occasions for communion as its joys and good times do.

Neither shared sorrow nor shared joy, neither blood relationship nor close acquaintance, guarantees communion or hospitality. Communion and hospitality are norms which actual relationships approximate to a greater or lesser degree. Many families, churches, fraternities, and clubs are pseudocommunities; many possess only the slightest solidarity. Many such relationships do manifest the principal elements of community. Normative terms serve to describe community at its fullest development and to provide a standard for evaluation of particular relationships which could or should be communal but which fall short in various ways. I do not mean to suggest, in using the terms as I do, that communion or hospitality is prevalent in the contemporary world. Community faces many dangers today, but we can only measure the dangers if we can understand community in its fullest senses.

The Bonds of Communion

If communion is an experience of particular kinds of relations between persons, then the structuring bonds must be examined. The task is not easy, since the discipline which should specialize in the analysis of such bonds has developed only very weak concepts of social integration which have attracted little consensus or empirical research. We can only attempt here to discern the most notable ties of communion by examining the elements commonly discussed and by exploring significant experiences of communion.

A few preliminary observations seem in order at this point. We may expect to find bonds of varying prominence in all kinds of communions. For example, communions entered into consciously by adults, such as friendships or work groups, will be quite different from communions into which individuals enter unconsciously or even without will, such as families. In the former case, the element of commitment will be quite prominent; in the latter, shared experience over a long period will take the lead in binding the persons, and commitments will strengthen slowly and almost imperceptibly. My purpose here is not to develop a typology of solidarity groups according to the proportions of the various bonds they exhibit but rather to explore the nature of communion by inquiring into its primary experiences of union.

I shall discuss four major bonds of communion: commitment, love, shared experience, and authority. Commitment includes loyalty and common beliefs, search for truth, moral norms, and symbols and rituals. Love includes the feeling of members not only for each other, but for some object. Shared experience refers primarily to work or action, though it may refer to passive experience as well, as in watching a movie with others. It also includes mutual responsibility. Authority, particularly that which is grounded in custom or tradition, provides the orienting element. The role of authority and its relation to community, however, is so often misunderstood and so essential for understanding political community that chapter 5 will explore it at length. Quite obviously, all of the bonds interpenetrate. A commitment may be a pledge of love. Love is a shared experience. Commitment to moral norms may be realized in common action to implement them or in common rituals which celebrate them. I believe, however, that these experiences are analytically distinct and may be discussed separately.

Commitment

Ignace Lepp points out that friendship properly understood is not jealous or exclusive. It reaches out to include others, yet it demands fidelity.[17] In reaching out to another, I may not abandon my friend. To save myself, I may not betray my friend. The same is true of other communions. Infidelity wrecks marriages. Comrades and colleagues have a right to expect that mutual commitment will mean mutual loyalty, trust, and confidence. Commitment is the basic bond of communion as well as the orienting principle of character.

Loyalty, of course, is not the same as conformity. Friends, lovers, and comrades will resemble each other in many significant ways, but I do not expect my friend to be exactly like me, nor do I expect my colleagues to think my thoughts, do the exact research I do, teach as I do, or vote as I do in departmental meetings. Lovers are often quite different in personality, preferences, tastes, and attitudes; yet they are committed and loyal to each other. Conformity can be compelled; loyalty cannot.[18]

To argue that commitment is essential is to imply that communion is always at least partially voluntary. Neither coercion nor deception can produce genuine commitment. Members must be committed to their communion and what it stands for. I do not mean that some persons may not be united to and obedient to a communion for other motives. Among the believers in a church there may be some who remain attached and obey its rules not because they are committed to its tenets or their fellow members but only because they fear hell or social ostracism if they do not belong. Persons sometimes remain attached to their families only because they are psychologically incapable of repudiating them, even though they wish to do so.[19] Can we say that such persons are members of a communion? I believe that such persons are *in* the communion but are not members of it. They experience conformity, and perhaps even alienation in outward conformity, not belonging and solidarity. Communions include both central and peripheral members. Because communion is a normative concept, it can recognize degrees of fullness, depending upon the percentage of peripheral members and the intensity of commitment of all. Ceteris paribus, a group is more fully communal the greater the percentage of central members and the more fundamental the commitment called for by the group. Participation in a number of communions does not necessarily lead the individual toward more peripheral memberships if the fundamental commitments of the groups are complementary, but it may make marginality easier.

Rosabeth Moss Kanter, in her book on nineteenth-century American utopian communities, has explained the relationship between commitment and communion with great care and insight. Kanter argues that successful utopian communities were those that built strong ties of various types among their members. Though her definition of commitment is deficient in stressing the need-love side of solidarity rather than trust and fidelity, she correctly argues that definite commitment mechanisms are necessary to sustain communal life over a long time and in the face of trial and conflict. "Abstract ideals of brotherhood and harmony, of love and union, must be translated into concrete social practices."[20]

Kanter identifies six basic commitment mechanisms. An attaching and a detaching (from other commitments and groups incompatible with the present group) mechanism is needed for each of three aspects of the social system. The retention of members requires instrumental commitment through the mechanisms of sacrifice and investment. Group cohesion requires emotional ("affective") commitment through renunciation and communion. Social control requires moral commitment by means of "mortification" and "transcendence." Kanter also discovered that successful solidarity groups allowed a certain personal freedom for each member and had some limits on commitment mechanisms.[21]

A brief description of the six mechanisms will reveal some of the dimensions of this bond.[22] Sacrifice refers to the abstinence and austerity often required in communions. More broadly, joining a group always limits a person's options for membership in other groups and for activities incompatible with the norms of the communion. In order to warrant these costs of joining, a person will commit himself to the communion. Investment also refers to a cost: the stake one has in a group, when he becomes actively involved in it, investing time and energy in its life.

Sacrifice and investment in Kanter's senses, it seems to me, are necessary parts of any social relationship. Her other four commitment mechanisms are more closely identified with communion. "Renunciation involves the relinquishing of relationships that are potentially disruptive to group cohesion, thereby heightening the relationship of individual to group."[23] Commitment demands renunciation of allegiances to values, beliefs, and symbols incompatible with those of the communion. Thus, for example, families concerned with the character of their children will often limit their television viewing and their circle of friends in particular cases that might undermine character. To renounce such activities and friends means a greater reliance on the group. More positively, such commitment to the group is fostered by "communion": by activities, work, and participation in decision making, which increase the sense of belonging and connectedness to the group.

Mortification refers to reducing the sense of separateness of self. Self-esteem is made dependent on the group. Mortification proceeds by means of confession and mutual criticism, sanctions against deviance from rules, and the erasure of distinctions between members. Obviously mortification is a major tool in producing conformity; yet all communion requires some reduction in the importance of the ego. Openness to a friend is impossible if I am too full of my own importance and my own needs. Thus communions have rules stressing awareness of the needs and feelings of others. "Johnny, if the toy is Andy's, you must ask him whether you can play with it."

Transcendence, in Kanter's sense, is closest to commitment to a common faith or truth as a bond of communion. With this word she refers to the experiences of awe, rightness, certainty, and conviction which come from commitment and to the experience of power and meaning residing in one's communion. Such experiences are generated through shared beliefs, references to higher principles, hierarchical authority, and charismatic leadership. A faith may carry a sense of conversion, and communions a sense of mission, which result in heightened commitment. The heart of all these types of commitment is a common faith, a reference to a sharing of basic beliefs and purposes.

The awareness among a group of persons of shared standards—honesty, pursuit of justice, the importance of Renaissance poetry, humane treatment of animals, and so forth—creates an internal bond among them. They hold meetings or seminars about the ideas to which they are commonly committed; their social occasions are dominated by "shop talk"; that is, talk about joint values. These occasions are the soil in which solidarity grows. The mutually acknowledged commitment sets this group apart from other individuals and groups; it makes them special and unique, individually and collectively, and becomes a stable root from which the growing plant of their solidarity sends out smaller and more densely concentrated roots. Aristotle most directly recognizes this moral side of communion when he calls the common discussion of justice the bond of the *polis*, which is a form of koinonia. Cicero defines the commonwealth as the people's affair, "the coming together of a considerable number of men who are united by a common agreement about the law and rights and by the desire to participate in mutual advantages"—not self-interest but justice is the bond of a republic.[24] I do not mean to suggest that every possible value may serve communal integration. Some values (sadism, for example) may create only conformity. Others (such as competition and achievement) may only separate people.

The more significant the common standards of a group of persons, the more likely that their commitment will bind them into communion. As persons share commitments to fundamental human goals and purposes, their unity has the foundation for deeper experiences of belonging, togetherness, and significance. George Morgan argues that the genuine meeting of persons

> has its being in shared esteem of worthy things . . . and shared knowledge of the denials and hardships, meaning and joy of man's life in the world. We commune with one another as we work for a common purpose; as we simply watch nature; as we enter into dialogue to find truth and struggle with its demands; and as we listen to music and our eyes meet in understanding. None of these things can occur without a community of values.[25]

Shared value cements any permanent relationship, but shared commitment to fundamental purposes and beliefs binds persons most deeply together. Fraternity and friendship, love and convivial order, are supported not by utility or mutual self-interest but by basic goals. Common purpose provides a context within which the ordinary frictions of human intercourse can be forgotten and forgiven, in which failures to achieve goals take on meaning. Thus incompletion, tension, ambivalence, and failure to achieve goals are the permanent conditions of communion. Shared belief and purpose, however, transform these seemingly divisive conditions into bonds of solidarity. Though we have failed, we have done so together, and jointly we can begin our pursuit again. Thus men are bound together in a quest which makes their irreducible differences assets in the pursuit of a shared goal given by a common faith.[26]

Truth about ultimate reality or the common commitment to the search for such truth and, therefore, trust in and loyalty to the reality which grounds truth, are the surest bonds.[27] Communions grounded in such bonds will be, then, the most significant in the lives of their members. Just as truth and honesty are required for personal character, so they are required if communion is to reach its maturity. Yet commitment to truth extends to the reality to which truth corresponds. Without trust and loyalty to the Ground of

Being beyond all beings which sustains limited communions and makes the search for truth one which may be fruitful, communion is doomed to frustration and disorder. Without such a faith, solidarity quickly succumbs to the blows of human conflict, time, and challenge from the external environment. Therefore, groups of real significance and solidarity in human life must have a religious dimension; they must at some point, whether acknowledged as religious or not, make contact with transcendent reality.

Because commitment to pursuing the intimations of shared faith is the most important bond of communion, equal treatment and equal conditions for all members are not essential. Communion does demand equality in the sense of equal worth and dignity in light of the ultimate ground of commitment. Hierarchies and differences of treatment, to the extent that they exist, will be instrumental to pursuit of common purposes rather then ends in themselves. Each person in communion has a place and a significance and dignity owing to his relation to the fundamental commitment. Thus a basic equality obtains. The idea of equal treatment, on the other hand, is rooted in societies of competition and exchange.[28]

Two of the most visible evidences for the commitment at the heart of communion are ritual and symbol. Communication between the members is possible only because of a common set of symbols, especially a language, but including also signs, dress, and gesture. Common participation in ritual is the reaffirmation of an original commitment. Utopian communities, for example, often promoted brotherhood and feelings of intimacy through ritual dances, "bees," worship services, and the like.[29] The world I share with others in communion is constituted by the language we use together to symbolize our experiences of morals, of commitment, of discovery, and of faith. Language legitimates the social reality we share. Sharing a set of symbols, whether speech, dress, or gesture, creates a sense of belonging. By learning the language and incorporating it into myself, I enter a world which only other members may enter. I belong there with them. Not to commit oneself to the symbols is to be excluded from the communion. The debasement of language and the decay of symbols are two fundamental reasons for the difficulty of creating communion in the modern world.[30]

Love

Love is the second major bond of communion. A common object of love, binding together members of a communion, is also a common object of commitment. Here love is indistinguishable from ultimate commitment. Such identity is the meaning of the famous lines: "No servant can serve two masters. Either he will hate the one and love the other or be attentive to the one and despise the other. You cannot give yourself to God and money"

(Luke 16:13). Similarly, "Wherever your treasure lies, there your heart will be" (Luke 12:34). The center of love is also that of ultimate trust and loyalty. Does the idea of love, then, add anything to what I have already said about commitment as a bond of communion?

Love has many dimensions. At one level it is simply emotional attachment. This is important to communion, as the following paragraph will show. Love is also erotic, passionate attachment to one object of desire and care, which is one type of communion. At another level love is a constant disposition toward the good of others, perhaps even those who are not liked. The injunction to love one's enemies is the highest form of this type. It is also the most difficult, since the good of my enemy seems somehow bound up with harm to myself. Love as well-wishing is obviously critical to the solidarity of a communion. At still another level, love is the passionate desire to know and to be united with the transcendent. The model here is the eros of the *Symposium* but also the love of the first and greatest commandment. Here love blends with faith but at the same time makes clear the passionate side of faith. Such love is the condition of the limited knowledge of the Ground of Being and of the truth which we have as well as the ground of our hope for greater understanding. We believe so that we may understand, but we must first be attracted to and desire union with the object of belief. Love, then, pervades all aspects of communion.

Love as a bond discloses the emotional ties among members of a communion. The members realize that the shared commitment has blossomed into affection. They look not only at an object of faith but at each other. Indeed, since a lived faith is characterized by constant cycles of ebb and flood, when faith is very low, persons often remain in a communion only because they care for their fellow members. Such direct concern for fellow members, not simply because the others happen to be similarly committed, helps such persons to live through the difficult times and makes the cycles less frequent, less deep, and of shorter duration.

The ties are not only indirect, through a common object of commitment, but also direct and emotional. Persons in communion are united by mutual sympathy, affection, mercy, and trust. They feel comfortable with one another, and the places where they gather seem like home. They stand ready to assist one another, to overlook faults and foibles, and to appreciate different talents. "Love as loyalty sustains the fabric of community by actions furthering the interdependence of man with man. Love as tolerance sustains the richness of variety in community in all complementary differences."[31]

The emotional, indeed, the libidinal, ties between persons in communion may frequently be more important than common commitment. Indeed, an outpouring of love overwhelms, at least for a time, all other bonds. Erotic love in its early stages certainly acts this way. Nothing seems important to lovers except each other. In time, as the caring matures, erotic attachment becomes balanced with other ties of shared experience, commitment, and love for children and kin. Friendship also has a large element of mutual affection in it. I appreciate my friend for who he is as well as for the commitments and experiences that we have shared. Such mutual appreciation despite differences is a strong bond of communion.

Shared Experience

Shared experience is the third major tie of communion. I refer here principally to common participation in decision making, to work in pursuit of communal purposes, and to mutual responsibility. These are the "active" side of common experiences, though significant "passive" experiences may also be shared and are the bonds which touch the heart most deeply. The experiences of birth and death, joy and pain are most significant. Living through an air raid or a hurricane together, huddled in fear, joins persons deeply. Suffering may join strangers, temporarily or permanently, but when such an experience is shared within an already existing communion, the members draw that much closer together. Because pain and fear are normally the most private experiences, two or more people who share them open a most intimate part of themselves to each other and can never again be strangers. A simple touch or embrace is thus more significant than words at critical times. Words, always unable fully to express experience, become inadequate. What we understand is then communicated best by the joining of bodies, which so powerfully expresses the merging of lives. The same is true, though perhaps less obviously, for moments of joy and birth. What do you say to your spouse when you hold your newborn child for the first time? What is important is the embrace and look in each other's eyes.

The same diminution of the importance of words is true even for some forms of active sharing. It is not without reason that lovers whisper sweet *nothings* during sexual intercourse. As the two become "one flesh," the most intimate and lasting of bonds is created. Thus, erotic love is the most exclusive of communions, and sexual fidelity in marriage becomes vitally important. Even common work is often carried on with long periods of silence or near-silence; yet it is nonetheless communion-building.

The first kind of active sharing involves a way of life, participation in the most significant affairs of the communion. Most elementary here are the ties created among persons by their common use of the knowledge and commitments transmitted by language and other communal symbols.[32] Each communion is a social world, separate and different from others, constituted by the communally created knowledge and symbols according to which everyday life functions. Thus all of a person's speaking and acting are textured by and bound to his groups through the language, symbols, gestures, and behaviors transmitted to him and in which he participates. This bond is so elementary that it is often not noticed. Imagine, however, a Catholic attempting to discuss his experience of salvation with a Baptist, and you will see that, despite the fundamental similarities between two Christian churches, the universes of discourse are very different and require a genuine and difficult effort of translation.

Ritual is a part of communal experience in two ways. First, ritual is itself a shared action. Expréssing common commitments through stylized and symbolic gesture, the communion acts together in the present, all members having a part. They partake together of the ritual meal, dance, songs, ceremonies, and chants. Second, ritual is most often a stylized remembrance of past experience. The experience recalled may be that of the founder(s) of the group, or of early heroes of the group, or of recent significant events in the communion's life. In sharing the ritual, members relive the experience, if it was their own originally, or live it vicariously, if it refers to the group's ancient past. Memory is a critical part of communal life, as the picture albums and nostalgic reminiscences which attend family reunions and Christmas dinners testify.

More obvious as a bond of communion is the process by which the group makes decisions. Such participation may be formal or informal, but the feeling of having an influence on the direction of common life ties a person more closely to it. Communal relations can scarcely do without this form of sharing. The successful communes of nineteenth-century America, for example, were by no means participatory democracies, but all had some forms of participation as integral parts of their commitment mechanisms.[33] Communal decision making takes us to the heart of politics, as we shall see in chapter 7.

Common work is an important and constant source of communal integration. A communion cannot be built directly but is, rather, a product of common work in the pursuit of the group's goals and purposes or of those around which prospective members have coalesced. Many contemporary communes have had very short lives because they set communion as their principal goal, not realizing that its realization has essential reference to commitments to ultimate goals and truths. C. S. Lewis points out:

> That is why those pathetic people who simply "want friends" can never make any. The very condition of having friends is that we should want something else besides friends. Where the truthful answer to the question *Do you see the same truth?* would be "I see nothing and I don't care about the truth; I only want a Friend," no Friendship can arise—though Affection of course may.[34]

Among those who see the same truth, "common action—and it must be positive action, as often as possible creative—is, in effect, the first condition for the formation of a community of friends."[35] Thus the relations among students and teachers in departments where common projects are often undertaken, such as theater and music, seem generally far more communal than in political science and history, where such group undertakings are rare. Empirical studies also suggest that cooperation in working toward higher goals more effectively brings harmony to groups with internal conflict than does social contact.[36]

Finally, a responsible person perceives particular obligations to the members of his communion and sees that they are in a similar position toward him. The web of mutual obligations to service binds communion and underlies common action and love. Love in action is responsible service to another.

Persons are responsible together, not only for each other individually, but also for the future of the whole communion. In a sense there is a communal responsibility which finds its counterpart in the individual.[37] Without such a texture of accountability, the persons move apart, and the communion itself simply drifts. Responsibility grounds common action and thus gives a dynamic thrust to commitment and love. Stagnant or drifting communions cannot hold their members.

Problems and Objections

Many objections can be raised to the picture that I have been drawing. I have attempted to construct a normative as well as a descriptive concept of communion. My account is descriptive in the sense that it reflects actual experience in communities characterized by solidarity that are committed to worthy goals. Certainly, frustration and failure occur as well, but they are endemic to all human life. The experiences I have considered distinguish communion from all other social relations and the picture, moreover, is normative; that is, it serves as a standard for human endeavor. To the extent that our communions fall short on this measure, we are enjoined to work toward it, realizing that failure will happen, but that in a good cause it can be as much of a bond as success.

There are three major objections to the concepts developed in these pages. The first is that communion is a romantic and unrealistic ideal. The second contends that conflict rather than harmony is the material of social relations. The third argues that the exclusivity of communion disqualifies it as a moral ideal.

The first objection aims at two ways in which communion has in fact often been romanticized: the idea of a future universal brotherhood based on historical progress and the idolization of the solidarity of the small, rural community. The universal brotherhood of the future stands in contrast with the strife and injustice of the present, which it wholly condemns.

The second sets the small community against the large, impersonal city.[38] Incidentally, the critics often reverse the latter comparison, committing just as serious an error as the romanticizers, by conceiving of the small town as rigid, unchanging, denying freedom, and enforcing conformity, while the metropolis is open, flexible, promoting freedom.

The characterizations in the preceding paragraph distort. Rural towns are not and have never been perfect embodiments of communion. They are divided by class and caste, by conflict and hostility, and by failure and frustration, just as large cities are. Neither, on the other hand, are villages the stifling places of uniformity sometimes pictured. Moreover, it is unrealistic and tragic to place all hopes on a future universal brotherhood, for to do so is to ignore the possibilities given in the present. Such opportunities for communion now may be limited and flawed, but they are all we have. My argument does not invest any particular past, present, or future community with all of the attributes of the normative idea. Rather, I contend only that the genuine experiences of communion, which do in fact exist, exhibit as their essential goal the qualities I have described. Many, if not most, communions are not at their best; yet they remain an essential requirement for the development of character.

The force of the objection I am considering comes from the frequent exaggerations of community in the history of political thought. Most recently, conservative thinkers have tended to distort the idea through organic metaphors. Contemporary radicals, perhaps imitating their nineteenth-century predecessors, also have been guilty of romanticizing, inventing a spontaneous, natural, harmonious community which is supposed to flower as artificial social constraints are removed. The objection gains additional force from the truth that the great temptation of communion is conformity. We are led to see togetherness as the only important value, to be maximized at all costs. Sentimentality and violence result when the experience of solidarity is loaded with ultimate expectations. When communion succumbs to this danger, it becomes frightful: conformity ensues, and the personal space and freedom of each member are trampled. Commitment switches from truth to a dogma, defining a "righteous" society. Love for the brethren becomes hatred of outsiders.[39]

These are the temptations of communion and those who believe in it, just as anarchism and meaninglessness are the pitfalls of liberalism. Neither group must succumb, though, sadly, some advocates do. My theory seeks to build resistance by stressing that communion, valuable as it is, is not everything. Individual character is, in the last analysis, the test of communion, measured by developing solitude, responsibility, and commitment in the members. Communion is judged as well by its own faithfulness to its transcendent goal which, humility teaches, will always beckon, since it will never be attained. Humility is the best defense against the lure of pseudocommunity.

The second major objection, similar to the first, protests that it is unreasonable and contrary to the evidence of society to build social theories on the idea of harmony. Interest conflict, rather, is the heart of human relations. Ralf Dahrendorf, for example, professes that power (particularly when it is unequal) and resistance are fundamental to social life and should be to social theory. Since harmony and equilibrium so rarely occur, nothing is gained by making them the basic assumption of political theory. The norms of society are to be explained by the interests of the powerful and by the sanctions which their power is able to bring to bear. Dahrendorf further argues that "equilibrium" theory also fails as a normative theory of politics, for its implicit assumption of certainty is a deadly weapon against freedom in a changing society. Conflict theory, on the other hand, incorporates freedom and change.[40]

Dahrendorf's objection misses the mark on a number of counts. First, the theory of communion outlined here does not purport to be a complete social theory. Attention to conflict may very well explain most social relations. My argument is simply that it does not account for all of them; the relationships described in this chapter do in fact occur. Further, I maintain that the deep importance of such relationships in the growth of character is often overlooked and that the goal of politics is to promote them. Second, I recognize that political order perhaps most often falls short of the pursuit of communion. Such failure does not disqualify it as a norm, just as man's repeated inability to love his neighbor as himself does not invalidate that commandment as a norm. Moreover, I recognize, as should be evident in my response to the charge of romanticism, that even communal relations will inevitably manifest coercion and conflict, as do all relations among finite men. Indeed, these forces are not essentially bad; they have a necessary and beneficial role in communion. Fully committed members of a scientific community may legitimately disagree strongly over the next step in their pursuit of the truth. Punishment of children properly proceeds from love. Yet conflict, disagreement, coercion, and resistance do not define the communion; they occur within a communion structured by solidarity, common commitment, love, and shared experience.

The third objection to communion is that it is narrow, defined as much by exclusion as by inclusion. Often persons are deeply hurt when they cannot join. Someone may unsuccessfully attempt to become part of a particular friendship, perhaps despite the best wishes of the friends. An Episcopalian is told that he may not receive the Eucharist (Communion) at a Roman Catholic service. A young woman who deeply desires to join a certain sorority is not admitted. A relationship which denies unity and causes so much pain cannot, it may be argued, serve as a social or political norm.

That community as solidarity is naturally exclusive cannot be denied. "Loyalty has an inherent propensity toward exclusionism and aggressiveness."[41] Fraternity and friendship as well require exclusivity, proceeding from two sources: the mystery of emotional ties and the requirement of commitment. The former is clearest in friendship and erotic love. Two persons may be similar in many respects, may share central commitments, may desire to be friends, and may even take steps designed to effect the liaison. Yet they may fail; some mysterious emotional spark is lacking. A man and a woman may be strongly attracted to each other and even wish to become lovers, but the chemistry is wrong. The reason for such miscarriages is a mystery, but clearly there is nothing evil or sinister about it.

Similarly, there is nothing bad about the exclusivity of communion based on commitment. Membership is intentional: one must accept the commitments which bind the group. Exclusivity's relation to commitment can be seen in the mechanisms discussed above. Renunciation, for example, requires that members sever relations which are incompatible with group unity. Sacrifice and investment (and often suffering) bring persons to the point where they must join or decline membership. Various initiation rites (baptism, for example) signal that a person is no longer an outsider. It is significant that affirmation of the goodness of the communion in fact more effectively promotes communal survival than does the supposed evil of those outside.[42]

When a person desires on many grounds to enter into communion with others and does not share the required commitment, his rejection is tragic, a sign of the finitude of human existence. Yet the lack is in him, not in the communion. Moreover, the wish to include others is often present in communities of solidarity. Indeed, the presence of such a desire seems to me an important sign of the worth of the object of commitment. Christian communities, for example, are called to be evangelical, to spread the good news, and to baptize all men. Communions built around political ideals are also characterized by their efforts to recruit new members. Large, extended families are often the ones most ready to welcome a stranger for dinner. Fifth-century Athens possessed a strong sense of identity and solidarity, yet it also contained a very sizable foreign population. Similarly, the city and the monastery in the Middle Ages were more ready than other social institutions to welcome outsiders. Communions are far less hostile to newcomers than are pseudocommunities or social groups. Thus, despite its natural exclusivity, the experience of communion also contains within it a reaching out to others under certain conditions. Moreover, the counterpart of the community as solidarity is hospitality.

Hospitality

"[Y]ou should make hospitality your special care" (Rom. 12:13). Why? We speak casually of southern hospitality, of hospitality suites at airports or conventions, and of hospitable hosts. Good manners enjoin hospitality, but what kind of special significance can it have? Hospitality, as I use the term in this book, refers to a form of community. It goes far beyond the ordinary meanings of kindness and comfort to the classical and biblical obligation to strangers who carry mysterious gifts and promises. Abraham's welcome to three "strangers" at Mamre is the occasion for the announcement that Sarah will give birth to a son. The actions of Baucis and Philemon earn them a special reward from Jupiter and Mercury.[43]

A major semantic difficulty, of course, is that English has no word for the relationship of mutual hospitality. The term is ordinarily used to refer to a personal disposition or behavior pattern denoting generosity and receptivity to guests. This meaning, of course, is central in my usage. I wish, however, to extend the word to cover the experience of mutual hospitality, a use of the term derived principally from Henri J. M. Nouwen but also equivalent to Tinder's use of "community."[44] I agree with Tinder that hospitality is a central form of community, but I believe that he neglects what I have called "communion" or community as solidarity.

As a personal quality, hospitality is generous receptivity to others, a fundamental attitude toward fellow human beings. As a relationship, it is an encounter of character between two or more persons with such receptivity. It is, Nouwen says, an open, free space where strangers may meet, live without fear, and become friends. In hospitality fearful newcomers can become guests, revealing the promise they bring with them in depth of character. Tinder, I believe, expresses much the same idea. "Through communication, persons associate with one another as independent and rational beings." In so doing, the essential qualities of persons, responsibility and veracity, become the grounds of union. "Community must come into being when the internal relationships of veracity and responsibility are externalized."[45] In the resulting relationship persons must be allowed the room or space to be themselves responsible and truthful.

What C. S. Lewis calls gift-love, or charity, is the center of this kind of community. Unlike the bond in communions, which always has a ground in some attractive quality of the other members, this love is a gift of self to another, no matter how "unlovable." Hospitality is thus unlike communion in important ways. The persons in such a relationship need not feel togetherness, belonging, or solidarity. They feel welcome (after all, "make yourself at home" is the most frequent initial expression of hospitality), but not necessarily because they feel bound to each other. Thus the bonds of hospitality are not those of communion. There is no common commitment, except to truth and responsibility; that is, each must have a developed character and bring it to the relationship. "When we want to be really hospitable we not only have to receive strangers but also to confront them by an unambiguous presence, not hiding ourselves behind neutrality but showing our ideas, opinions and life styles clearly and distinctly."[46] But persons in such a relationship need not believe the same things, be committed to the same faith, or possess the same values, purposes, and goals. Hospitality is impossible if I require continual tests of ideological purity.

In the same way, the emotional attachments characteristic of communion need not be present in hospitality. Host and guest, clerk and customer, teacher and student, need not feel affection, eros, or friendship for each other. They can nevertheless be mutually open and receptive. Certainly, such a community need not possess shared experiences, work, or participation. It need not have rituals or symbols in common. Indeed, when hospitality occurs between strangers, such past sharing is obviously impossible. Even lack of a common language is no barrier to hospitality, as the experiences of hosts receiving visitors or refugees from other countries demonstrate.

Because hospitality differs in these important ways from communion, it is safe from the dangers associated with pseudocommunity. An open and free space is required for encounter; therefore, I cannot attempt to reduce the other to a simple role or mask of his character. To do so would be to avoid a genuine meeting with him. Shared commitments, loves, and experiences cannot tempt the members of such a community to destroy the freedom demanded by hospitality. The host who destroys this space by attempting to fill his guest's every moment with talk, activity, and entertainment is not hospitable but fearfully insecure.[47] Because hospitality is room for the encounter of characters, each of which is formed by commitments, the possibility of conversion is always present, but to demand conversion as the price for hospitality is to deny its very essence. Exclusivity plays no part in community as hospitality.

Thus hospitality is different from communion. Yet since both are forms of community, they are the same in significant ways. First, each relationship unites persons in essential being. Communion is a union in solidarity and significance, hospitality in communication of heart to heart. Second, hospitality may be transformed into communion. Indeed, the more open, or hospitable, a person, the more likely he is to have friends. Friendship does not inevitably or even frequently result, but it may do so.

Third, while hospitality does not necessitate communion, communion does require hospitality. I must be hospitable not only to strangers but also to friends. Indeed, the "stranger" who needs my generosity may often be found in my own home.[48] Forgiveness and reconciliation, the healing of broken communion, is the special province of hospitality. If I reach out only to strangers and neglect my own family, trusting to solidarity to sustain the relationship, either it will decay and communion disintegrate, or so much demand will be placed on solidarity that conformity will begin. Uniformity is the temptation of community as solidarity, which is overcome by hospitality. Thus there can be no question of "balancing" communion and hospitality. Hospitality is so closely linked to the requirements of character that it is a foundation of communion, related to it because truth and responsibility are bonds and requirements of each.

A few words should be said here about the requirements and bonds of hospitality. Hospitality requires, first of all, tolerance, not in the ordinary sense but rather in the sense developed by Tinder.[49] Tolerance here is not the principally negative phenomenon of not interfering with a person, which often degenerates into unconcern for the other. Rather, it is a personal attitude or a social condition of attentiveness. If hospitality is the encounter of two persons, then each must be receptive to what the other brings; each must attend to what the other is saying or feeling, which may mean listening to implications as well as to the words.

Because it requires such presence, tolerance or attentiveness should not be confused with an image of the open person as merely an absorbent sponge. The attentive person genuinely considers what the other brings but responds from the depth of his own character. Tolerance means not unconditional acceptance, but a concern for the other which entails a genuine consideration of the offering.

The mention of response indicates that tolerance demands responsibility, which is communal, since one must be prepared to answer for the way he is going, for who he is, and for what he believes. Thus responsibility is a bond of hospitality just as it is of communion. Unlike communion, hospitality is necessarily inclusive. It welcomes the stranger and recognizes that he is entitled to a response expressing genuine concern for him as a human being. I must be prepared in every interaction with another to acknowledge this claim on me, to acknowledge the other as a whole person. Most often, simply a kind word, a smile, a helping hand will do, but sometimes more is asked. A student, responding to attentive and receptive teaching, may ask for advice about some personal trouble. An exchange of greetings between airline passengers may lead to a discussion of personal significance for each.

Hospitality insists that those encountered daily be treated as persons, not as machines, roles, servants, or obstacles. Obviously this is extremely

difficult when life is hectic, when social relations seem deliberately impersonal, and when we are frequently obstinate and closed to response.
Tolerance and hospitality thus require great patience, prudence, humility,—and solitude, for there the habits of listening and receptivity are
developed.[50] So often the plea of another for dialogue seems only a
maddening interruption in a neatly planned schedule. Solitude transforms
life into more than a series of tasks. Hospitality also requires solitude as
the space in which a person encounters his own fears, desires, self-
doubts, and hostilities. I must recognize and deal with them before I can
be hospitable. Without such inner knowledge I can only regard the
stranger as a potential thief who will rob me of my precious possessions.
Thus to be poor in spirit helps, since it takes away fear that our precious
possessions, spiritual or material, will be lost in the encounter.[51]

Finally, community as hospitality requires openness to the truth. First,
attentiveness assumes that the other brings something of value to the
encounter. It assumes that the truth to which I have committed myself
may be incomplete and in need of correction, or even transformation,
from the truth the other may carry. Often, of course, the other may care
little or nothing for the truth, but when both persons in a relationship of
hospitality do care, then a real union between them is possible. "Only in
the supposition that most people are disposed toward truth essentially as
you are yourself is there any sense in opening yourself up to them in
fairness and tolerance."[52] A community based on free discussion is
necessarily committed to the search for truth. The second reason why
truth is a bond of hospitality is that the appeal and the effort required to be
attentive to other persons depend upon a sense of eternity. In classical
mythology and in Scripture, strangers seeking hospitality are usually
gods in disguise. Hospitality assumes that there is a transcendent reality,
accessible to the search for truth, because the existence of such a reality
is the only justification for treating each person with the respect and
reverence that each being deserves.[53]

As described, hospitality is a burdensome attitude for an individual.
Because it is so difficult to sustain, it is relatively rare. Openness to
another, particularly to a stranger, is awkward, because his separateness
must be fully recognized. He may reject me, mock me, or harm me for the
commitments I have revealed. It is much easier for me to keep myself
closed or to ignore the other's separateness and to assume that he is just
like members of my circle. It is also for this reason that hospitality must
extend even to members of our communions. Though they are like us in
fundamental ways, our fellows always retain a separateness and uniqueness which must be acknowledged.

Hospitality is not, then, simply a blessing.[54] It demands acceptance of
social differences, idiosyncrasies, estrangements, anxieties, and ten-

sions which we may strongly wish to erase or ignore. Tolerance and hospitality are not easy to sustain between persons who, individually, wish to flee the relationship or to smash the necessary barriers to communion. Hospitality demands a sense of finitude, a readiness to forgive, and commitment (as well as tolerance of differences of commitment). Yet it must become a fundamental orientation if personal relations are to be more than indifferent, impersonal, and pseudocommunal.

There are, then, two valid conceptions of community important to political and social theory: communion and hospitality. Each signifies a genuine experience of union, but their characteristics demonstrate how each is necessary for the development of character and how character is a requirement for building and maintaining them.

4

Character and Community

In chapter 2, I considered man alone; more precisely, I examined the character of man in solitude, commitment, and responsibility. To embrace solitude and its dialogue, to be committed to truth, and to be responsible is to be human. In chapter 3, I considered man in community, in the solidarity of communion, and in the encounter of hospitality. Solitude, commitment, and responsibility were seen as part of those relationships also. Now I shall bring these themes together. Throughout the previous chapters I have hinted at reciprocity, but I have avoided developing the theme because it was not possible to do so until the fullness of character and community had been disclosed.

My analysis has four principal parts. I shall demonstrate that communion is essential to the development of character. Persons deprived of communion will fail to find solitude, commitment, and responsibility unless they encounter frequently those rare displays of hospitality which can midwife the birth of character. Second, I shall argue that communion is impossible unless its members possess the qualities of mature character. Pseudocommunity is the normal result of solidarity among persons lacking solitude, responsibility, and commitment. Third, I shall consider how hospitality contributes to the formation of character. Hospitality confirms the results of nurture in communion and, in rare cases, may substitute for communion. It allows space for persons to develop solitude, to test and examine their commitments, and to treat each other with the usages of responsible persons. Finally, I shall indicate how hospitality is possible only between persons who possess maturity of character or are growing toward maturity.

In what follows, as in what has preceded, I use the terms character, communion, and hospitality in a normative sense. Character is never fully formed; we are never completely responsible, never fully at home in solitude. Thus when I speak of character as the condition of communion, I use a shorthand way of saying that only persons with a certain degree of character, persons striving toward the norm, are capable of entering into communion. Similarly, communion and hospitality are never complete. Even the perfect host occasionally does too much or too little for his guests. Mature persons sometimes shrink from interior dialogue. Carey McWilliams means something close to this:

> Fraternal relations do not reveal identity to the individual: they provide him with the assurance of identity which is necessary for him to seek to know its nature. . . .
>   . . . the possibility of moving forward in the search for identity requires the support of persons who assure our identity anew—not as authority might, by giving us the conviction of a new, "known" self, but by stimulating us to seek the self which remains unknown.[1]

There are varying degrees of achievement of character, communion, and hospitality, but a substantial degree is the condition for the possibility of the relations described below. Finally, I do not contend that character is entirely shaped by community. Each person is ultimately responsible, unless insanity or severe mental retardation intervenes, for his own life. My argument is that community is a necessary condition for the emergence of maturity.

The importance of community for maturity is suggested by the human needs for belonging and significance. These are not elements of character, but their centrality to human life may serve as an introduction to our theme. Individuals dominated by the need to belong acutely feel the absence of affectionate relations with others and seek an established place in group or family.[2] As a result we have seen the tremendous increase of communes and intentional communities in recent years. Communities of total commitment provide the psychic rewards associated with the need to belong. The "battle brotherhoods" desperately sought and formed among soldiers in combat also bear "pathetic witness to the fact that individualism is not enough, and that men will seek for some modicum, even a phantasm, of fraternity."[3]

The need to belong, then, is profoundly important in human life, demanding communion and hospitality, a place where one can be at home. When we feel the pain of not belonging, we do not require objects but the warmth, recognition, and acceptance which only another person can give. Anyone who has shared such relations deeply and for a substantial part of his life knows that he belongs, even when he is apart from others, even when he is rejected by some. One who has not is likely to seek acceptance in pseudocommunity.

Closely associated with belonging is significance. Persons also need to feel that they have a special place and an important role in social life, that somehow their achievement has contributed to the well-being of a group.[4] The acceptance, love, and affection of communion, as well as its shared commitments and experiences, inculcate in the individual the sense that he is needed, that his presence makes a difference in the life of the group. The tragic cry "Nobody cares whether I live or die" points to the centrality of the search for significance and the care which satisfies it. Such care can be provided also in the context of hospitality, but the effort required is greater. The foster home, the psychiatrist's office, and the confessional frequently must be the occasions for the long and difficult task of helping another to recognize that he is important, that he can make a contribution, and that others care for him.

Hospitality also has a special role here. The evaluations of me made by kin and friends are obviously biased. Nevertheless, they are too important to ignore or reject; on the other hand, I cannot depend wholly on these valuations. Praise from a source itself respected for its objectivity is often more important than that from parents. The giver of esteem must be respected by the beneficiary; otherwise the kind words will be received as flattery or loquacity.[5] The context of hospitality, then, in which strangers meet on a common ground of acceptance and respect, can play a most important role in meeting the need for significance.

Communion and Character

Human life is irresistibly social. Individuals are conscious of themselves as persons only in social contexts. It makes no sense, therefore, for someone to regard himself as the center of the universe. Even individual talents and achievements are, partially, at least, gifts of society. Am I healthy? Who taught me to eat properly? Am I intelligent? Who introduced me to the world of signs and symbols, words and books? Am I in love? Who taught me to love? I can claim very little credit in such matters. Family, friends, and schools have led me into these realms. As Ortega y Gasset says, "The essence of living is that man is always existing within an environment, that he finds himself—suddenly and without knowing how he got there—projected into and submerged in a world, a set of fixed surroundings, into this present, which is now about us."[6] Thrust into a world, man is forced to interpret it; he does so using the ready-made symbols which culture has provided and which he necessarily confronts. Of course, such a view is not new. Aristotle knew that a man outside the polis is either a beast or a god. To be human is to be in relationship with others. The Judaeo-Christian tradition goes further than Aristotle, affirming that it is God's nature to be in community. Israel showed "that the real God is the God who can be addressed because He is the God who addresses."[7]

That man is essentially social is a commonplace, but it is often denied in thought and practice. In chapter 1, I pointed out various intellectual positions espoused by people who seek a self apart and attempt to evade all social roles and responsibilities. The effort is either futile or productive of mental illness and misery, but it is nonetheless real. So a few words should be said about the sociality of man before I turn more specifically to his communality.

Persons first meet the larger society in the neighborhood, because there they first experience persons, social rituals, and experiences beyond the narrow limits of family. In this encounter the personality of the child is strongly affected. If we do not believe so, why do we seek to live in "good" neighborhoods with "good" schools? As Ruth Benedict has said: "The social arrangements are never just something outside the individual. The possibilities or impossibilities they create become his possibilities or · impossibilities; they are internalized in men and women."[8] Such internalization is entirely normal and necessary. Without limits, character cannot be shaped. Though the possibilities provided by society do not determine character, they define it, provide it with alternatives and models without which character could not exist. If there could be human beings without social restraint, without character, we could never recognize them as persons.

Such language demands care. People are not simply collections of roles. In chapter 2, I argued that the dialogue between role and center, the commitments which ground roles, and the responsibility with which a person lives the roles accepted define character. On the other hand, roles make it possible for society to exist, both by forming individuals and by making it possible for social institutions to exist.

Character grows as a social product, its emergence mediated by "significant others." They induct the person into rituals and experiences, teach him his roles and responsibilities, and monitor his development. Human activity becomes, to a large degree, habitualized and institutionalized. To deplore the process is a mistake, because it has the important purpose of providing a stable background against which important choices can be made and of freeing time and energy for creative action. Only total routinization is to be regretted. Without regular, socially defined habits of scholarship, I could not write this book, nor could you read it. The importance of models of behavior is well known, even in social psychology.[9]

The most important means of participation in the life of society is through symbols, particularly language. Nisbet argues, "We must think of symbolic interaction as forming the very stuff of human personality, character, self, and identity. Only through communication in terms of shared symbols is it possible for each of us to acquire his sense of self, character, and identity."[10]

Speech, the most important form of symbolic expression, brings a broad range of social activity into my experience, enabling me both to understand and to participate. Language helps me locate myself in the world and know myself better. Thus, according to Aristotle, man is ultimately distinguished from other creatures: he is fully himself only in the polis, which is constituted by common speech about justice and injustice.[11] Susanne K. Langer affirms the same truth: "Symbolism is the recognized key to that mental life which is characteristically human and above the level of sheer animality."[12] And symbols are inherently social. You cannot, like Humpty-Dumpty, make words mean what you alone say. Like other symbols they are created by communication about common experience that uses signs possessing a jointly agreed-upon meaning. And the meanings define the world experienced, so that different languages describe different worlds.[13]

The creation of language is not simply the making of a tool, for example, a hatchet, the use of which produces greater individual benefits. Rather, language is the indispensable means for developing both character and community. It enables me to carry on the dialogue between center and masks which establishes character. Through symbols, I define, understand, and explore my commitments, interpret the claims which others make on me, and reflect on my responsibility to respond to them. At the same time, language is a medium of pure companionship. When friends are together, their speech is a bond of communion between them. "Language was the outcome of man's need to affirm solidarity with his own kind."[14] Commitments are put into words, and experiences are shared when men talk about them. The contemporary debasement of language and the loss of a community of discourse, therefore, have dangerous consequences. Without a common language, men face each other as strangers, as potential enemies. Simone Weil observes, "To clarify thought, to discredit the intrinsically meaningless words, and to define the use of others precisely—to do this, strange though it may appear, might be a way of saving human lives."[15]

Thus far, I have shown only that human life is essentially social, not that it is communal. In general terms, there is evidence for dependence on communion in everyday experience. The mature, responsible individuals we know seem to have been raised in an atmosphere of love, care, discipline, and responsibility. They have had the benefit of a strong and healthy family life or, lacking it, have been fortunate to find these qualities in friends, teachers, or counselors. Such observations are confirmed by the child psychologist Selma H. Fraiberg, who states that the development of self-esteem, conscience, and responsibility is a product of family. Children raised in institutions do not develop these qualities as rapidly or as fully as people raised in families.[16] Conversely, we can see the importance of communion for character in the pathologies of modern mental illness. These are reflected in the phenomenal growth of therapeutic communities—communes, religious sects, and encounter and sensitivity training groups. Such groups can be viewed as part-time or full-time communities or quasi-communities designed to repair the psychic damage inflicted on character by a society in which the "natural" communions of family, church, locality, and friendship are disintegrating. Sociologists and psychologists have long seen mental illness, confusion, loneliness, and frustration as resulting, at least in part, from the breakdown of community, family, and the moral web of social life. Daily observation affirms that many lonely, confused, and insecure individuals have tragic family histories.

The argument just stated is open to the objection that experience also acquaints us with mature individuals who have grown up in very stifling families. In addition, over time we see persons of extraordinary strength who have emerged from situations of crisis and conflict, even of tyranny. Alexandr Solzhenitsyn comes first to mind. At the same time, "fine" families occasionally produce severely disturbed persons. Is the connection between communion and character essential or only a probability or even folk wisdom? A number of replies can be made. First, while family is of prime importance in shaping character, it is not the only influence. Persons whose families are anticommunal often find communion among friends, within a church or other social group, or in school. Communion in such settings can make up many deficiencies in family life. Second, the emergence of character in tyrannical societies should not be surprising, since communion cannot be wholly suppressed. The combination of strong communion and adversity may, in fact, tend to produce a few individuals of singular, even heroic, character. Third, the emergence of weakness or of severe personality disorder in seemingly excellent families may be accounted for by deceptive appearances, by the negative influence of other groups and individuals, by severe psychological trauma, or by physiological/genetic disorders. Finally, the general assertions stated in favor of and against the connection of communion and character all remain general and impressionistic unless supported by theoretical arguments grounded in the essential elements of character and of communion, which do supply strong reason to accept the connection.

Solitude might seem to be the quality of character which owes the least to communion and in fact might seem to owe nothing, being wholly occupied with the soul. Yet without communion, solitude becomes loneliness. To show why communion is so important, I shall first examine prayer as a particular activity of solitude. Prayer is often but not necessarily an activity of solitude; there are various forms that are common. Nor is prayer the only activity of solitude. Yet our most frequent images of places of prayer are solitary—a quiet room, hermitage, mountain, forest, desert. "He went up on the mountain by himself to pray" (Matt. 14:23). When we pray alone, the dialogue of center and masks reaches out to include God. What had formerly seemed part of the center of character is now seen as mask. Masks which had seemed compatible with center are now seen as false. Such discoveries about character are frightening; their acceptance requires courage. Though in the New Testament God can be addressed as a loving Father, in the Old Testament the danger of contact with Him is clear. "When he heard this, Elijah hid his face in his cloak and went and stood at the entrance of the cave" (1 Kings 19:13). "Then I said, 'Woe is me, I am doomed! For I am a man of unclean lips, living among a people of unclean lips; yet my eyes have seen the King, the Lord of hosts!' " (Isa. 6:5). The dialogue of prayer in solitude allows no illusions about character; it seems to break all securities and certitudes.

For this reason, prayer requires communion. "Just because prayer is the most precious expression of being human, it needs the constant support and protection of the community to grow and flower."[17] In a common faith lie the "protective boundaries" where the person of prayer can heed his deepest longings, listen for God, and find the courage to accept and the language to understand that Voice. It is also in the communion of faith that the person learns how to address a Father, just as a child must learn how to communicate with its parents.

Prayer and solitude are the occasions for spiritual growth, but models and guides are needed. All mystical traditions, the Eastern and the Western, stress the importance of a director, a guru, for anyone who would embark on the journey. The same lesson is evident in the lives of the towering spiritual figures of history—Buddha, Socrates, Moses, Elijah, Jeremiah, Christ, St. Francis of Assisi, and the Hasidim of Elie Wiesel's *Souls on Fire*. All were marked by a direct and soul-shaking encounter with God, but all were trained for it in communions of faith, and all formed communions around themselves. Thus Simone Weil can say: "Nothing among human things has such power to keep our gaze fixed ever more intensely upon God, than friendship for the friends of God." She says so despite her belief that the soul must detach itself from all worldly things to meet God and to love universally.[18]

Solitude transcends the masks of character without abandoning them. Such transcendence is always a response to a call, a vocation to go beyond the superficial layers of life to encounter what I am beyond my masks. Such a call must be mediated by intimate others, who care for me despite my poses. They encourage me to become the mature person I am potentially, and they teach me the language of the dialogue of solitude. Society indeed forms me, but its purposes are served if I merely wear the appropriate mask at the appropriate time. The fellows of my

communions, however, cannot be satisfied with that, because they realize that we are jointly called to seek the truth and explore the dimensions
of our common commitments and experiences. Masks alone cannot
answer such a challenge.

Self-knowledge does not come from self-scrutiny; it is a gift from others.
In solitude we open that gift. The person of character can enter solitude
because his participation in a communion of love, inquiry, worship, or
friendship is the foundation of his transcendence of the masks of character. This participation is also the ground of his ability to unite the various
parts of himself in harmony with what he has discovered in the experience
of solitude. His communion provides models of others who have achieved
self-knowledge. Those persons of solitude who seem like aliens in their
own society can be understood from this perspective. Their alienation is
not that of lonely and isolated persons who desperately seek affection,
esteem, and security but are afraid of relationships with others. Rather,
they are whole persons who are called out of conventional society by the
higher values of a better communion.[19]

The support and the symbolic language learned in communion assist
solitude in another way. They allow us some distance from ourselves, a
place to stand in judgment. Conscience, for example, is at least partly the
ability to judge oneself and is facilitated by the distance we can achieve
from our masks.[20] Such distancing is a prerequisite for the solitary dialogue. For all of the reasons above, solitude depends upon communion.

Commitment, too, grows in the context of communion. Commitment to
truth and to ideals and principles, confidence in and loyalty to a center of
value, is not only a bond of communion but also communion's gift to
character. Schaar observes:

> Loyalty, then, is a great good from the standpoint of community. It is equally
> good from the standpoint of the individual as it gives him an ease of com-
> munication with his fellows and a set of goals which help impart purpose to
> his life. Through loyalty one becomes related to something outside of and
> larger than himself. And, through this connection, life acquires meaning and
> direction.[21]

The commitments to a communion and to a truth are correlative. In other
words, the ability to commit oneself to truth which forms character is
possible only by committing oneself to others who honor the same truth.
Saint-Exupéry says:

> Happiness! It is useless to seek it elsewhere than in this warmth of human
> relations. Our sordid interests imprison us within their walls. Only a comrade
> can grasp us by the hand and haul us free. . . .
>   No man can draw a free breath who does not share with other men a

common and disinterested ideal. Life has taught us that love does not consist in gazing at each other, but in looking outward together in the same direction. There is no comradeship except through union in the same high effort.[22]

Brothers teach us our ideals and hold us to them.

There are two reasons why commitment requires a communal context. The first is practical. Adherence to the truth and to the ideals implied in commitment is difficult. Falsehood is a constant temptation. Support, then, is required to teach and exhort the person to uphold and follow his commitments. The communion also provides models of persons who have succeeded in adhering to the faith. And it provides emotional stimuli as well. The believer does not want to let down his fellow believers, and he fears the shame and reproach which may follow from his failure. Such communal support is particularly necessary in a pluralist society, because countermodels and constant temptations are immediately available. The dilemmas of the college freshman away from home for the first time are instructive.

The second, theoretical reason why commitment demands communion turns upon the relationship of communion and authority to truth. Alone one cannot discover or pledge loyalty to truth or a value center. Faith is essentially communal. The basis of this assertion is Polanyi's epistemology, of which this principle is a central tenet. "[O]ur adherence to the truth can be seen to imply our adherence to a society which respects the truth, and which we trust to respect it."[23] Persons never discover truth unaided and never commit themselves to it without at the same time committing themselves to a communion of fellow believers.

The discussion of this assertion can be foreshadowed in a consideration of what Berger and Luckmann refer to as symbolic universes, "bodies of theoretical tradition that integrate different provinces of meaning and encompass the institutional order in a symbolic totality."[24] Commitment to a center of worth is mediated by the symbolic universes developed by different communions. Access to the object of commitment is possible only through such a universe. Thus commitment as a fundamental element of character is necessarily linked to communion. The symbolic universe is a social product, but it is transmitted to a person and maintained in him through his particular communions, through those whom Berger and Luckmann call significant others, who represent the universe. In other words, friends, neighbors, relatives, and fellow members initiate the person into the basic principles of his commitment. The Ground of Being can be discovered not alone but only with the assistance of the symbols of a tradition of faith and inquiry, as mediated by the members of particular communions committed to the same faith.

The centrality of communion can be seen as well in the experiences of revolt against one commitment and of conversion to another. As Elie Wiesel reminds us, "The revolt of the believer is not that of the renegade; the two do not speak in the name of the same anguish."[25] The believer suffers but remains in the communion; the renegade must undergo the additional anguish of rupturing his bonds with his fellow believers. Thus conversion to a new symbolic universe requires attachment to new significant others. The potential convert leaves his old world of family, friends, and comrades and becomes immersed intellectually and emotionally in a new one. Thus Moonies seem like strangers to their parents.

The centrality I have been discussing does not mean that the person may be a member of only one communion defined by a particular faith and excluding all others. Since communions centered on the ultimate object of faith tend toward universality, involving the whole person and integrating his most significant experiences, one communion will tend to occupy the most prominent place in a person's life. But the person may and should, at the same time, be a member of a number. Such multiple membership has the advantages of pluralism; the memberships will not be dissonant so long as their commitments are the same or complementary.

Responsibility, too, is essentially grounded in communion and related to truth, just as commitment is. Character demands truthfulness to self and to others. Truthfulness toward others is learned first in communion. The lie is so destructive of communion because its basis is intimate sharing. Intimacy is destroyed or blocked when deception and falsehood permeate a relationship. To lie is to close communication in order to hide the self. Thus in families, in friendships, and in other intimate associations, the growing person learns the effect of falsehood when he commits it himself and when he is victim.

Responsibility, moreover, involves the ability to listen to the other, for responsibility means the virtue of answering in truth the call of the other. Learning to listen and to identify sympathetically with the other are characteristics of communion because the members can most easily see themselves in another's place. They are like one another in important ways. "John, how would you like it if your brother took your bat and ball?" The family teaches responsibility and empathy first. The most difficult part of moral responsibility is to transfer this empathy from friend and brother to stranger and enemy. But it cannot be transferred until it has been learned. "Charity begins at home," not merely because our first duty is to our brother, but because unless we have learned to love him, we cannot love others. Love for the brother is by no means a given, since he often becomes an enemy, but it must be learned as the condition of responsible character. Love is the greatest gift and the greatest responsibility, demanding an ability to recognize itself when it appears and to recognize its proper embodiment when it is required.

Communion is a place to learn responsibility, so that action may reach out beyond the limits of self to other men, both within and outside communion. But community is also a refuge when I fail and when I am afraid. I can never be perfectly responsible. Invariably, emotion or desire, sin or failure, inattentiveness or preoccupation, will prevent me from responding as I should to the claim of another. Then I need the support of friends and comrades to bear me up and to give me the confidence to try again.[26] Communion, unlike pseudocommunity, gives me space and freedom and thus responsibility. It enhances my capacity for responsible action. So it rejoices with me when I succeed and weeps with me when I fail.

Communion also calls forth responsibility because it depends upon common participation. Such participation, of course, takes many forms—decision making, a place in a ritual dance, soldiering, motherhood, and so forth. Participation contributes to character formation because it places responsibilities on the participant. One who takes part in a communal decision must take responsibility for it; indeed, he will be held accountable. One who has a role in ritual or liturgy knows that its success depends upon him. Acceptance of the roles of parent or lover, worker or warrior, means acceptance of the responsibilities implied. Indeed, acceptance of a role in the community may inspire a person to levels of excellence not otherwise achievable as he rises to fulfill its duties. A soldier, for example, may learn bravery; a parent, self-sacrifice.[27] The communal context is central here, because duties are undertaken voluntarily and maturely, because of the freedom associated with community. Pseudocommunity and other forms of social relations may involve duties, but they are imposed rather than accepted and so have no necessary relation to responsibility.

"With all its difficulties, fraternity is vital to anyone who would find himself and who knows that no one can do so alone."[28] Communion does not account for the whole of character but is vital in its formation.

Character and Communion

I have attempted to demonstrate that character is formed in communion. The converse is also true. The intimate associations of persons possessing or developing maturity of character tend to be communions. Immature persons tend to create pseudocommunities, or they fail to unite intimately at all. As Plato observed, human associations grow not from stones and trees but from the souls of their inhabitants.

This generalization is confirmed by ordinary experience. Individuals who, insofar as it is humanly possible, are totally caught up in one or more social roles fail to form communities of solidarity with their fellows. Such persons always meet on the surface of life; they are incapable of solidarity, whether of communion or pseudocommunity, because they are incapable of sharing themselves or giving themselves. They give and share a handshake or even an embrace because their roles call for it or their passions demand it, not because they wish to experience unity with another. Such is the case of the wife who submits to sexual intercourse with her husband "because a good wife is supposed to satisfy her husband's needs." It is also the case of a father who takes his children on an outing "because a good father spends some time with his kids." The saying "but his heart was not in it" reveals a deep truth. Such relationships may from the outside appear to be communions, but inside they are full of division, pain, and sadness. And acquaintances, surprised by the divorce proceedings, say, "But they seemed like such a happy family."

I do not mean to condemn adhering to roles and their duties. Man cannot live without roles. It is better for a wife or husband to follow a role than to hate or ignore spouse and children. But living merely in this way is not fully human life, and unless it is integrated with the heart, the center of character, through solitude, commitment, and responsibility, the relationship cannot be communal. Even persons who join together with the explicit goal of creating a community will fail if they individually lack commitment and responsibility. In theological terms: "Sin denies fraternity because sin denies humanity and dehumanizes. And since sin is the first condition of man, man by himself is a stranger to his brother."[29] Irresponsibility lies at the heart of sin, as the story of man's first sin demonstrates. The person who merely plays his roles and follows his duty never knows his brothers.

Communion thus requires its members to be persons of solitude, more than mere collections of roles. A person who knows himself through the dialogue of center and masks has a heart which he can share with others in communion. Because he can give himself in intimacy, he can receive the gift of another and form a communion with him. Nouwen says:

> When we do not protect with great care our own inner mystery, we will never be able to form community. It is this inner mystery that attracts us to each other and allows us to establish friendship and develop lasting relationships of love. An intimate relationship between people not only asks for mutual openness, but also for mutual respectful protection of each other's uniqueness.[30]

There is a further reason why persons of undeveloped character are incapable of communion. Some persons are dominated more by their basic needs for security, self-esteem, and belonging than by their social roles. Such persons desperately seek or demand friendship, love, and togetherness in order to fill the empty space in their hearts. When such persons find each other, they cling together fearfully in dread of the emptiness outside. Such persons cannot allow others any room, privacy, or solitude, for fear that they will slip away. Honesty and truth are also frightening, because they might lead away from the group, might leave one alone and subject to ridicule. Hence they are sacrificed for the sake of uniformity. Commitment and responsibility, which depend on honesty and truth, become impossible. The attachment of individuals to pseudo-community rooted in a desperate belonging need is a mockery of the genuine commitment of character which facilitates the mutual commitment and responsibility of communion. Again, examples from family life are only too familiar: the adult who is a psychological cripple unable to act independently of his parents because they, in a terrible need to be needed, never allowed him any freedom of action or decision.

So far I have given negative arguments, showing that communion is impossible for persons without maturity of character. Now I shall show how mature character contributes to communion. I shall argue that character furnishes the requisites for commitment, love, and shared responsibility. Since I have already said something about how solitude contributes, and since commitment and responsibility are traits of character as well as bonds of communion, the argument need not be protracted.

Truth, honesty, and love are basic to human character. A person is defined by what he loves. A person cannot be responsible or committed to a center of trust and loyalty unless he is honest. But of course, love and honesty are social virtues. I cannot be honest with myself if I am dishonest with others. I cannot love the truth if I hate my neighbor. This is why the second great commandment is like the first. The connection between love as a quality of character and as a bond of community can be readily seen in the great description of love in 1 Corinthians 13:3–7. At its best, the love binding members of a communion is gentle. The members of a communion seek the same truth and love the same object, so they gently encourage each other but are patient with failure and slowness. Jealousy and snobbery are divisive, as are rudeness and self-seeking, which Paul also condemns. Love is also not prone to anger or to brood over injuries, both of which are fatal to communion. Similarly, the communal bonds can be seen in the fruits of the spirit: "love, joy, peace, patient endurance, kindness, generosity, faith, mildness, and chastity" (Gal. 5:22–23). Conversely, the destruction of communion lies in the fruits of the flesh, which are the qualities of immaturity of character and lack of love: "lewd conduct, impurity, licentiousness, idolatry, sorcery, hostilities, bickering, jealousy, outbursts of rage, selfish rivalries, dissensions, factions, envy, drunkenness, orgies, and the like" (Gal. 5:19–21). When love is at the center of character, the person can give himself to others and so form associations of intimacy, sharing, and permanence. Without love, the "I" gets in the way of relationships.

Commitment to communion is always voluntary. Because space always remains for character development, a door always stays open for one who wishes to go. This is true even of the communions into which a person is born. Hard though it might be to leave, it is always possible, because members are trained for freedom. Thus all communion is by choice,[31] and the commitment at the heart of communion must match that which is fundamental to character. The loyalty and confidence which form character must be congruent with the pledge to comrades. The faith which grounds a person's life becomes shared, grounding a life together in pursuit of its intimations and responsibilities.

Because this faith is voluntary, the person can make the sacrifices required by the commitment mechanisms of communion. Although they restrict the person, the limits are implicit in a freely accepted faith, so members strengthen one another—and their communion—in their resolve to make the sacrifices. Freely pursuing the truth which he honors, each person must be honest with his fellows, reinforcing the commitment to veracity which they share.

Responsibility is also social. The responsible person responds to others in terms of his fundamental commitments, so that common experience, work, and participation run smoothly. When responsible persons holding the same commitments act together, communion is created or strengthened, and no one individual feels the need to appropriate for himself alone the fruits of shared work. He can take his place in the ceremonies, rituals, or labors of the group without the desire to dominate or to achieve special status.[32] Moreover, the mutual responsibility and service which are bonds of communion obviously cannot exist unless members are individually responsible persons. The whole in this case does not contain more than the parts. The mutual responsibility which makes action possible is only the responsibility which each person brings to the task. Irresponsible persons are not capable of the deep sharing of experience, ritual, work, and decision making which constitute the daily life of a communion.

The greater the personal maturity of character among the members of an intimate association, the more the qualities of communion. Obviously, I must warn again, as I have done throughout these three chapters, that neither communion nor character is ever complete. There will be discord and irresponsibility, but these result from the inevitable failures of character of members. The more perfect they are, the more fully will their association take on the qualities of communion.

Hospitality and Character

I turn now to the relationship between character and the form of community which I have called hospitality. Just as with communion and character, an intimate and reciprocal relation prevails between hospitality and character.[33] Hospitality is a relationship between persons of character. Martin Buber affirms this reciprocity in his discussion of "dialogue," which is closely related to my notion of hospitality:

> Certainly in order to be able to go out to the other you must have the starting place, you must have been, you must be, with yourself. Dialogue between mere individuals is only a sketch, only in dialogue between persons is the sketch filled in. But by what could a man from being an individual so really become a person as by the strict and sweet experiences of dialogue which teach him the boundless contents of the boundary?[34]

I shall treat first the side of the relationship in which hospitality helps to form character.

A hospitable encounter necessarily involves treating each individual as a person of character. In so doing, I assume that the person is responsible, thereby helping him to become so. I treat him as a person of commitment, thereby assisting him to have faith. I respect his solitude, thereby helping him to enter it. How hospitality acknowledges character can be seen in the everyday uses of speech and silence. In all but a few contexts, speech with another recognizes the humanity of the other, while silence denies that humanity.[35] Compare the icy silence of a quarrel to a verbal battle. In the latter, the enemy is at least recognized as someone who can be hurt or changed or persuaded. In the former, his existence is ignored as completely as possible.

The discussion of hospitality in the previous chapter showed how such a relation is a meeting of character. It goes beyond the superficialities of most encounters and invites each person to be at home, to respond and present himself from the depth of character. Evidently, then, the most complete form of hospitality is that between mature persons, who are open to each other in their commitment and responsibility. They may even share their deepest thoughts and feelings and so may enter each other's solitude. In such a case, it can hardly be doubted that solitude, commitment, and responsibility are reinforced. Maturity of character grows first in communion but is reinforced, refreshed, and nourished in hospitality. Indeed, character can hardly be said to be mature if it shuns hospitality and constantly remains in the relative security of communion. Moreover, hospitality is often needed among members of a communion. Comrades and family are often taken for granted; hurts or doubts in friends often go unnoticed. As an occasion of special attention beyond the warmth of communion, hospitality brings friends and comrades, hurts and doubts, to joint recognition. Hospitality heals communion and thus reinforces its character-building qualities. Hospitality is also a testing of the character formed in communion, when it occurs between persons of different communions and commitments. In encounter with a stranger, a person learns more about himself.

Communion and hospitality have an important relationship. The former is one of the meeting grounds for the latter. Communions provide places, institutions, festival days, and language for dialogue. Some of these occasions may be customarily open to the general public; thus, wider dialogue may take place. On the other hand, hospitality reminds the members of a communion not to take each other for granted. And in constantly recognizing the "otherness" of each member, it also keeps communion from encroaching on the person's space for freedom.

Yet hospitality also brings to bear on character special qualities lacking in communion. These qualities are an essential supplement to character formation and, in very significant encounters, may possess a therapeutic efficacy in healing the wounds inflicted by failures of communion. This is certainly the intention behind encounter group therapies, as mixed in success as they are.[36] Thus hospitality has its own special excellences to bring to personal development.

Hospitality has a special role to play in the unfolding of solitude. Communion's contribution to solitude is limited. It gives the person the freedom and privacy—that is, the opportunity—to enter into dialogue. It teaches roles, and it builds faith and responsibility, thereby providing the essential discourse with material. But there communion stops; it is incapable of going deeper into character. Yet the person alone is also incapable of solitude. Introspection fails to see the whole person, and it alters what it does see. "Man remains a mystery to himself, and to attempt to elucidate that mystery by delving into one's mind is merely to increase its perplexing obscurity."[37] Indeed, we are afraid of entering into solitude by ourselves. Quiet is distracting because it invites solitude, so we turn on the radio or television, or reach for a book or magazine.

Entry into solitude requires a guide. This person may be someone from within my communion or outside it. But he must be one who begins a dialogue with me by recognizing my character and by opening his to me. Because he is a gracious host, he leaves me free to continue the dialogue by myself, to enter into solitude. The hospitality we share begins the dialogue; when we renew it or when I share such hospitality with another, further solitude is encouraged.

A major lesson of the Socratic dialogues is that Socrates always speaks directly to the character of the other persons in the dialogue. His words are chosen to appeal to particular kinds of persons, not to all in general.

The Socratic dialogue is a picture of hospitality. If its result, on the intellectual plane, is often uncertain, this is because its point is to continue the dialogue in the solitude of the participants, including the reader.[38] Such an invitation can also be extended by the spiritual director, the psychiatrist, the counselor, and the friend. Indeed, in genuine solitude the person is never alone. The questions I address to myself receive an answer from outside myself. The exchange between center and masks takes place in the presence of One beyond them. Prayer is the explicit recognition of this and is thus a form of hospitality as well as of solitude.[39] Since solitude is an essential part of character, hospitality has an essential role to play in character development.

Hospitality contributes to the growth of character in other ways as well. Truth is a bond of hospitality; falsehood and deception absolutely block it. To commit oneself to hospitality is thus to honor truth. The truth met in hospitality calls forth truth in character. I must be honest with myself in order to be so with another, as the other in hospitality will demand. Hospitality thus assists in the development of truthfulness.[40] The other listens to me, attentive to my answers; to lie or hide is to disappoint him and end the reciprocity necessary for a relation of hospitality between us. Even if I fail, as I often will, the pain may teach me the value of truthfulness.

Hospitality demands a firmness of faith as a corollary of its demand for truth. In hospitality whole persons meet; their wholeness includes their commitments, so that faith is deepened or a reconsideration of faith inspired. In the ordinary meetings of life, automatic responses are the rule. Men reply to each other conventionally, even if the forms do not jibe with their faith, because faith is in the background. In hospitality, it is in the foreground, even though it may not be an explicit topic of dialogue. Automatic responses are ruled out, and each word and gesture should come from the center of character.

Just as truth calls forth its counterpart, responsibility calls forth responsibility. The responsibility basic to hospitality and that essential in character demand one another. Hospitality teaches responsibility because it requires each participant to listen to the other and to respond from the heart to that gift of self. In conventional meetings, such responsibility is not normally demanded because conventional replies normally supply all that is required.

The tolerance and attentiveness called for in hospitality also reinforce responsibility. Indeed, attention is the first prerequisite, because one cannot respond properly to the call of another unless he first listens carefully and openly. Tolerance is also crucial here and indeed is closely linked to attentiveness. The tolerant person is available to the other.[41] Such a relation among persons means that each listens, despite the possibility that the other represents an abhorrent way of life or a competing faith;

each will respond to the other genuinely rather than stereotypically. The responsibility demanded and practiced in tolerant hospitality may then permeate the entire life of the person.

Hospitality has the great advantage of bringing character down to earth. The plurality of life opens new vistas for character, makes new demands of solitude and commitment, and provides tests for responsibility. Without such experience, the person is in danger of becoming too comfortable in communion, too abstract in his beliefs. Unless faith is tested in the uncertainties and risks of the concrete activity of life, it is not firmly grounded. More significantly perhaps, where a person has lacked the opportunity of communion or has found only pseudocommunity, hospitality will prove the only salvation of a broken life.

Character and Hospitality

The preceding section so stressed the reciprocal contributions of hospitality and character that the argument of this section may be briefly made. Hospitality as a relationship is possible only among persons of mature character. This condition, which we saw was true of communion also, is based on the necessity of psychological availability. Unless a person is truly open to another he is not free to give himself to another, and he is unable to enter into a deep relationship of either communion or hospitality. The person dominated by needs or lacking a center to hold his masks cannot permit himself the risk of meeting the character of another. Such an encounter would expose, most of all to himself, his shallowness. Thus men develop a multitude of disguises, excuses, and evasions in order to avoid genuine encounter with each other.[42]

The person dominated by the needs for belonging, love, security, or self-esteem is afraid to open his home in hospitality. He is afraid of the strangeness, the "otherness," which must always be accepted in hospitality. Some trivial thing which he treasures as a substitute for human contact might be stolen. Because he needs the other so desperately, such a person cannot give himself.

The responsibility essential to character is obviously essential also to the relationship of hospitality. There cannot be encounter without it. As Tinder says, "Autonomy is going one's own way, while responsibility is being prepared to explain—to respond for the way one is going."[43] Responsibility requires attentiveness to what is directed to us in everyday life and makes the dialogue of hospitality possible.

Honesty and faith also are required of each person in a relationship of hospitality. Without them there can be no encounter. The tolerance which is a bond of hospitality demands receptivity, but one should not hide his convictions in order not to offend the other. Such deception destroys the basis of hospitality by presenting to the other a role rather than wholeness. Faith does not get in the way of hospitality, rather it gives solidity to the meeting. Nouwen notes, "Hospitality leads only to a congested home when nobody is travelling anywhere."[44]

Faith contributes to hospitality in another way as well. Hospitality involves both the acceptance of risks and the knowledge that neither community nor character is ever complete or perfect. Faith overcomes the fear of risk taking because it involves hope and confidence in the center of commitment. Trusting in the ground of faith, the person can take the risk of opening himself to the other, confident that the encounter will mean growth, not destruction. Any wounds sustained will be healed, and any pains will be those of growth. Similarly, hope and confidence allow the person to bear the pain of distance and estrangement which can never totally disappear in hospitality.[45] These can be tolerated because faith reveals that the relationships entered and sustained in an imperfect world are not the totality of existence. Misunderstandings and harm occur even when openness to hospitality is as complete as possible on the part of all persons involved. If hospitality were the purpose of life, such pains could not be borne. Since it is only one goal of life, however, and since it contributes to the formation of character centered on a ground of meaning which transcends human limitations, pain can be borne and harm forgiven. Without honesty, faith, and trust, hospitality would falter from fear and incompletion.

Finally, hospitality requires solitude. First, an occasion for developing the habit of listening is needed; a person must come to be attentive to the dialogue of his heart and to the voice from beyond his heart. "Waiting patiently in expectation is the foundation of the spiritual life," says Simone Weil. In solitude distractions and fears can be put aside, and a quiet, patient attitude developed. Then, when a word comes, it can be heard. Just so, the ability to listen is the heart of hospitality. Weil refers to "that moment for pausing from which alone our consideration for our fellow proceeds."[46] Until a person has learned to pause in solitude of heart, he cannot receive his fellow man. Second, solitude is the place to learn poverty of spirit, which is essential to hospitality and depends first on the quieting of desire, on teaching desire its appropriate place within a responsible life. In solitude desire for many possessions is confronted and made a partner in dialogue between center and masks.

The person of solitude is, moreover, tolerant, and we have seen that this quality is a condition of community as hospitality. Solitude engenders toleration, because the struggles, doubts, and dialogues which occur in solitude can be recognized in others. Insight into my own heart sharpens insight into another's. Compassion is a product of solitude; when I can see beneath my own poses, I can envision the heart of the other beneath his masks. Aspects of the other's bearing and commitments at odds with mine are seen to proceed from a life with joys, sorrows, and experiences which I too can enter and may have experienced. Though love demands far more than tolerance, we could paraphrase the second great commandment: "Tolerate your neighbor as you tolerate yourself."

Without wholeness of character, including solitude, faith, and responsibility, hospitality is impossible. Without it, encounters between persons remain conventional, socially regulated. The deeper and more enriching levels of human relationships remain undiscovered, and life is the poorer for it.

Conclusion

We have reached the end of a long, though necessary, journey. I have tried to argue carefully and to provide as much detail, reason, and illustration as possible, because I believe that the position I have defended is unfamiliar to most and distrusted by many to whom it is familiar. Character and community are not mutually exclusive, nor need they be seen in any kind of opposition. The last three chapters have attempted to defend that proposition. Indeed, I have tried to support an even stronger argument: character and community are so essentially connected that the development of one requires the emergence of the other.

In order to support this thesis, I have described the nature of human character and in particular three essential qualities: solitude, commitment, and responsibility. In chapter 3, I defined two forms of community, communion and hospitality, discussed their essential elements, distinguished them from pseudocommunity and from each other, and considered various objections to the concept of community. Finally, in the present chapter, I drew together the strands of a complex argument and showed, first, the reciprocal necessity of communion and character, and next, the reciprocal necessity of hospitality and character.

Though I believe that the particular arguments and the combination of concepts are original, the perspective I have defined is neither new nor idiosyncratic, as the references to ancient authors suggest. The stand suggested here is as much recovered as discovered. It matters little whether my meaning is new as long as it is true.

My aim has been to develop a view of person and community which will support a way of looking at politics. Because political theory ultimately depends on a philosophical anthropology, a valid statement about politics cannot be constructed upon an invalid anthropology. An overview of politics was impossible until an idea of man was elaborated which appreciates both each person's character and the coresponsibility of persons in their most significant human relationships.

In the following chapters, I turn directly to two concepts which form bridges from character and community to political life. Authority and freedom, mentioned in these last three chapters in relation to both character and community, are obviously also key political concepts. Just as community and character are often erroneously viewed as being in opposition, so are authority and freedom. The following chapters will discuss freedom and authority, show how they correlate with each other, and place them in the context of politics.

5

Authority

Authority has become, since the seventeenth century, the key political concept. Yet discussions of authority usually put the cart first, since they are ordinarily posed in terms of obligation, which cannot be discussed before consideration of the nature and foundation of authority. Indeed, a certain air of futility has marked the recent literature of political obligation and the literature of civil disobedience, its most obstreperous offspring.

The present chapter serves two related purposes. First, it completes the development of the theme of communion begun in chapter 3. The bonds of shared experience, ritual, participation, affection, and commitment are joined by authority. Communions order themselves, formally or informally, tightly or loosely. A communal group requires a mechanism of authority to maintain itself as it moves through time, facing internal and external challenges to its existence. Authority is also required to direct the group toward the objectives specified by its commitments. Communion-like associations appear constantly—persons sharing a tragedy or a short-term political objective or rallying around a winning team—but they just as constantly pass out of existence unless the emotions, objectives, experiences, or commitments which united them are reinforced by a structure of authority.

Second this chapter will develop a concept of authority capable of acting as a key concept in a theory of political order. Conflict, pride, and power demonstrate the need for a structure of authority to maintain a minimum level of peace, as does the function of government as the ultimate legitimate wielder of coercion in society. In short, it is generally acknowledged that provision for authority is an essential feature of any comprehensive theory of political order.

Yet authority is the most widely misunderstood concept in political theory and, indeed, in political life. It is even more subject to misinterpretation than community. It will therefore present a difficult hurdle to the reader who has followed me this far. Yet it is vital that the barrier become a bridge, for authority clearly links the preceding chapters with those ahead, showing how my theory stands. My discussion thus far may be totally convincing, but it can contribute nothing to the following argument unless the concept now before us is clearly developed.

My exposition is divided into four parts. First I discuss some misconceptions about authority and the reasons for them. The second part defines and describes the concept itself. Such a task is most difficult, given the reputation of authority today, so the argument is lengthy. Third I show how authority is a necessary bond of communion. The final section distinguishes the political from other types, starting with the general concept, which is needed before the specific form can be appreciated. Therefore the full concept central to a theory of political order emerges only gradually.

The Problem of Authority

The problem of authority in the modern world is both theoretical and practical. From a theoretical standpoint, authority is often confused with power, force, or coercion. Thus it is viewed with suspicion. I intend to demonstrate, however, that authority does not add something to power; rather, it transforms power. When it is understood to depend upon communion and right, then its radical difference from power should be clear. Like power, force, and coercion, authority is directive, but in a quite different way.

The practical difficulty is more striking than the theoretical. Men can live comfortably with considerable looseness in their conceptual language, but the existential consequences of the problem of authority present serious dangers to modern public life. Weak commitment to authority produces three related consequences. First, the decay of authority means the demise of political legitimacy. If its citizens perceive a state as legitimate, then, ceteris paribus, they will feel themselves bound by its laws, regulations, and rules. Yet in the modern world, as Schaar has written, "we are nearing the end of an era . . . [because] the philosophical and experiential foundations of legitimacy in the modern states are gravely weakened, leaving obedience a matter of lingering habit, or expediency, or necessity, but not a matter of reason and principle, and of deepest sentiment and conviction."[1] Authority depends upon standards of right and on cultural values that justify the power which states do exercise. To the extent that community has given way to a society of separate individuals and groups, authority loses its ground and turns into an equilibrium of power. Common commitment to values and norms is replaced by interest-group accommodation.[2] The legitimacy of policy so created is called into question. Of course, it is also true that to the extent that those in authority simply make power compromises, community is undermined and fragmented into conflicting individuals and groups.

Second, the practice of morality is made difficult by the crisis of authority. Moral principles may be discovered by individuals in solitude. This is a lesson we learn from Socrates and Christ. The practice of such principles, however, requires social support. This we learn from the outline of the just polis in the *Republic* and from the early Christian communion in the Acts of the Apostles. Authoritative institutions provide a supportive context in which the practice of virtue by individual persons is reinforced and made a fixed disposition.[3] As the modern world succumbs to the temptations of moral individualism, moral integrity becomes more and more difficult.

Finally, suspicion of authority ends in the decay of visions of the good society. Emphasis is placed on the value of freedom and on its use to satisfy private wants, thereby glossing over the question of the best way of life. Yet obligation and authority are difficult to reconcile with such a view. Obligation becomes simply one more strategy for interest maximization.[4] Any conception of a common way of life as a candidate for the best way of life is excluded. If authority is to have any meaning, it must be grounded in a public conception of the best life and of the good society, which may serve as valid reasons for obedience to laws designed to pursue them.

Carl J. Friedrich has contributed the best known theory of authority in modern political science. Consideration of its strengths and weaknesses will prepare the way for a fuller understanding, especially because Friedrich's account ties authority closely to community.[5]

Friedrich distinguishes authority from power. Both enable one person to direct the actions of another, but in the former case the direction is one of a natural conformity of wills, while in the latter conformity is manipulated by force, deception, or eloquence. In the case of authority, goals are shared by leaders and followers. In the case of power, aims are simply those of the powerful. Thus power is naturally unstable. The ability of one person to impose his ends on another is never simply given but must constantly be renewed. As a result, the parties to a power relation remain forever uncertain of their relationship and so strive to increase their power vis-à-vis each other. More constant in human life than power itself is the unlimited struggle to acquire it, which ensnares each in its devices. Authority, however, remains stable so long as the community among those involved remains intact. The fact that authority must at times use power indicates that community is always imperfect and that wills falter.[6]

Authority is defined by Friedrich as the capacity to issue communications permitting reasoned elaboration in terms of the values, beliefs, and interests of the political community to which they apply.[7] Friedrich traces the word "authority" back to the Roman *auctoritas.* The Roman Senate added auctoritas to popular laws by "augmenting" them with traditional or religious truths. Auctoritas was advice which could not properly be disregarded. Authority for Friedrich is connected with reason; its first property is the potential for reasoned elaboration of any communication, law, rule, or decision. The reasoned elaboration need not be carried out; the potentiality for it, and the recognition of this potentiality, are all that need be present. The elaboration may be termed reasoned because it contains adequate reasons for the recipient. It includes a careful consideration of alternative courses of action. The reasons given need not be conclusive. "But whether they are set forth or not, these reasons exist, and they are what gives law authority."[8]

Such capability of reasoned elaboration refers to a set of values which the person possessing authority shares with his followers. Here for Friedrich is the link between authority and community. "What matters is that this capacity to issue communications which may be elaborated by reasoning is there, that it exists, and that as a consequence a community of opinions, values, and beliefs, as well as of interests and needs, is manifested in such communications."[9] Community serves as the foundation of authority, and authority exists to relate particular judgments to the basic values of a community. Authority, and the power based upon it, has a fluid quality, because it is founded upon values, beliefs, and interests which constantly change in response to changes in the environment or to creative innovation.

The genesis of authority in the shared values of a community suggests authority's connection with tradition, an important carrier of value. Reasoning from tradition is a key method of authority; a heritage of values, beliefs, and information thus passes from one generation to another. Yet because of the need for interpretation, change is possible, though tradition may hinder it on occasion. Accordingly Friedrich notes that tradition is related to the very basis of politics. While brief periods of revolutionary fervor may do without tradition, even revolutions soon look back at their own past. Friedrich is careful to distinguish tradition from traditionalism, an ideology absolutizing tradition.[10]

Friedrich has made a significant contribution to understanding authority by showing that it adheres in communications capable of reasoned elaboration and by demonstrating how this capability must be rooted in communal values and, in most cases, in customs embodying these values. Yet something is missing. Communal values and traditions point beyond themselves; they are, or claim to be, warranted by their accord with truth and a reality which transcends them and of which they are only immanent manifestations. Even authority itself points beyond tradition and community, as when the people of Capharnaum marvel about Jesus that he "taught with authority, and not like the Scribes" (Mark 1:22). They recognized that he spoke not only within the rabbinical tradition but as though he had direct access to the reality to which it pointed. An authority, then, must be a witness not only to a tradition, but to the truth which validates it.

Friedrich himself senses the need to go beyond tradition and communal values in his discussion of authority as the link between justice and power. Justice is defined in the political sense as

> the epitome of all that is in conformity with the communal values, opinions and beliefs, and more particularly therefore with what can be authoritatively stated as satisfying the demand for equality.
>
> The bald statement that political authority is just provides a shorthand expression for the fact that authority in so far as it is the capacity of reasoning upon values provides the bridge between power and justice. In that perspective it would be possible to assert the proposition that authority justifies power, provides power with an explicit argument for the relations to values prevalent in a given community.

Friedrich senses that the definition of justice makes it, and authority, relative to any system of values. Therefore he immediately adds that "truth is one of the key values to which authority in many contexts is linked." Yet Friedrich illustrates this relation only with an allusion to scholarship and states that authority in its connection to truth is subject to the limitations of human reason.[11] Friedrich thus seems to develop two different ideas of justice without adequately explaining their relationship. On the one hand, he ties justice to transcendent values; on the other, he limits it to the value judgments of a particular community. Since authority is tied to justice, the problem affects his analysis of authority.

The crux of the difficulty with Friedrich's definition is that ultimately it relates authority solely to the fluid, changing values and interests of the political community. This definition means, as Friedrich admits, that Hitler and Stalin exercised true authority.[12] It does little good to say that they did so only in relation to their followers, for this is true of all rulers. For a communication to be authoritative, it must be susceptible to reasoned elaboration in terms not only of the relative value judgments of the community but also of the truth. This assertion implies only an openness to reality and truth on the part of the one in authority, not the possession of absolute truth. By "truth" I mean an insight into reality, which is capable of being understood and communicated through symbols. The insight may be religious, scientific, human, aesthetic, or political. By "absolute truth" I mean a claim about reality which purports to embody it, or some aspect of it, fully and completely in a doctrine, dogma, proposition, or law. It is the ideologist's imitation of the authority's knowledge.

Grounding authority in truth and reality does not lead to arrogance or totalitarianism, as some might claim, but only makes authority a normative concept. Reality is always fuller than we imagine it, and it can never be defined or packaged by our theories. Thus truth is always partial and personal, as I shall argue more fully below. Realizing the real but partial quality of truth serves to make authority humble about its claims. At the same time, the anchor in truth and reality provides a standard for assessment, a measure more sure than the changing values of a particular part of society. This openness to appraisal places an inherent limit on authority and denies the title to those who claim to wield it but who in reality serve only their own interests or those of a certain class. Finally, the dependence of authority on reality provides its executors with insight into the limits of their directives. Reality includes the stubbornness and self-seekingness of human beings, qualities which undermine obedience to authority and restrain lawmakers in their efforts to lead or restrict the members of their societies. These considerations indicate that proper understanding of the dependence of authority on truth implies not "authoritarianism" but limited government.

While Friedrich seems to recognize a relationship between authority and truth, he still clings to a concept of the former that is rooted in the relative judgments of the political community. Thus he does not appear to take his own examples of authority to heart. He refers to the Roman Senate, the doctor, and the parent; yet in all of these examples, and in that of the teacher, we see that authority does not rest wholly upon ties with the judgments of the populus, the patient, the child, or the student. Indeed, in all these cases it rests primarily, as Friedrich admits about the doctor, on greater knowledge and better reasons.[13] Clearly the parent draws primarily upon a knowledge of certain truths which the child does not have and which the parent wishes to communicate to the child. The situation is analogous regarding the teacher, the doctor, and the Senate.

Authority's Foundation in Communion

Despite its failure on the issue of truth, Friedrich's discussion of authority does powerfully support its connection with community. To define the link further and to prepare the way for a definition of authority, I shall discuss the two most profound modern theorists of authority, Yves R. Simon and Michael Polanyi.

Simon's theory achieves the openness to truth missed by Friedrich and is undoubtedly Simon's most significant contribution to political philosophy.[14] Simon observes that authority today has a bad name; it is distrusted and contrasted with liberty. It is associated with unequal exchange and with arbitrary assertion of truth. Authority and authoritarianism are seldom distinguished. Liberal and democratic thinkers have tended to conceive of social progress in terms of liberty, and liberty in terms of self-determination or self-government; yet authority implies government by others. Therefore the growth of liberty should imply the decay of authority.[15] Moreover, the concept of authority confronts what Simon calls the "deficiency theory of government," which holds that only defects in men make government necessary.[16] As education and better institutions remove shortcomings, a mechanism for governing will become less necessary. Yet liberals today tend to believe that substantial government activity is necessary for the preservation and normal growth of all the benefits which society stands for. Progress seems to call for more, not less.

Simon admits that the deficiency theory is plainly applicable to parental authority, which is necessarily substitutional and temporary. It aims at making up deficits of knowledge, virtue, or experience and therefore at bringing about its own disappearance and the creation of autonomy in the child. Simon goes on to assert that this self-liquidating quality of paternal authority is a principle of justice in all kinds of political systems (e.g., colonial government).[17] He next asks whether any case can be discovered in which authority is not substitutional but essential, as it will be if unanimity of opinion about the end of and means to the common good cannot be attained even in a community of intelligent, informed, and virtuous persons. If Simon can demonstrate that even such a society needs authority to direct it, then he will have demonstrated an essential function of authority.

Taking first the determination of the means to the common good, Simon observes that if there is only one means, then unanimity about it will arise naturally in a perfect society; authority will not be necessary.

> When the means to the common good is uniquely determined, affective community supplies an essential foundation for unanimous assent; unanimity is, then, the only normal situation, and, if everything is normal, authority is not needed to bring about unified action. Unity of action requires authority in so far as not everything is normal, in so far as wills are weak or perverse and intellects ignorant or blinded. The function of authority remains substitutional. But when, on the other hand, there is more than one means to procuring the common good, there is no foundation whatsoever for unanimity.[18]

Unanimity, Simon observes, may be all-important. It is, for example, literally a matter of life and death that all drive on the same side of the street. Yet intelligent, virtuous, and informed men may disagree on which side it should be; there are two possibilities, so the means to the common good is not uniquely determined. Authority is needed to make the determination. As deficiencies decrease, in societies or in individuals, the number of available choices increases. Simon thus concludes, "The function of authority with which we are concerned, i.e., that of procuring united action when the means to the common good are several, does not disappear but grows, as deficiencies are made up; it originates not in the defects of men and societies but in the nature of society. It is an essential function."[19] The deficiency theory does not hold in this case; authority has an essential role.

Simon's examination of authority does not end with the discovery that it has an essential function in determining the means to the common good, for the question of the determination of the goal of social action remains. The answer at first seems obvious: if society is composed of stupid and vicious people, authority is clearly necessary. But if it is composed exclusively of good and enlightened people, it seems that they will spontaneously intend the common good. Yet the question is profoundly difficult. In his attempt to answer it, Simon uses the Scholastic distinction between matter and form, distinguishing formal consideration of the common good from material consideration. The issue then becomes how the members of society are related to the matter and form of the common good.

Simon is not satisfied with a sharp distinction between private and common goods; the citizen must be devoted to the common good at all times. Yet it also "matters greatly for the common good itself" that particular persons properly defend particular goods. Simon argues that the distinction between form and matter resolves this difficulty. The private person must always will the common good formally understood. That is, he must place the common good and whatever specific policy it might demand before his private advantage. Yet as far as content or matter goes, he is to will and intend private goods. The obligation of the public official is different:

> But the public person is defined by the duty of willing and intending the common good considered both in its form and in its matter. And because the service of the common good normally involves an arrangement of things private, and sometimes requires the sacrifice of private interests, the subject of the public capacity exercises authority over the private person, whose business it is to look after particular matters.[20]

Since the private person is concerned with only one particular aspect of the common good, there must be above him a person or group of persons properly involved, formally and materially, with the whole of the common good. This concern develops into a direction of society by public reason and will toward the common good. In other words, authority is essential in the determination of social goals and priorities.

In summary, then, three functions of authority may be distinguished: the paternal or substitutional, the essential (unifying common action when the means to the common good is not uniquely determined), and the most essential (procuring the intention of the common good, materially considered). The latter two would be necessary even in a "society composed exclusively of clever, virtuous, and fully mature persons." Authority is, for Simon, fundamentally linked to the common good of a community. For him the binding power of authority is derived from its moral cogency, its relation to the common good. It elicits a distinctly ethical motive for obedience. For Simon, then, the community and common good are central to the concept of authority.

Community and common good are intimately related—community being defined as a society relative to a common good.[21] Society does not exist to serve individual needs alone, for the daily life of the community transcends the limitations in duration and diversity of individual achievement. Man is sometimes a part of a community, sometimes not. When he is, the common good is greater than the private, and the latter may have to be sacrificed, as long as the common and the private goods are of the same order. The common good is not ultimate, absolutely speaking, but only in an order which itself is not ultimate. It does not take priority, for example, over the individual's relationship with God.

Simon's theory, then, strongly supports my thesis that authority is possible only in community. Politics for Simon attempts to secure or to pursue what is beneficial for men in community. Authority is not an external force commanding an individual against his will. Rather, because it proceeds from communal life, which is a shared internal life, it speaks to that which the individual member of the community shares with other members. It is thus compatible with liberty.[22] Authority also makes possible the continued existence and growth in excellence of the community by forming and perfecting new members and by assisting the old. Such excellence is facilitated in two ways. First, the person grows when he follows a leader toward a truth or good which he cannot discover on his own. Second, the person grows when he participates in authority himself, exploring the dimensions of truth and common good and attempting to manifest them in rules of action for the entire community.

Although Simon grounds authority in community, he goes beyond Friedrich to refer it to a common good measured by standards which transcend the immediate values or beliefs of any particular community. In Simon's conception, an authority is a witness for the common good, which will always build on what the community is and on its object of commitment but will always call the community to become something it has not yet become.

This notion of authority as witness is especially important in Simon's discussion of the theoretical judgment, that is, in the realm of theoretical knowledge. "When the issue is one of truth, not of action, the person in authority has the character of a witness." So understood, Simon argues, authority has a large role to play in the cognition of theoretical truth and in its social teaching. Yet, Simon goes on to say, the function played by authority in the realm of theoretical truth is substitutional, not essential. It "plays a part which under better circumstances would pertain to the object."[23] Simon seems to be saying that when a person is directly confronted with truth, no mediating authority is necessary. When a person falls in love, he does not need anyone to tell him what it is like. Similarly, when a person faces truth, he needs no one to tell him what it is. Yet, if I understand Simon correctly, I believe him to be mistaken in calling authority substitutional in the realm of theoretical truth. I agree that its role differs from its function in the determination of the means to and the matter of the common good, but a stronger term than "substitutional" is required here. In the practical realm, for example, the sphere of parents and colonial officials, the goal is to bring the child or the colony to the point where it no longer needs the authority. Yet authority in the discovery of truth can never be dispensed with. Reality always exhausts the efforts of those who seek truth; it has ever new secrets to disclose. As I hope to show below, it will disclose them only to a communion structured by authority, which thus remains essential, or at least indispensable, in the discovery of theoretical truth. The role of authority in the province of scientific and abstract knowledge poses profound difficulties but is seldom treated. Simon here touches it, but he does not explore it in depth. Michael Polanyi, however, has probed these issues in a most creative way.

Polanyi has framed an epistemology and a philosophy of science directed against methodological limitations on science and against the restrictions on knowledge imposed by the modern paradigm of Cartesian skepticism. This theory of knowledge can be summarized here only briefly. According to Polanyi, the old epistemological dichotomies dependent upon the notion of critical doubt, absolute/relative, and subjective/objective do not characterize knowledge. Moreover, the methods of induction and deduction do not adequately describe the process of scientific discovery. Polanyi replaces these with the new dichotomies of subsidiary/focal awareness and of tacit/explicit knowledge.[24] He maintains that man knows, not by means of induction or deduction, but by the integration of his subsidiary awareness of particulars with his focal awareness of the whole through active perception. He integrates fragments into a comprehensive whole. The significance of the particulars cannot be explicitly known or stated. All knowledge thus has a tacit dimension. The norm of objective knowledge is an impossible one, for it attempts to eliminate the tacit or unspecifiable part of knowledge. It attempts to make all knowledge explicit and thereby readily communicable, so long as each knower is abstracted from all "subjective" hindrances. It calls for detachment which, Polanyi argues, is impossible, because the tacit dimension is essential in the discovery, validation, and communication of knowledge. The knower cannot be detached; rather he must "indwell" the particulars. He takes meaning from the subsidiary terms by entering into them and making them a part of himself. All knowledge, Polanyi argues, is personal, arising from the commitment of the knower. "According to the logic of commitment, *truth is something that can be thought of only by believing it.*"[25]

Though knowledge is rooted in personal commitment, it is not thereby subjective.[26] The knower indwells in order to appreciate reality, not a structure created by the self. The ultimate honesty of his personal commitment ties him to reality. This honesty is derived from intellectual passions which lead the knower to search for and to identify reality by its preciousness; therefore he knows and communicates with universal intent.

If, then, all knowledge is personal knowledge, what is the place of authority, communion, and tradition? Since knowledge is the result of tacit operations passionately supported and cannot be formulated in totally explicit definitions, rules, maxims, or procedures, it must be transmitted tacitly; that is, as part of a tradition and an apprenticeship structure of teacher and student. "The transmission of knowledge from one generation to the other must be predominantly tacit."[27] Knowledge is like a skill or an art; it must be passed from master to apprentice. The tradition in which the two craftsmen operate serves as a guide to what others have found to be rich in the representation of reality. Tradition is not valued for itself, then, but for its transparency when it allows reality to shine through.[28] But tradition depends upon authority and community (or "convivial order" as Polanyi calls it).[29] The learner must affiliate himself with a communion which cultivates the tradition of knowledge to which he aspires and which appreciates its values and strives to act by its standards. Such a convivial order makes fellowship, communication, and participation in joint activities possible. This, of course, recalls the idea of community in Simon. Even more striking in this regard is Polanyi's adding to the idea of convivial order the idea of authority in the achievement of the common good. In the case of scientific communions, of course, that good is knowledge. Authority, then, is necessary to keep the communion together and to keep it directed toward its end, correcting deviation through mutual control; even more basic, however, is its dynamic function in pointing to new possibilities for discovery within the tradition. The acceptance of authority is the recognition that what appears meaningless has a significance which can be discovered by the same kind of indwelling practiced by those who have gone before. It is a joint celebration of the structure of the convivial order. Thus "the effect of Polanyi's argument on behalf of traditional knowledge is to suggest that *belonging* to a community, *believing* in its traditions, and thereby *understanding* the experience which engendered them are all part of single process, i.e., the acquisition of knowledge."[30] Unlike Simon, Polanyi sees an essential connection between authority, communion, and the acquisition of theoretical knowledge.

Authority for Polanyi has two aspects: the horizontal and the vertical. The former refers to the fact that only recognized scientists establish the tradition and authority of science by forming a scientific consensus which is a "chain of mutual appreciation."[31] Each individual is responsible for maintaining watch over the traditions in his own area; yet since fields overlap, a network of authority is formed. In many ways this is what Friedrich says about authority. A scientific communication is authoritative because it is capable of elaboration in terms of the consensual values of the community, which are embodied in a dynamic tradition. Yet there is a vertical dimension also, an orientation toward the truth, which we saw in Simon.[32] A scientific communication is authoritative also because it is in principle universal, because it makes contact with reality. It is genuinely knowledge and makes a claim on each person, not just those within the tradition. Such a claim is made with universal intent; yet since the contact with reality is personal, it is in fact meaningful only to a community of similar persons. Like Socrates' claim to authority in Athens, which was based on his insight into reality but was understood only by his followers, any knower's claim to authority has these two inseparable aspects.[33] When we speak of society, the universal (or vertical) aspect of authority must be the common good. To the extent that society is a convivial order (communion) committed to seeking the common good, authority directs it toward that common good. Thus, Polanyi's epistemology is congruent with Simon's political philosophy but demonstrates more profoundly the dependence of all authority upon truth, communion, and tradition.

Certain conclusions and a definition of authority may now be drawn from this discussion of Simon and Polanyi. First of all, the connection between authority and common good in Simon and between authority and reality in Polanyi helps to dispel the strangeness which at first glance surrounds the claims to authority of Socrates and Christ.[34] They are comprehensible in terms not of power or of widespread following but only of a personal contact with transcendent reality. The vertical aspect overwhelms the horizontal in these two cases. These extreme cases confirm the insight of Polanyi and Simon, *pace* Friedrich, that all authority is rightful, that a higher source than common values must validate any claim to it. The person "in authority" is always an authority *on* something and always a witness to the truth. There are right and wrong ways of doing things in a communion, and authority is justified by its insight into the right ways, which is also embodied in the language and traditions of the communion, especially the symbols of its origin and its goals.[35]

But Christ's speech and action draw on the traditions of the Law and the Prophets, and Socrates' speech draws on those of Athens and of philosophy. Moreover, each man gathers a group of disciples around him. Thus their authority is meaningful because it appeals to a communion of seekers of truth and draws on the traditions of such a search. It follows that a horizontal aspect is always present. This is the second conclusion to be drawn. Authority is possible only on the basis of communion and tradition. Outside his communion, the communications of the authority are unintelligible. This personal quality of authority and the necessities of communication demand communion as a system of shared values of action and speech. This is why attacks on the rituals and even the language of a communion do so much to undermine authority. Authority is difficult to attack head-on, so the attacks often come indirectly, on the communal foundations of its support. Thus long hair and dirty words were an important indirect threat to authority in the 1960s.[36] The authority as witness must be part of a communion which makes possible his reaching beyond its horizon. In any one case, either the vertical orientation to truth and reality or the horizontal relation to the wisdom of the communion may predominate. Perhaps in the majority of cases it will be the latter. Yet both must be present in every authority and in every authoritative pronouncement.

Third, the creation by Socrates and Christ of followings extending to the present teaches that the existence of communion requires authority. Friedrich, Simon, and Polanyi also teach this. Persons may experience occasional moments of spontaneous sharing, love, and trust. While such an experience may linger long in the heart, the unity it creates will not last unless it is maintained by some form of authority.

We may think, then, of authority as the reflection, within a communion of persons pursuing a common goal set by their shared tradition, of the tension between the given and the demanded. Authority as insight into the demanded directs the communion from where it is to where it ought to be. Its directions are in the language and symbols of the tradition, while at the same time it subtly reforms them in conformity with the demands of truth. Authority, then, may be defined as that faculty which directs a communion, of whatever kind, toward its proper end through insight into the requirements of the communion's basic commitments. Thus authority refers beyond communion, since it refers to a dynamic faith, but it is rooted in communion because of that faith and because it speaks in the language of traditions, experiences, and norms. Power need not have these connections, though the "power of persuasion" may, for example, make use of the symbols of a communion. It uses the symbols without being rooted in them. Authority may use persuasion or even force when necessary, but not for its own ends: its ends are exclusively those of the communion.

We now approach the reasons for the crisis of authority today. All three grounds of authority, personal knowledge, communion, and tradition, are weakened and under attack in our time. The Cartesian paradigm of systematic doubt predominant in epistemology cuts the link between authority and truth. Its effects can be seen in Friedrich's theory. The impact of individualism and the idea of personal autonomy have weakened belief in and ties to communion. Communions, of course, exist and will continue. Yet autonomous individualism undermines their foundations in common commitment, trust, memory, collective ideals, and discipline. Finally, tradition and the ceremony, ritual, and emotion connected with it have acquired a bad name in the contemporary world. They are associated, often rightly, with traditionalism, reactionary politics, and obscurantism. The attack on tradition as such, however, is fundamentally an attack on history, an attempt to escape the necessarily historical, and therefore limited, existence of man. Tradition makes historical existence bearable by giving some meaning and perspective to the distance between the given and the demanded. "Tradition is the living faith of the dead; traditionalism is the dead faith of the living."[37] Political theorists can do little, perhaps, to respond directly to the practical crisis of authority. Yet ideas have consequences, and this crisis has roots in the undernourished soil of our theoretical understanding of authority, tradition, knowledge, and communion. Thus the task of political theorists becomes twofold: to reformulate and improve our understanding of such concepts and, drawing on them, to speak to the political dislocations of our time.

Authority as a Bond of Communion

I indicated above that the lessons of Socrates and Christ teach that communion requires authority as an essential bond. The pursuit of truth is authoritatively symbolized by Socrates, and his spirit animates the philosophic communion formed according to his way of pursuing truth. Hence, his presence is demanded in the dialogues composed by his followers. Christ's work and example, of course, serve as authoritative referents for the communions formed in his name. Even the most loosely organized Christian sects maintain authority structures rooted in Scripture and in their traditional ways of interpreting Christ's example.

That authority is a bond of communion follows from the definition of authority given above and from the understanding of communion developed previously. Communions are built around commitments to truths which transcend the lives and experiences of their individual members. Common action according to the demands of these commitments marks communions. Authority is that which directs them in common action, pointing out paths from the actual to the demanded. If authority, then, depends upon the communion's faith, it is equally clear that faith is weak and ineffective without authority's ability to make it live in the daily actions of the members. Without authority a communion cannot achieve its purpose, which is fidelity to the reality which calls its people together.

If shared belief is one bond of communion, authority is another, because authority maintains shared belief. Churches, clubs, and societies pronounce principally about the beliefs of the group. Parents concentrate on the teaching of moral, religious, social, and economic beliefs. The authority of scientific communions, as Polanyi shows, fundamentally concerns the identification of acceptable statements about reality within the various disciplines. Without authoritative standards about reality communicated through the convivial order of scientists from one generation to the next, no scientific progress would be possible.

Similarly, Simon's theory of authority shows how it is essential to the pursuit of the common good, not only in the determination of its nature and the means to it but also in binding the communion together for the common pursuit of that good. James MacGregor Burns suggests the same in his consideration of leadership. The true leader, he contends, moves the public to higher moral levels by creating an authentic relation with the genuine needs of the society.[38] The true leader will have a deep understanding of truth and its demands which he will articulate in such a way as to direct his followers more surely to the truth to which they are loyal. The absence of such leadership is a prelude to the decay of authority and communion. "The death of a culture begins when its normative institutions fail to communicate ideals in ways that remain inwardly compelling, first of all to the cultural elites themselves."[39]

Before discussing more fully the idea of authority as a bond of communion, I wish to enter two cautions in order to avoid misunderstandings. First, the question of the need for authority is separate from the question of the forms which it may or should take.[40] What I have said above could possibly be read to imply that every human group must have a clear, hierarchical structure of authority. Since many examples of communions without such a structure can be adduced, it will seem that I am wrong about this bond of communion. Absence of hierarchy, however, does not mean absence of authority. The right to exercise authority does not naturally lie with one, few, or many. A communion organized according to the principles of direct, fully participatory, egalitarian democracy—be it a friendship, a commune, or a genuine New England town meeting—still manifests authority and obedience. In such a case, all organize themselves periodically in a public way to determine the direction of the group. Once it is decided, each must equally obey the directives issued. Authority is present, then, whether the decision-making procedures are hierarchical or egalitarian, formal or informal. Most communions are more or less hierarchically organized. Still, the issue of the best way to organize authority is separate from the issue of the need for it.

The second cautionary point I wish to make is that authority plays no essential part in relations of hospitality. Since hospitality does not depend on shared faith, authority is seldom present. In hospitality persons open themselves to each other, attentive to the truths which may be revealed. But these are not necessarily common truths, and the revelations need not eventuate in common action. Thus there is no ground for authority. Such a relation may develop into a communal one, or it may happen that one person places himself under the authority of the other or that they jointly decide to pursue some action as a result of the hospitality shared. In such cases authority could come into the relationship, but as a consequence of the change, not as a necessary feature of the hospitality. Thus, my remarks about authority apply only to communion, not to the special form of community I call hospitality.

The ways in which authority binds communion may be more fully elaborated by considering service. This is an unusual standpoint, because our contemporary misunderstandings of authority lead us to see it chiefly as mastery. Confused with power, authority seems more readily apparent in the actions of the master than in those of the servant. Indeed, it must be admitted that those "in authority" far too often deny the nature of their authority and transform it into mere power. In doing so, they forfeit their moral right to govern. Yet genuine authority is best seen in the way it can bind a communion by performing essential services for it. In some communions, moreover, authority is still defined in terms of service, even though its authorities may often fail to serve.

> Jesus then called them together and said: "You know how those who exercise authority among the Gentiles lord it over them; their great ones make their importance felt. It cannot be like that with you. Anyone among you who aspires to greatness must serve the rest, and whoever wants to rank first among you must serve the needs of all. Such is the case with the Son of Man who has come, not to be served by others, but to serve, to give his own life as a ransom for the many."[41]

One of the traditional titles of the Pope is *servus servorum Dei* (servant of the servants of God). The greatest scandal comes when his authority of service is perverted into an exercise of ecclesiastical power.

The true visage of authority is service, which can be manifested in a number of ways, most obviously, by guiding communion toward its proper end. Those in authority do not serve their own special ends when they direct the communion toward its common good. Rather, they truly serve, because the great temptation of persons in authority is to identify their particular needs or desires with those of the whole. "What's good for General Motors is good for the country."

In addition, however, to this general service, authority unifies the communion by creating and sustaining order and stability. Genuine unity must be freely created by the voluntary choice of members. Coerced unity and conformity deny communion, because faith, participation, love, and shared work are meaningless if they are imposed from outside. Faith and love cannot be imposed. Yet freedom, as I shall attempt to demonstrate in the following chapter, requires a stable order to ground it. Unless some possibilities are foreclosed, free choice is not possible. Unlimited freedom is impossible because each free choice forecloses other free choices. Moreover, responsible choice defines character, and responsible choice is always choice subject to limits. The order created by authority does not deny freedom of choice; nor does it impose faith and love. It provides the background, or the boundaries, which make choice responsible.

The order created by authority also serves to bind communion together by protecting each member from harm from outside or from other members. No communion is perfect; each member is tempted, and frequently succumbs, forgetting his faith and love and satisfying his desires at the expense of his fellows. While such wrongs can never wholly be prevented—and this failure is one of the great tragedies of communion and one of the signs of the radical imperfection of the human condition— authority can make such occurrences less likely and less dangerous. It promotes trust and settled expectations, which facilitate unity and harmonious living together. Such maintenance of order, of course, is the most familiar function of authority and the one most clearly focused upon by early liberal political theorists. Authority here most frequently employs sanctions, and it is this aspect which seems most political.

In addition to this general protective service, authority has a special service to protect and strengthen the weak within a communion,[42] whether the shortcoming is physical, spiritual, psychological, economic, or mental. Each member suffers from one or more of these weaknesses. Authority here serves communion by building it up, by vivifying the attachments of those whose faith is weak or whose love is losing its vigor. It protects those too shy or inarticulate to participate freely by giving them a role and by shielding them from the scorn of the assertive.

It is evident, of course, that authority often fails in this respect. Here, again, is the tragic face of communion. Yet when authority does exhibit compassion for the poor, it can draw persons together in a most striking way. Here the example of many families caring for a mentally or physically handicapped child is instructive. Because the parents use their authority to bring that child as fully as possible into the life of the family, they reinforce and deepen the love among all its members.

Authority also serves by initiating young and new members. There is no opposition between authority and rationality.[43] Polanyi's account of authority and knowledge forcefully demonstrates this point. The rationality of science depends upon a basic faith in reality and in the methods of science and upon a tacit understanding of the principles of particular scientific communions. Such faith and understanding are the conditions of knowledge; yet they can only be passed on from teacher to pupil or master to apprentice, by means of relationships which inherently involve authority. In such cases authority makes rationality possible. The same is true of schooling in general (normally a function of authority in a political community) and of the parental role. Churches, fraternal organizations, and other communions also initiate their members by authoritatively passing on their systems of belief and practice. Thus the communion is further bound by the integration of new members and by the reinforcing of the commitments of established members in the acts of teaching, initiating, and accepting.

Those in authority represent the communion, acting on its behalf in its internal and external business. Such a function is one of the basic meanings of representation and also a service which can reinforce the unity of a communion. Despite internal differences, in normal circumstances the members of a group tend to unite behind their representatives when it is a question of confronting other groups. Such unity is generally the case as well when authority represents the communion in disciplining its own members. Counterexamples are, of course, frequent, but the extent of communion in the group is problematic when such examples occur. In general, those in authority act for the communion in those instances where the group as a whole is not capable of acting for itself.

Finally, authority serves by transforming "spontaneous" into lasting communion. Most persons have experienced luminous moments of spontaneous solidarity in their lives. Strangers meet and share common action for a few days by marching for civil rights or against war or by fighting disasters such as floods or tornadoes. Strangers may form a bond by suffering together in war or in some natural or man-made crisis. Lately stories about similar moments have surfaced among persons trapped in elevators, offices, or subways by power failures. The kinds of sharing, talking, helping, and acting together characteristic of these experiences are important instances of communal contact in a fragmented world. They are long and fondly remembered, despite the suffering frequently involved. Yet such persons do not form lasting communions unless they organize themselves, appoint officers and meeting places, and establish at least informal bylaws, that is, unless they set up a structure of authority. Otherwise, despite exchanges of addresses, nothing beyond the moment is shared. I mean to suggest not that all such groups should organize themselves but only that authority can serve unity by doing so, thus preserving and strengthening bonds first spontaneously created.

Such are the principal ways in which authority serves as a bond of communion. The mere citation of such essential functions is forceful evidence that authority is an essential bond. The key to seeing things properly is to see authority as a servant, not as a master. Service may go awry, but it is essential to human living together.

Political Authority

I have not spoken directly about political authority, though much of the foregoing is drawn from discussions of it, because I believe that all authority must be grounded in transcendent standards and in communion. Yet authority is shaped and manifested in different ways in different contexts. Political authority is related to the common good and to common political ideas, experiences, and goals, while scientific authority is related to reality and the shared assumptions and methods of the scientific communion. Parental authority is oriented to standards of maturity and responsibility and to the beliefs, commitments, and experiences of the family. Authority, in its various contexts, may be exercised by one person, a few persons, many persons, or even all persons in a communion. The nature of authority, which must not be confused with the manner of its exercise, is to direct an activity to its proper end. The right to direct is not necessarily lodged in one, few, or many. The type of communion, activity, and end will determine the manner of exercise of authority.

Consideration of the general case suggests the particular definition of political authority as that which directs the political order to its ends of justice and the common good. The locus of authority is left open because it may be any of a variety of institutions or persons. Clearly, such a definition cannot be completely appreciated until the concepts of political community, justice, and common good are discussed, and so the definition must remain somewhat formal until chapter 7.

My definition of political authority draws largely upon Simon's, so there is no need to expand it at great length. Let me simply recall that this understanding of political authority gives it an essential part to play in the life of the political order. While it may be necessary in some cases for authority to substitute for the political immaturity of citizens, this is an accidental, even if frequent, requirement and is to be strictly temporary. In every political communion authority performs the essential task of guiding toward its common good. Therefore, authority is as essential for political order as for communion. To pretend that authority will wither or disappear as communions improve is to mistake its essence.

At this point someone might object that I have drawn a very idealistic account of political authority. After all, politics involves power and force. Political authorities most often use a near-monopoly of force to command or direct persons to do or to refrain from certain actions. To be able to cause to act or refrain from acting is itself a kind of power, one especially characteristic of the state. I do not wish to deny that this is so; I wish only to reemphasize that authority may employ power but is not itself power. Power is the ability of one person to cause another person to do something he would not otherwise have done. Authority entails the right to employ appropriate instruments to cause persons to work for the common good. In some cases, given human weakness and imperfection, authoritative directives will use coercion or the threat of coercion or material incentives, such as tax credits, in order to move persons.

Authority, then, justifies power. Of course, not infrequently power unjustified by authority reigns in a political order. Persons in "positions of authority" often direct the association to their own ends or those of various influential groups rather than toward the common good. To acknowledge this, however, is only to admit that the presence of authority in laws and regulations cannot be automatically assumed. When public policy serves the interests of a part while excluding the whole, it lacks authority and is supported only by power. To the extent that policy lacks authority, it lacks moral foundation and obligatory force. The concept of political authority justifies political resistance.

I must also point out that since authority depends upon communion, political authority depends upon the existence of political communion. In the absence of such communion—that is, in liberal partnership society and in pseudocommunities—authority has no foundation. Power remains unjustified, and obligation remains a matter of expedience or convenience. Liberalism attempts to justify power by reference to fair procedure, consent, and participation, but this cannot be done unless it is claimed that procedure, consent, and participation lead to better decisions than would have been made without them. A moral standard is implicitly introduced, but because it remains implicit, it cannot provide solid ground for a liberal theory of political obligation, hence the notorious disagreement among liberal theorists on questions of political obligation and civil disobedience. The concept of political authority makes such grounds explicit and can support a more coherent theory of obligation, though such a theory cannot be developed within the scope of this book.

The central idea of political authority as direction toward a goal hints at a distinction between leaders and followers, that is, it suggests that political authority is inevitably hierarchical—and indeed imperfection characterizes all communion. Since we are speaking of unions of those who share a faith and a set of norms by which they are judged, it is inevitable that all members fall short in some degree and so require each other's support. Communion thus requires authority to guide it from imperfection toward perfection. Because some members will invariably be closer to perfection, of stronger faith, or will have greater experience, intelligence, and insight than others, it would seem that political communion must always structure authority hierarchically.[44] I believe that such will usually but not always be the case. Yet as Simon teaches, authority would be required even were all perfect.

The prevalence of hierarchy should not be taken to mean that democracy and authority are incompatible. Representative democracies include executive officers, legislators, judges, and administrators possessing authority in varying degrees vis-à-vis each other and the general public. Moreover, in a democratic system the people have some share in authority, depending on the extent of their participation. Participation, hierarchy, and authority are compatible. Indeed, I would argue that a genuine participatory democracy with daily rotation of officers would be the only form of democracy without hierarchy, though it would still have authority at its center. Even unanimous, direct democracy is a form of authority. The people in their role as leaders give directives to themselves in their role as followers.[45] Participation, I have argued, is a necessary feature of communion. It is impossible that such a necessary element is incompatible with another necessary element, authority. The truth of the matter is that authority may be institutionalized in many forms of participation and in many varieties of the hierarchical principle. We should strive to make political institutions more participatory, and we should not be misled by those who argue, either in sorrow or glee, that greater participation must mean weaker authority. I shall conclude this account of political authority by pointing out briefly how its functions for the political community parallel those of authority outlined in the previous section, that is, how political authority protects the weak, teaches morality, and represents the community.

In political community, as in all others, some members are poorly integrated into communal life because they lack education, wealth, status, or the qualities of character requisite for full participation and sharing. In America the poor, racial minorities, and the uneducated do not participate in political life as fully as their opposites do. Political authority, especially in its orientation to justice, has the duty of protecting such persons from the depredations of others and of drawing them more fully into the whole.

Authority must work to remove formal, legal barriers to their participation but also to promote in these individuals the material and personal resources which facilitate full participation. Simultaneously an effort must be made to alter those attitudes of dominant groups which obstruct full participation.

Each of us is weak in one way or another, and politics becomes remote and forbidding unless authority protects our participation. It does so by creating an order that safeguards the role of the individual. Moreover, authority's task is to provide the various freedoms, such as speech, press, assembly, protection from arbitrary arrest, which shield each person. More positively, authority should see to it that the person's participation influences the direction of the community. That is, it should promote representative and participatory institutions, accountable bureaucracies, and local institutions which are both salient to and easily penetrable by the ordinary citizen.

Political authority also contributes by teaching the specific political morality of the group and by reinforcing the total set of moral norms of the community. Authority, as I have described it, is a moral concept, directing moral life toward its proper goals. Thus all authority concerns morals.[46] Such a conclusion does not demand that political authority take a direct hand in all moral matters. It should not. Rather, political institutions should abide by and should initiate ordinary citizens into the specific rules of political morality: legitimate means of participation, honesty in elections, care for the common good, and so forth. Moreover, political authority and the institutions it controls or substantially influences, such as schools, armed forces, nationalized industries, and public programs, are to promote the major moral goals and principles of the community, such as justice, freedom, and equality. These assertions raise substantial issues of freedom and the scope of politics with which I shall deal only after direct consideration of the concepts of freedom and political community in the next three chapters.

Finally, and least controversially, authority represents or speaks for the community in relations with other communities and with internal individuals or groups. The authoritative institutions and the persons who staff those institutions stand and act for the entire community. Indeed, some political units often define themselves or understand themselves principally with reference to these institutions and the commitments they represent. Fulfilling such a role, political authority orders and promotes community in a critical way. It becomes a symbol of the self-understanding of the society and the entire principle of that understanding. It becomes the vehicle for the society's action in history.

Such a contention raises once again the question of freedom, because it seems to exalt political order at the expense of the individual person. I have argued throughout this book that only communion and hospitality can promote the full development of the person, but the suspicion of denial of freedom still lingers. Now, however, I am prepared to confront it directly.

6

Freedom

Freedom is not something
you get as a present. . . .
You can live in a dic-
tatorship and be free—
on one condition: that
you fight the dictatorship.
Ignazio Silone,
Bread and Wine

In the next realm, where
things are clearer, clarity
eats into freedom. We
are free on earth because
of cloudiness, because of
error, because of marvelous
limitation, and as much
because of beauty as of
blindness and evil. These
always go with the
blessing of freedom.
Saul Bellow,
Humboldt's Gift

The thematic quotations above present contrasting views on freedom. Silone links it with right choice. A person is free in a tyranny only when he takes the proper stance toward the tyranny—resistance. Any other attitude produces enslavement. Here there is no "cloudiness," no perplexity about the nature of the regime. Governed by a dictator, the citizen's responsibility is clear. Bellow, on the other hand, associates freedom with uncertainty, with the errors and frailties of life which multiply choices and obscure consequences. Earth is the school of freedom because it spawns endless options.

Though contrasting, both perspectives are anchored in human experience. Some situations do demand a particular response. If that response is not made, whether from cowardice, pride, or error, freedom shrinks. Behavior becomes more subject to external control. Yet it is also true that human experience associates freedom with situations where no particular response is demanded, where any one of a range of alternatives is open. The example of a child in an ice cream shop with his own dollar bill is readily appreciated. It would be, then, arbitrary to reject out of hand one of these experiences and to declare the other the true experience of freedom. The concept must be able to accommodate both. Yet this conclusion leaves open the untidy possibility of widely differing types to be incorporated into one concept. While there is, perhaps, no a priori theoretical reason why there should not be at least two contrasting sorts of freedom, the attraction of parsimony is strong. Every attempt to reconcile the contrasting experiences should be made before accepting the theoretical paradox. After all, freedom is worth pursuing, and it helps to know whether to do so in cloudiness or clarity. One may doubt whether a regime is truly tyrannical. What then? Does freedom lie in fighting it, in some other response, or in any particular response at all?

I intend in this chapter to sift these and other issues in order to create a concept of freedom both true to experience and theoretically coherent. This task requires full consideration of whether there is one type of freedom or more than one. Also to be considered is the idea of restraint. Do conditions internal to the actor (e.g., psychoses) place a restriction on freedom, or do only external conditions count? If internal conditions may diminish freedom, which are they? Must external restraints be deliberate to be curbs on freedom? Are individual or social omissions to be regarded as checks?

Another set of issues is suggested by the preceding chapter. There it was argued that authority and communion do not stifle freedom. Why not? Part of the answer rests in the discussions of authority and communion, but a complete answer awaits explication. Thus this chapter will unfold the idea of freedom and relate it to authority, community, character, and politics. It will show how communion and hospitality encourage and support freedom, how the free person makes authority part of himself, and how freedom is inseparable from responsibility and commitment. We start with the following preliminary idea of freedom: a person is free to the extent that he has and exercises the ability to make choices which bring him nearer the goals set by his fundamental commitments, these choices being unrestrained by external forces or by internal fears, delusions, and weaknesses. Responsibility is always linked to freedom, providing the connection between options and goals or commitments. At its highest, freedom is the responsible use of choice. If this is so, then hospitality directly promotes freedom; communion, including authority as a bond of communion, also does so as it aids development of the qualities of character on which freedom depends. Freedom, then, cannot be understood apart from human character.

In order to unfold these themes I shall, first, consider various well-known conceptions of freedom. From these a new theory will be constructed. Second, I shall explicate the relationship between authority and freedom in light of the new understanding of freedom. Third, I shall discuss the relationships between communion and freedom, and hospitality and freedom. Finally, I shall close the chapter with a consideration of politics and freedom.

Definitions of Freedom

There are four common but erroneous definitions of freedom which claim most contemporary allegiances. Each is associated with individualism, for the criterion of free action in each makes no reference beyond particular actors.[1] These four ideas of freedom are not introduced as a comprehensive account of contemporary thinking about freedom, though most influential views of freedom are contained in them.

First is the idea of freedom as spontaneity. In this conception a person is free when there are no restrictions on his expression of whatever is in him. He is free when his wants, desires, feelings, or behaviors flow without inhibition, preparation, or determination. This idea is captured in the term "free spirit," one who constantly surprises, who seems to have no inhibitions, no care for social pressures or conventions which might claim to govern his behavior. Moreover, spontaneity refers to the absence of conscious internal controls on behavior. Feelings, desires, or behaviors do not conform to a plan or a conscious set of rules. Action is not thought out in advance. The person free in this sense "does his own thing," whatever it happens to be at the moment.

This understanding of freedom has the obvious deficiency of failing to acknowledge that feelings, desires, and behaviors which seem spontaneous may have points of origin outside the immediate control of the actor. Certain spontaneous behaviors are the result of prior conditioning. Some free spirits always get drunk and make passes at the opposite sex during cocktail parties. If Freud has taught us anything, it is that seemingly unpremeditated feelings or behaviors may actually be the result of psychological compulsions which are anything but free. Even more elementary, a blink may be spontaneous, but it is neither voluntary nor free in the usual sense of these terms. This definition simply does not discriminate clearly enough among those experiences of unrestraint which are clearly free and those which only seem free but which careful analysis reveals to be constrained in important ways.

To preserve as much as possible of the first definition of freedom while taking account of its weaknesses, some have come to understand freedom as the ability of a person to do what he wants to do.[2] Here the focus is on conscious wants. Behavior resulting from subconscious impulses or biological determinisms is not considered free. This view places no restrictions on what may be consciously desired. Wants need not fit into any plan or set of principles. As long as the actor consciously wishes to do something and is unhindered from doing it, he is free. Liberty comprehends license.

The fundamental flaws of the first definition, however, remain in the second. Even though it restricts the motivations for action to conscious wants, this idea of freedom also allows the possibility of considerable coercion or restraint on the actor consistent with his ability to act upon his wants.[3] In the first place, a person's wants clearly can be manipulated by others in various significant ways. Social pressures, ideological appeals, deceptions, and socializing agents may largely determine many of a person's wants. Suppose a salesman uses deception on a susceptible customer in order to lead him to want refrigerator A when the customer needs only refrigerator B and, indeed, would realize this were it not for the salesman's deception. Yet he now consciously wants refrigerator A. If he buys it, would we say that he acted freely? No. The external manipulation has introduced an element of constraint at odds with the experience of freedom. Yet the definition could take account of this only by moving from a concept of wants to one of needs or of "real" wants. The third and fourth definitions of freedom considered below make a move similar to this.

The second flaw in the definition of freedom under consideration is that it does not count internal constraints as interfering. A person under the domination of mental illness or severe psychological tension can still consciously desire a thing, the death of a spouse, for example. Under such a circumstance, however, we should be reluctant to say that the want and the ability to act upon it are an instance of freedom.

The third and fourth notions attempt to overcome the difficulties with the idea of freedom as the ability to get what is wanted by stressing reason and intention. The third definition of freedom conceives it as the ability of an actor to choose and to act upon his choice without internal or external constraints. Choice in this understanding implies reason and intentionality. The object or state pursued must be consciously chosen in light of alternatives generally or easily available. Any manipulation of desire or any interference with reason or the normal range of choices available to the actor diminishes freedom. Moreover, impulsive behavior rooted in feeling, desire, or wants does not meet the conditions of free choice.

William E. Connolly, building upon the definition of Gerald C. MacCallum, Jr., expresses this idea of freedom well.[4] Connolly views freedom univocally, rejecting the well-worn distinction between negative and positive liberty. Freedom contains both positive and negative elements. A person is always free from something in order to do something else. What should be stressed, Connolly believes, is autonomy. "A person is autonomous to the extent that his conduct is informed by his own reflective assessment of his situation."[5] Thus Connolly offers the following definitions:

> X is free with respect to z if (or to the extent that) he is unconstrained from conceiving or choosing z and if (or to the extent that), were he to *choose z*, he would not be constrained from doing or becoming z. X acts freely in doing z when (or to the extent that) he acts without constraint upon his unconstrained and reflective *choice* with respect to z.[6]

For example, I am free with respect to lunch today if no internal or external forces have forced me to choose where to eat it and if, having chosen to stay at home, nothing would prevent me from doing so. Connolly makes some very perceptive comments on what counts as a constraint, describing various kinds of manipulations, impulses, or interferences with normal ranges of choice. But the key to his concept of freedom is his stress on reflective choice as the ground.

The fourth definition of freedom adds to the third the existentialist notion of a "project." Benjamin R. Barber, for instance, argues that persons are free when they act consciously and intentionally in pursuit of their projects.[7] Such a conception can even acknowledge that coercion occasionally may enhance freedom by helping to raise the actor's consciousness. The crucial distinction is between action (intentional) and behavior (nonconscious or reactive). The "autonomy" or "self-actualization" involved in this understanding demands only that projects conform to a self-set way of being. Freedom, in existentialist terms, is a potential for being in the world in a variety of ways, when the choice of a way or ways is not interfered with. A free act is creative; it produces something new, a new way of life or a new path of action in pursuit of one's project.[8]

The last two concepts are an improvement upon the first two, but they still fail to capture the distinctive flavor of freedom or to comprehend entirely its temper. A sound definition must make some reference to human character in the sense specified in earlier chapters. If freedom means anything more than simply following one's desires and merely feeling free, then the character of the person in question becomes relevant.[9] The concept of "project" is a diluted form of the concept of faith, just as life-style is a watered down version of a way of life. Such terms imply the false notion that fundamental commitments to ways of being in the world may be changed as easily as last year's fashions or the various short-term projects each of us undertakes from time to time. The latter two theories are correct in associating freedom with reason and intentionality, but these concepts in turn must be associated with judgments about the ultimate value of different ways of life. A way of life in commitment to truth and reality is more free than one at odds with truth and reality. A particularly telling example of this fact is the depiction of the voluptuary life in the film *Carnal Knowledge*. Here the intentional pursuit of his project leads the protagonist to ultimate enslavement to his sexual desires. The conceptions of freedom offered by Connolly and Barber significantly advance the understanding of freedom beyond fruitless debates between advocates of "positive" and "negative" liberty and beyond the primitive notion of freedom as want fulfillment, but they fall short of a complete account.

Freedom Defined

Responsibility is the key to the connection between freedom and character. Freedom and responsibility are inseparable, for to be free is to be responsible for the good and the evil one does. To be free is to be subject to praise and blame. In chapter 2, responsibility was linked to freedom and accountability. Without freedom there is no responsibility. Commitment too is linked to freedom, because the accountability owed by the responsible person refers to his basic commitments.

Freedom cannot be defined without reference to responsibility. Connolly himself suggests such a reference in pointing out that the language of constraint, intentionality, and choice demands that of responsibility. For example, to determine whether a constraint on choice or action interferes with freedom, we ask ourselves, among other questions, whether any person or group has caused the constraint.[10] The human being's inability to run sixty miles per hour is not an interference with his freedom, because it is a natural limitation. No person or group is responsible for it. Similarly, the idea of autonomy at the heart of freedom as the ability to make intentional choices evokes the idea of responsibility. To say that persons are capable of forming intentions, of deliberating about alternatives, and of choosing courses of action is to say that they are responsible. If a person is compelled by irresistible psychological or physical force to perform an action, he is not responsible for it. If a person acts "thoughtlessly," that is, unintentionally, we do not hold him directly responsible for the consequences of his deeds, though he is normally held responsible for the thoughtlessness itself. Thus freedom's features must include first responsibility and then commitment. Freedom is defined in one respect by the absence of constraint and in another by the commitments to which accountability is referred.

This analysis of freedom, responsibility, and commitment and the discussion of the various conceptions of freedom in the preceding section suggest three different but related phenomena within the general experience. First, we can distinguish the voluntary. This type corresponds to definitions 1 and 2 above. Action is voluntary if the actor has the ability to do what he pleases without internal or external compulsion. Here what one pleases or wants may be manipulated by others, but it is not determined by them or by any psychoses or gross mental defects. The customer in my earlier example who buys refrigerator A acts voluntarily though not completely freely. There is undeniably a value to voluntariness. It encourages the availability of a wide variety of options for individual choice. More importantly, it is beneficial for persons to be able to do just as they please on occasion. All work and no play makes Jack a dull boy. Voluntariness, however, is subject to all of the limitations discussed above and so is incomplete as an account of freedom.

The second phenomenon is Connolly's idea of freedom as the ability to choose among alternatives. It introduces responsibility, because it demands that selection among alternatives be made consciously, rationally, and intentionally. Simply following one's pleasure will not do. This type may be called freedom of choice, or "initial freedom"; it finds its home in the experience referred to in the quotation from Bellow. The cloudiness of the alternatives available in this world calls for conscious, deliberate choosing. This freedom need not be exercised in conformity with goodness, virtue, or fundamental commitment, though it may be in accord with one's project. One may make the wrong choice and still be free in this sense. Whether used properly or abused, this remains freedom. All that is required is that the actor make conscious, intentional choice among his alternatives. He may then be held responsible; he may be praised or blamed for his choices.

But to say that a person is held responsible or simply is responsible for his actions is not to say that he is a responsible person.[11] Such a person must habitually make proper use of his freedom, that is, he must tend to make choices which are harmonious with his commitments and which advance the goals specified by his faith. The person who follows only his desires is generally held to be irresponsible. The person who chooses consciously but not in accord with a fundamental faith is responsible for his choices. He fulfills some of the demands of responsibility—rationality and intentionality—but lacks the ability to ground his decisions consistently upon a fundamental commitment. He may possibly lack fundamental commitment itself.

These considerations suggest a third and most complete experience of freedom, that of the responsible person. Here we are concerned with the ability to choose properly in freedom situations, according to the demands of faith. This is called (in terms to be developed) "terminal freedom" and corresponds to the experience embodied in the quotation from Silone. Living under a dictatorship, a person committed to freedom and justice might choose consciously to collaborate with the dictator. This is an exercise of freedom, but its result is unfreedom in the terminal sense. Such a person is free terminally only if he chooses the proper course, that is, to resist. If freedom is a virtue and if initial freedom is its only variety, why do we excoriate quislings and praise the Resistance? I suspect that it is not only because we believe the former to have abused their freedom but also because we dimly realize that in a fundamental sense the latter are freer than the former.

There is a very weighty objection to adding the concept of terminal liberty to voluntariness and freedom of choice to express the fullness of freedom. D. D. Raphael voices it when he criticizes the view that liberty is to be identified with doing the right thing.[12] Acting correctly may very well lead to inner peace and harmony, the objection runs, but what do they have to do with freedom? Freedom of choice is real and does not suddenly vanish when a wrong choice is made. Others take the objection to terminal liberty further, arguing that such an idea runs the risk of imposing tyranny in the name of freedom. If freedom is doing right, then is it not likely that regimes convinced of the rectitude of their causes will seek to impose their views upon society, thereby substantially diminishing freedom of choice?[13] Liberalism is far more comfortable with "One man's freedom to swing his fist ends where the other's nose begins" than with "You shall know the truth, and the truth shall make you free" (John 8:31).

The latter saying is, however, a genuine insight. Terminal freedom is, indeed, the most complete form of freedom. To see why this is so, let us first take truth in the relatively narrow sense of honesty. I suppose that each of us has had the experience of telling a lie that seems to trap us. We are afraid of being caught, so other lies become necessary. Circumstances seem to conspire toward revealing the deception, and a web now seems necessary to hide it. The result of that prevarication, originally told so that we might be in control of a situation, now demands a network that ensnares us and leaves accidental circumstances in control of us. To break out by finally telling the truth, painful though it may be, is a liberating experience. In doing so, we regain a measure of control of our lives. No longer needing to hide, we have broadened our options. Originally, we were free to lie or not. The wrong choice, however, resulted in a diminution of freedom. To tell the truth, then, makes or keeps us free.

This illustration is an example of the general point intended by Simone Weil when she identified sin with gravity.[14] Sin means the loss of freedom because, like gravity, it weighs a person down, subjecting him to the necessity of its own logic. It leads the person away from where he would really want to go, from where he would be happiest. Sin implies choices without or contrary to commitment. Virtue, on the other hand, is that ability which enables a person to keep sight of where he really wants to go. Bernard J. Cooke says, "It is love that frees a person to be truly honest and genuinely himself; it vitalizes his experience so that he lives fully; it stimulates and brightens his consciousness and his thought."[15]

The phrases "initial freedom" and "terminal freedom" come from

Jacques Maritain and Yves R. Simon.[16] The most basic experiential base for understanding the concept of terminal freedom is the feeling of mastery which accompanies a free act. At such a moment I am conscious of being in control of myself and of my reactions. When I am not free, I am conscious that others, or circumstances, or some limited part of myself (desires, compulsions) drag me through situations.

"Terminal" refers to goals. Such freedom enables the person to achieve his ends in the daily choices he makes. As Simon says:

> Freedom is the power to make a choice between the means offered to our activity. Now, there are authentic means, those which lead to the end, and illusory means, which lead us away from our end. Freedom to choose illusory means is itself only an illusion of freedom, for a means which does not lead to the end is not a means.[17]

To choose an illusory means is a genuine exercise of initial freedom as long as it is conscious and intentional, but in leading away from the end, it subjects one to its own gravity and makes proper choice the next time more difficult. To choose a true means is an exercise of both initial and terminal liberty, because in leading to the end, this choice makes it easier to choose properly the next time. It helps the person to achieve mastery over the various means to his ends. A sports analogy may help understanding here. The person just learning a game such as soccer is mastered by the ball and the game situation. Though he is free to attempt a variety of moves with the ball, he is nevertheless reacting to it and to the other players. The good player, however, makes the ball and, to a certain extent, other players, subject to his own ends, such as scoring a goal or stealing a pass. Free to attempt a variety of moves, he selects the ones best suited to his purpose.

The person free in the terminal sense, then, does not have his choices determined by extraneous circumstances or by fascinations attaching to means themselves; rather, his choices are determined (Simon calls this freedom superdetermination) by his goals. Such a person's faith commitments achieve a mastery over his desires and passions and over his environment. The scholar, for example, having committed himself to learning, must master his own laziness, gluttony, pride, and other weaknesses as well as the blandishments of friends, the inadequacies of research facilities, and so forth. Only by doing so will he be free to reach the goals he has set.

Simon points out that terminal freedom is promoted by any background which "gives the individual more firmness, more coolheadedness, more self-control, more clear-sightedness, a more lucid insight into his own aspirations and the end he has to pursue."[18] Yet what are these qualities but the features of responsibility? To act clearheadedly and firmly in conformity with the requirements of faith is to be free and to be responsible. Such responsible action frees the person from error, weakness, the determinisms of the psyche, and domination by others.[19] Truth makes free because it indicates the path to be taken and instills the courage to travel it responsibly.

Connolly's discussion of freedom moves in the direction I have specified by introducing the idea of responsibility, but as I indicated, he does not go far enough. S. I. Benn and W. L. Weinstein suggest something similar to the idea that the responsible person is free when they argue that the language of freedom assumes that man is a responsible being and that responsibility is a status to be achieved.[20] Neither, however, captures the full dimensions of freedom and responsibility, because neither links responsibility to commitment. It is not enough to set any goals and to pursue them in one's choices. Goals must be set by commitments guided by a concern for truth and reality. To commit oneself to the life of a libertine and to choose means well calculated to that end is not to achieve terminal freedom. The result of such a commitment is enslavement to lust, not freedom. To reject the fullness of reality, committing oneself only to part of it, is to subject oneself to the natural necessities of that part and to deny the ground of one's being. Commitments themselves must be responsible. The assertion that the self is its own ground is the beginning of the cycle of unfreedom. The idea of freedom as choice in terms of a "project," then, will not do, unless the project refers to a faith open to truth and reality. The concept of freedom developed here thus includes all of the experiences associated with freedom—voluntariness, choice without constraint, and mastery.

The concept of terminal freedom has one additional advantage over theories which stop with the idea of initial freedom, if we again call to mind Silone's dictum. Most theories have a difficult time handling situations of coercion.[21] Clearly a person threatened with bodily harm if he exercises the right to vote has had his freedom obstructed. Just as clearly, he is free to comply or not. Moreover, the person who defies it seems to be free in Silone's sense of the word. Persons may act freely and responsibly within a very narrow range of choices. The responsible answer to the threat "Your money or your life" is to hand over your money. The responsible answer to the threat "Your faith or your life" is to hand over your life.

In the theory I have articulated, initial freedom is always a matter of degree. There are normal social and natural limitations on choice. To the extent that threat or coercion interferes with the normal range of choices, the person is unfree in the initial sense. Freedom of choice is always a matter of degree; choice is never unlimited. Moreover, the range of choices deemed normal may vary historically. Cultural and technological progress expands alternatives. Despite these complicating factors, however, it is clear that choices may be narrowed by coercion from individuals or social institutions. Such narrowing is a denial of, or at least, an interference with, initial freedom. From the point of view of terminal freedom, however, such limitations are the kinds of tests of responsibility and faith that should be expected in an imperfect world. Terminal freedom is responsible action within limits. Both Socrates and Christ, for example, were masters of their situations and acted responsibly in circumstances of massive coercion. They could be described as acting freely in unfree situations. Terminal freedom makes no assumptions about the number of means available to attain one's goal except that a choice is possible. Since terminal freedom is the responsible fulfillment of commitment in situations where choices must be made, fundamental commitments give guidance in decision making where choices are few and perilous, as in cases involving coercion. Coercion is not to be welcomed by those who believe in freedom, but it does not annihilate the experience of terminal freedom discovered by those who choose responsibly in the face of peril. To say that tests of responsibility are to be expected is not to treat them lightly or to diminish our condemnation of their interference with initial freedom. It is only to say that a theory of freedom must have the concepts available to handle such common experiences.

Naturally, the extent to which a particular individual is to be praised or blamed for his meeting of a challenge is a function both of the severity of the threat or coercion and of the strength of character which can reasonably be expected. Moreover, modern uses of brainwashing and torture, psychological and physical, remind us that coercion can interfere with terminal liberty if it is of such intensity that it severely damages, temporarily or permanently, the will and reason of the persons subject to it. The point at which different persons break under such extreme coercion varies; indeed, some individuals' strength of terminal freedom is sufficient to carry them through the most extreme measures. Such persons are, however, rare. The concept of terminal liberty does not demand heroic action from those whose natural endowments or training have not prepared them well for challenges to their faith. It does suggest, however, that a society which does not prepare its citizens for challenges to faith has failed in its responsibilities.

Freedom and Authority

The understanding of freedom developed above allows me to treat the relationship between authority and freedom more systematically than in the previous chapter. I have just shown how coercion may limit initial freedom without necessarily interfering with terminal freedom. Since the two types are not necessarily congruent, it becomes possible to argue that on occasion a decrease of initial freedom may actually increase terminal freedom. Authority may justifiably limit or interfere with a person's choices in order to train character for the exercise of terminal freedom. This happens frequently in raising children, and it is common with adults, too. Indeed, individuals often threaten themselves in order to strengthen their own sense of responsibility. Dieters are a good example.

Virtually everyone who advocates the notion of negative freedom or who would limit freedom to the initial form discussed above acknowledges that there must be limits on freedom. Some restriction of choice is legitimate. Authority has a place in the social world. But such advocates would deny that limits lead to a higher or truer freedom. Such ideas are thought to smack of Rousseau's infamous dictum that he who does not obey the General Will must be "forced to be free." Limits on freedom, it is argued, are justified only to make freedom of choice more equally available or to prevent one person's intrusion upon another's freedom of choice.

Some go much further and see an irreconcilable conflict between freedom and authority.[22] They take this position because they identify freedom and autonomy, defined as moral self-legislation. The autonomous man defines the moral law for himself and obeys only his own law. Since authority requires the surrender of moral judgment to others, it is incompatible with freedom.

The first thing to be recognized is that the idea of autonomy at the heart of this argument proceeds from a false conception which attempts to sever character from its communal moorings. Moreover, the idea of autonomy as self-legislation has internal problems as well. Presumably, the autonomous person is obliged to obey his self-made laws. But suppose he legislates erroneously and then realizes it? To obey would be to act irresponsibly. To disobey would violate the obligation. It would not do to argue that the obligation can be set aside whenever the author discovers an error, because there would then be no grounds for any idea of the obligations of an autonomous person. Without firm ideas of truth and commitment, on what warrant could the self certify an error to itself? The temptation to certify an error would be overwhelming when the self-made laws become burdensome. "Error" would become a universal and unchallengeable appeal and the idea of self-legislation simply a disguise for self-will. The real dilemma involves not authority and autonomy but authority and responsibility.

Wolff is correct in seeing that authority involves a surrender of personal judgment. When I submit to the command of a person that I perform or not perform some action, or to the teachings of a religious, moral, or scientific master, I surrender (temporarily, at least) my private judgment about the matters at hand. But it is critical to understand that I do so because I recognize, or believe I recognize, that the person in authority is entitled to deference.[23] The foundation of this belief is the basis of authority in reality. Contrary to Wolff, to surrender private judgment is frequently the most responsible action. It is appropriate in a fire to accept orders from a fireman. It is entirely proper when learning Greek or chemistry to defer to professors of Greek and chemistry. Of course, such surrender never totally displaces my own insight into reality. Firemen sometimes give faulty orders, and professors occasionally talk nonsense. Yet even in challenging, where appropriate and necessary, the orders of one who is suppposed to be an authority, the challenge is issued partially in the name of the authority of common sense or of other authoritative opinion. In short, the common challenges to the compatibility of freedom and authority rest upon a misunderstanding of one or both of the concepts. To set the matter straight, I shall consider in turn the relationship of authority to initial and terminal freedom.

First, authority certainly does place constraints on potential choices. The rules of political authority, for example, make persons less free than they would otherwise be to purchase certain products, perform actions sanctioned by criminal law, and engage in particular callings. These rules encourage certain potential choices and discourage others. Yet it would be mistaken to say that authority simply restricts initial freedom. The constraints which authority places on potential choice assist the person to be intentional and rational in the choices he does have. The constraints thus cultivate qualities of initial freedom.

The explanation of this paradox lies in the relation of pure voluntariness to initial freedom. The traditions, laws, and moral structures of society channel the chaotic desires of the person in particular ways. If he lacked direction, the wants of the individual would govern his life, which is to say that those persons most able to influence his desires would control his life.[24] His action would be voluntary though not free because not conscious and intentional. A person with some guidance by authority, that is, with some ability to think and to choose, is able to resist those who would control his life. The person who lives only to satisfy his desires has no standing from which to resist those who would manipulate his desires. Authority, then, provides an essential structure to freedom of choice and sustains it so that it does not decay into mere voluntariness.

As Peter Winch has most effectively argued, choice is meaningless without rules.[25] If the game "Monopoly" had no rules, what would be the point of trying to decide whether to buy Boardwalk or Park Place? Authority is a precondition of liberty in the initial sense because we must live by rules which give meaning and structure to potential choices. Without the laws, customs, and expectations of modern society, what would be the point of trying to choose between marriage and the single life or between college and trade school? Indeed, without such rules, would the distinctions be possible?

This is not to say that all of the rules, customs, and expectations of a social order are good and unqualifiedly promote freedom of choice. Many do not. Some rules take away with one hand, as it were, what they give with the other. Providing structure in sexual and occupational matters, for example, they may make certain occupational choices impossible for each gender. Remember, however, that I am discussing the role of authority in promoting initial freedom. Authority, I have contended, must be connected to reality. Its directives must be issued in accordance with truth. Not all social rules are authoritative, and not all support freedom of choice. But each social order requires authoritative directives to make freedom possible within its boundaries.

Next consider the relationship between authority and terminal freedom. Since both are intimately related to truth and to the demands of faith commitment, they are essentially connected. They mutually reinforce the ability of the person to act in conformity with his commitment. Authority teaches and directs, setting the demands of faith before the person and calling him to account for failure to live up to them. Terminal freedom refers to the person's mastery of situation and circumstance such that he is able to make choices fulfilling the demands of faith. A dramatic account of the dialectic of authority and terminal freedom is the history of the Hebrew people. In the Old Testament God continually frees His people from famine, war, and oppression, yet, at the same time, He constantly demands obedience to the Covenant and its Law.[26] Indeed, fidelity to the Covenant is required if the chosen people are to remain free.

This affiliation of authority and freedom to commitment is the key to explicating Arendt's insight that authority implies an obedience in which men retain their freedom. When the responsible person defers to one genuinely in authority by obeying his directives, the law becomes part of his own character. That is, he obeys not because the law is an external force that will threaten sanctions if he disobeys but because the law is part of himself, expressing the requirements of his own faith. In terminal freedom, mastery has become so much a part of the person that it has become ingrained, a habit. Deference to the one in authority is a product of loyalty, based upon recognition of the link between truth and the person in authority.[27]

My point may be most clearly seen in the authority of parents over children, though the substance is the same in any authority relation. Parents attempt to teach their children basic commitments, for example, to a religion, to honesty, or to fairness. At the same time, they attempt to inculcate the habits of church attendance, truthfulness, and fair play.

Indeed, the commitments cannot be taught apart from the conduct. Actions speak louder than words, and children pay little heed to teachings unconnected with requirements for behavior. Thus the teaching authority of the parent extends to demanding habitual behavior which will manifest the requisite mastery of circumstance in situations where the direct authority of the parent is absent. Commitment to honesty and the speech it demands are products of the interior appropriation of authority. Habit, as Aristotle tells us, is second nature and the principal part of virtue.[28]

A skeptic reading this account of authority and terminal freedom might wonder how internalization of law differs from brainwashing. The individual who has been brainwashed or, to put it more broadly, conditioned to act in certain ways, habitually behaves in those ways. Can we detect any difference between him and the terminally free person? Terminal freedom does not abolish initial freedom. The person who has made the law part of himself may do so imperfectly or may choose wrongly despite deep commitment and training. Honest persons occasionally lie. Responsible persons sometimes act irresponsibly. Such freedom of choice is what is denied, at least in attempt, in brainwashing or conditioning. These aim at total control by the conditioner. This external control is precisely opposite to interior appropriation of law and precisely opposite to the experience of mastery characteristic of terminal liberty. Moreover, action on commitment is free because, in addition to the freedom of choice enjoyed by the terminally free person, the commitment on which action is based is free. The commitment at the center of life must be freely accepted; otherwise it is not a commitment. Brainwashing and conditioning operate in the absence of commitment or through the destruction of the controlled person's ability to make one. The principles upon which the conditioned person acts are those of the controller and are, as such, alien to him.

It should now be clear, then, that authority and freedom, both initial and terminal, are not only compatible but also mutually reinforcing. The latter becomes possible only when the former orders choice possibilities. Authority can fulfill its purpose of directing persons to the demands of faith only when it is freely accepted. Authority cannot be imposed, because there is no congruence between the commitments of those in authority and those subject to it.

Freedom and Community

Given what I have said to this point, it should come as no surprise that freedom and community are intimately connected. This idea, of course, cuts across the grain of a substantial part of contemporary thought, which prefers to view community as an oppressive weight upon individual originality and spontaneity. There is certainly some truth in this, since community does impose restrictions upon spontaneity and upon the unbridled expression of feeling and desire. Yet these, according to the argument of this chapter, are not to be fully identified with freedom. Community does, indeed, restrain spontaneity, but in doing so it enhances initial and terminal liberty.

Many aspects of the relationship between freedom and community have already been developed in chapter 3; therefore my discussion here can be brief.

First, and most clearly, hospitality promotes freedom because it recognizes persons as responsible beings, capable of intention, rationality, and conscious choice. Thus hospitality is most clearly affiliated with initial freedom. A relationship of hospitality naturally evokes considered choice, because it treats each party as capable of it. It is a fundamental rule of human life that persons will tend to live up (or down) to what is expected of them. By encouraging high expectations of responsible action, hospitality promotes initial freedom.

Hospitality has some connection as well with terminal freedom, because it is a space in which persons meet in their essential being. In it commitment encounters commitment. It is, therefore, a place where commitments are developed, explored, and changed. Thus hospitality tends to encourage the speech and action which spring from fundamental commitment, yet it does not attempt directly to train for terminal freedom. But since hospitality is possible only to the extent that the persons involved are responsible, hospitality will be a field on which terminal liberty will be practiced. And practice is training for virtue. Because hospitality evokes responsibility and honesty, an opening to terminal freedom is always available. Since hospitality exists to bring out the best in persons, it indirectly inspires terminal liberty.

Of course, not all, or even most, encounters between persons are encounters of hospitality. Many meetings are dominated by the participants' attempts to gain or assert power over each other. Discussions become debates in which the object is to "win." Romantic encounters degenerate into sexual power plays. In such situations, initial freedom suffers because each party is attempting to limit the other's options. Terminal freedom suffers because the other is regarded as a means rather than a person of character and commitment. Given the power games present in most meetings, hospitality, to the extent it can penetrate and restrain them, can only serve to enhance freedom.

It should be added that hospitality imposes only minimal restrictions on freedom of choice. Since persons may meet in hospitality who have fundamentally different faiths, hospitality allows wide latitude of speech and action. It outlaws only choices which would violate its requirements of honest and responsible mutuality.

Community as solidarity also supports freedom. Communion makes authority possible, and authority facilitates terminal liberty by encouraging interior appropriation of the law. Communions attempt to train their members in the right, and hence in the proper, use of freedom of choice. After all, the growth of responsibility and faith is fundamentally dependent upon the support and nurture of communion. Since freedom depends upon faith and responsibility as well, freedom depends upon communion. It is a serious mistake to see the two as being antagonistic. Benjamin R. Barber expresses this view when he contrasts liberty in a Swiss canton with the liberal ideal. In Raetia, he asserts,

> freedom never came to be thought of as a commodity that might be enjoyed in the loneliness of the private arena, that condemned men to a solitary sanctuary where only the alienated were considered free, where the most irrational behavior, so long as it was unimpeded by physical constraints or public coercion, had to be regarded as free, and where the most rational and moral behavior, if it conformed to the dictates of law and the public will, had to be deemed bondage.[29]

On the contrary, freedom there was thought of as conscious and intentional participation in the decisions of the canton.

Communion, in short, fosters the development of the qualities of character which are essential to freedom. In doing so, it may repress impulses or desires inimical to character, possibly using coercion and removing or constraining particular choice potentials, but the result is enhanced reason and responsibility, which are more central to freedom than impulse or desire.[30] Community as solidarity teaches and strengthens the faith essential to responsible choice. It teaches the responsibility which is an essential component of freedom of choice, and it fosters the solitude in which the use made of freedom can be examined and improved.

Recall also that communion, as opposed to pseudocommunity, leaves an important area of open space, of privacy and solitude, for each of its members. Communion does not stifle initial freedom in the interest of terminal freedom. Communion is secure enough to dedicate a considerable amount of civil and political liberty to its members. Such is the result also of the requirement of participation in the life of the whole which is an essential bond of communion. Obviously, there is a dialectic of restraint and freedom operative in the life of communions. Some forms of behavior are restrained so that other forms may prevail and in order that freedom, in both senses of the term, may have a wide scope. Freedom requires both the space for appearance and the common norms and traditions against which new beginnings are visible.

Finally, we may ask with respect to the relationship between freedom and community as solidarity whether freedom supports communion. Here again the answer is "Yes." In the first place, as Simon points out, the free person has made his own the requirements of authority. Since authority is essentially related to the common good of a communion, the terminally free person promotes the common good, thus augmenting the life of the whole.[31] Such freedom must be pursued in communion. To seek it for one is to seek it for all, for the life of a group devoted to increasing the freedom of only one or of a few would hardly meet the criteria of communion. In a genuine communion, freedom itself can become something to be shared in common. Indeed, this is the essential foundation of the bond created by shared participation. Moreover, since joining is itself a free decision, the freedom of choice characteristic of the act of affiliation also strengthens communion.

Because of their rationality and responsibility, free persons are best able to contribute to communion and hospitality. The free person has resources and talents to bring to the common work of communion and to the encounter of hospitality. Such gifts as inner resiliency, dedication to goals and mastery of the means to goals, conscientiousness, and responsibility are not to be despised. Indeed, the responsible person is essential to communion and hospitality. Since he has now been identified as the free person in the highest sense, it is clear that freedom makes a major contribution to community.

Of course, it is obvious that freedom of choice is often misused, that persons acting consciously and intentionally make mistakes and commit evil deeds, and that responsible persons fall into sin and error. Such things promote neither communion nor hospitality. Yet even here freedom of choice is good. The opportunity to make mistakes is critical to the members of any communion, even though the errors can be harmful. Communions must leave wide latitude for exercise of initial freedom and must tolerate abuses and mishaps in its use, for initial freedom is a good. But such freedom is not to be without any limits. That surgeons make mistakes is no reason to ban surgery, though it is reason to regulate it. Similarly, freedom is not the greatest good. Its imperfections make it subject to regulation in the interest of the common good. Here again is an example of the dialectic between freedom and restraint.

Politics and Freedom

When we move into the arena defined by the concepts of freedom and politics, we move into a troubled and cloudy area. Here we must contend not only with the complications of personal freedom but also with the difficult idea of political liberty. We must ask whether a concept of communal or political liberty has any validity or whether politics simply affects for better or worse the freedom of particular persons.

The preceding section suggests the direction we might take to find an answer to this question. Since community promotes freedom in important ways, it seems plausible to believe that political order and freedom are not only compatible but even allied in principle. Despite a most influential heritage of perceived opposition between politics and freedom, such opposition is more illusory than real. Certainly it is abundantly clear that throughout history governments have not made freedom a prime goal and indeed have been at times its principal enemies. Yet this is not a matter of essence. At bottom there is mutual support between politics and freedom. Barber hints at this notion in discussing communal liberty in the Swiss context: "For [Anglo-American political thought], freedom and political community have represented antagonistic parameters of an essentially anarchistic scale moving from individualism (freedom) to statism (political community, thus nonfreedom); in Switzerland freedom has been understandable only within the context of community."[32]

To explore the framework in which politics and community are mutually reinforcing, I shall divide the subject into three parts. First, I shall look at the idea of a "free society," the extent to which politics affects freedom in many areas of life. Second, I shall examine the meaning of specifically political freedom. Third, I shall consider the relationship between politics and terminal freedom.

In its most elementary sense a free society may be considered one in which the maximum possible latitude of freedom of choice is open to the individual members of society. Such a society will as well provide a wide area for freedom as spontaneity, that is, as much as possible it will leave persons alone to do as they please. This idea is obviously very close to the liberal conception. The terms "maximum possible" and "as much as possible," however, are qualifiers introduced because of the intrinsic limitations of choice and because freedom must be reconciled with other fundamental principles. In other words, political freedom does not refer merely to choice; terminal liberty also has a political dimension. Moreover, the extent of freedom of choice and spontaneity available in society must be compatible with justice, community, character, and common good. Even liberal theory recognizes this, permitting restrictions on range of choice in the interest of justice or other aspects of freedom. For example, freedom to join or not to join a union may be restricted in the interest of the economic justice promoted by the union shop. Mail may be censored in wartime in the interest of national survival. In this respect, the chief differences between my view of the free society and the dominant liberal theory are that I am willing to accord other principles a higher value vis-à-vis freedom than most liberals and that liberals tend to try to translate these values into terms of freedom when it is a question of sacrificing freedom to gain them. "Economic justice," for example, might become "freedom from want" or "economic freedom."

How does politics affect a free society? First, as liberals have long recognized, politics leaves persons alone as much as possible. Politics in this view refrains from intrusions into the economic, religious, moral, and social life of citizens. Often such government restraint is mandated by constitutional provisions. By not interfering, it leaves open many areas for free choice which past governments closed. In addition, politics according to this view serves a protective function, also acknowledged by liberals. It does intervene in certain areas of life—for example, in physical injuries, enforcement of contracts, and protection of personal property and of the integrity of national borders—to protect the individual from the depredations of others. Such protection promotes freedom by giving persons peaceful areas of movement so that they may actively exercise their wills in ways of their own choosing.

This is all very well known, as it is that later liberal theory found another role for politics that caused liberals to part company from conservatives. Politics, from this new perspective, may increase options available to freedom of choice by removing constraints in the economic and social environments. Freeing persons from economic oppression, racial and cultural stereotypes, poverty, and dependence upon similar forces beyond their control provides for them a broader area of choice than they would otherwise possess. This is the basic liberal justification of social welfare programs. Why the same logic does not apply to restraints originating in the moral environment has always been one of the great paradoxes of liberalism, one which ritual appeals to *On Liberty* have not been able to resolve.

Given the qualifications mentioned above and below, these two general descriptions of how politics promotes a free society are valid. Of course, there are problems in reconciling the two principles in practice. A particular program of government intervention to remove an economic restraint on persons may violate the injunction that government must leave people alone. One of the advantages of the theory presently being outlined is that it provides principles to which to appeal in such dilemmas. Moreover, to these two liberal principles of the free society must be added the idea that politics promotes a free society by bringing persons together. That is, politics, as we shall see in the following chapters, makes community possible. Politics protects not only individuals but also communities, facilitating the growth of both. Since freedom of choice requires, as I have argued, basic qualities of character, and since character requires community, politics indirectly promotes freedom of choice by promoting community and the qualities of character essentially related to it. This function of politics also promotes terminal freedom, as I shall argue below.

The free society defended here, then, differs from the liberal idea in a number of ways, but most importantly in seeing politics as related not only to individuals and their freedom or lack of freedom but also to the flourishing of community within the social order. A properly functioning polity will, then, frequently uphold the authority of a communion against the claim to freedom of an individual citizen. More positively, it will promote a diversity of communions.

The principles outlined above may be made more specific through consideration of some other concepts often connected with the idea of a free society, especially tolerance and pluralism. Tolerance, according to the principles developed in this book, is a communal principle expressive of the value of hospitality. A free society will practice tolerance as an active concern for the character of each member. It will promote the social requisites for the encounter of character by actively permitting differences of communion and commitment. In other words, politics is not indifferent to the beliefs of its members but cares enough about them to protect the freedom necessary for such persons to meet in hospitality. Such a politics will promote the freedom of each to go his own way, not because it does not care which way people go, but because it hopes their paths will cross. Indeed, it encourages publications, universities, political parties, and auditoriums where paths are likely to cross.

Moreover, since responsibility is the key ingredient of freedom of choice, political society should be tolerant, because tolerance as an active principle calls forth responsibility. A tolerant society makes persons responsible for their own views on political, religious, artistic, literary, moral, and economic matters. Tolerance here promotes freedom by treating people as free; that is, as capable of responsible choice in such matters. Tolerance is thus a part of freedom and a social virtue encouraging wide freedom of choice.

Liberal theory also values tolerance, but it does so individualistically rather than communally. As Barber points out, in liberalism "tolerance appears as a compromise between a predilection for anarchistic autonomy and a realistic recognition of the minimal requisites of public order—not, of course, as ends in themselves but as necessary weapons in the struggle for individuality."[33] Putting tolerance in this framework provides a sound theoretical foundation for the decisions which, not uncommonly, must be made to limit tolerance. If the value of tolerance lies only in the freedom it allows to individuality or to spontaneity, then it is difficult to find sound principles upon which to limit tolerance, even when public order is severely undermined. If, on the other hand, tolerance is rooted in responsibility and community, substantial harm to community or the prevalence of irresponsibility may constitute ground for refusing to tolerate some actions or expressions of opinion.

For example, obscenity and pornography, though not nudity or eroticism per se, encourage, indeed celebrate, irresponsible choice in sexuality. They undermine as well communal sexual bonds and encourage treating partners as objects of individual gratification, interfering with both communion and hospitality. A free society may, then, be justified in imposing restrictions on the ability of citizens to choose to buy and sell obscene and pornographic materials.[34] A free society will not be embarrassed to impose limits on the range of choice where restraints are critical for protection of the common good or the society's pursuit of its basic commitments, because it is the existence of communion which makes responsibility and therefore freedom of choice possible.

Such an argument does not imply that the political order must always and with utmost vigor suppress pornography. It only provides a theoretical justification for doing so consistent with the values of freedom and tolerance. Whether to suppress, and how firmly, are prudential matters to be settled by references to these principles and to the circumstances of each society.

A free society is pluralist as well as tolerant, though it is not pluralist in the sense that politics is dominated by the struggle of interest groups. Rather, its politics is pluralist in encouraging a wide variety of types of community to flourish. Just as communion does not demand total conformity, so a free society promotes freedom by making a wide variety of communities available for the responsible choice of its members. Indeed, diversity is a requirement of stable political life just as it is essential for the survival of a genetic and ecological system. The more diverse a natural ecological system, the less fragile, because it allows the effects of mistakes to be dissipated. A political order should exhibit a similar diversity. Freedom, moreover, as Robert A. Nisbet is fond of noting, is located in the interstices of authority.[35] In a political order a plurality of authorities based upon a plurality of communities allows a greater freedom of action and choice than a system of authority grounded in one or a few communities only.

Second, it is clear that political freedom is not fundamentally negative, that is, it is not absence of restraint or governmental noninterference in private life. Political systems which allow political freedom may interfere substantially in the economic, moral, and social lives of their citizens. On the other hand, political freedom may encourage extensive economic, moral, and social freedom. Democracy and the absence of restraint are not logically connected.[36]

The most important part of political freedom is communal participation, by which I do not principally mean voting or lobbying efforts which, though part of political freedom, are normally highly individualistic activities designed to express preference or protect self-interest. In its fullest sense, however, political freedom is tied to participation in the ongoing common life of a political community. It requires loyalty to the common good and the competence and the opportunity to make a significant contribution to it. Genuine political freedom is exhibited by the ancient Greek democracies and by the direct democratic institutions of the Swiss cantons rather than by the institutions of Western liberal democracy. The last named exhibit the basic minimum requirements and perform a most valuable service in protecting them but rarely exhibit the fuller possibilities of political freedom.

Just as an individual is free in the fullest sense when he makes responsible choices in light of his aims, so a political order is free when its citizens elect together the means to their common goals. Such choice, of course, requires the basic freedoms familiar in liberal democracy, the rights of speech, press, assembly, and religion, the vote, choice among a variety of candidates and policies, and so forth. Yet even more is needed. Such choice also demands small-scale institutions in which a citizen may have a real impact and may genuinely encounter other citizens, debating and deliberating with them about a common destiny.[37] If freedom involves mastery, then it is clear that its political form can come only when citizens participate together in authentic shaping of their future and when they know that their contributions matter.

Third, we must consider the contribution which politics makes to terminal freedom. This subject leads directly to the following chapter, which takes up the nature of political community and human character, and also follows directly from the idea of political freedom. Since political freedom involves, at its fullest, extensive participation in the life of a community and involves persons in encounters with others, political freedom is intimately associated with communion and hospitality. Therefore politics can make a contribution to terminal freedom because it builds up the social requirements for character formation. Both political authority and political freedom importantly contribute to character, communion, and hospitality.

This perspective is unusual. It seems to give politics a more extensive involvement in personal life than most are willing to grant it. It seems to demand lofty virtue of institutions which normally display human imperfection in its most blatant forms. It seems, in other words, to be a wholly optimistic and hence unrealistic picture of politics. It is true that I have heretofore considered politics at its height, in its fullest development. My perspective, while couched in descriptive terms, has been fully normative. It is now time to confront politics directly and to examine its nature and its relationship to character and community. Is there any sense to the term "political community"? What is the place of political loyalty in the whole pattern of a person's loyalties? Such questions are fundamental to an understanding of the relations among politics, character, and community. The understanding and explication of these topics will require as well full examination of topics touched upon only briefly in this chapter: political participation, political freedom, and pluralism. It will also require discussion of the fundamental goals of politics, justice and the common good. With these topics we arrive at the heart of a theory of political order.

7

Pluralism and the Common Good

There is no guarantee for democracy, or for the protection of the person against the collectivity, without a disposition of public life relating it to the higher good which is impersonal and unrelated to any political form.
Simone Weil,
"Freedom of Opinion"

Since communion, hospitality, and character are the central normative principles that we have established, the central question becomes: how, if at all, does politics promote character and community? The worth of politics must be measured by its contribution to the human good. All political theorists have explicitly or implicitly taken this view. This chapter and the next examine the role of politics.

I shall treat separately the questions of how politics is related to community and of how politics is related to human character. First, I consider the potentially misleading idea of a "political community." Second, I consider the notion of a direct contribution of politics to human character. This idea must be almost totally rejected as explaining how politics promotes character, but we may learn from it important lessons about the limits of politics. Finally, I discuss at some length the proper answer to the basic question, developing the fundamental political ideas of the common good, pluralism, tolerance, and participation. These concepts provide the keys to unlock the relationships among politics, character, and community. They tell us what it means to be a citizen, a member of a political community.

Political Community: The Body Politic as Community

The idea of the body politic itself as a community is especially tempting in an age of nationalism in which the communal aspects of the nation, such as language, symbols, and traditions, become assimilated into the political system. We tend to see the body politic or its representative, the state, as an object of faith and loyalty and to build it into a pseudocommunal unity. Sebastian de Grazia develops a version of this idea.[1] De Grazia's plea for increased allegiance to the political community and reduced allegiance to commercial values is premised on the absolute necessity of a political faith and loyalty superior to all other loyalties. This last, he believes, will make brothers of all members of the political community. Conflict of the political with other faiths separates persons from one another and causes anomie, simple or acute, in members of the community.

The purpose of politics in such a view is to promote community among all citizens of the nation-state. Note that this is an idea of communion. Hospitality has as yet no part to play. Despite its great temptations in an individualistic and anomic age, this view is heavily flawed. Though it does contain a partial truth, acceptance of this version of political community would likely produce an oppressive and ultimately despotic political regime. In order to show the truth as well as the danger of this idea, I shall proceed by discussing the nation-state's claim to be a communion in terms of the principal bonds of communion established in previous chapters.

1. The most obvious bond of national political communion is shared value and commitment. Whether they refer to a basic creed, a political faith, or a civil religion, many have argued that a central commitment to shared political values lies at the heart of the bond between citizen and state. As Aristotle observed, a polis is defined not by a territory but by a constitution, that is, a way of life. Obviously the degree of commitment to such shared values, the number of such values, and their degree of particularity will vary from nation to nation and from time to time. There will be tensions within the system of values, as, for example, in America, where commitment to individualism tends to weaken commitment to the political order and its demands upon citizens. Though a vast sea of social science literature attempts to document national consensus, to test its limits, to define the requisite degree of commitment, to mark its impact on public opinion, and so forth, it seems at least clear that the modern nation-state does stimulate a substantial commitment to basic values, institutions, and purposes. For better or worse, deeds are done in the name of nations which in other times would be performed for the sake of religions or heroic ideals. Politics does seem to be related to communion through its bond of shared commitment.

2. Closely tied to shared values are symbols and rituals. Here again, we find elements of communal unity. Citizens draw on important political and cultural symbols, celebrate common rituals, and remember important collective histories. Flags, anthems, independence days, rulers' birthdays, and dates of uprisings symbolize and evoke feelings of solidarity and significance. They provide occasions for common participation in communal life and belief.

Just as consensus on shared values varies according to time and place, so devotion to symbols will vary. Flags mean more to some than to others. Nevertheless, such common customs form a critical part of whatever degree of solidarity is present in political societies. Without them the life of nations would be cold and bloodless. We find, then, that on at least two counts there is reason to view political society as communal. This finding is the ground of the partial truth in the idea of the body politic as communion. Other bonds of communion, however, are not as prominent as common commitment and ritual.

3. Authority is a critical bond of communion. Certainly, it would be a mistake to claim that authority is absent in nation-states, but the crisis described in chapter 5 is the more striking phenomenon. To be authoritative, policymaking must be oriented to the common good of a community, not to the private preferences of competing interest groups. Today, not only does policymaking generally follow the latter model, but, even more striking, attempts are made to develop that model into a normative democratic theory. Citizens are increasingly, and rightly, skeptical of politics and its practitioners who operate according to such theories. Their obedience to policy becomes a matter less of deference to authority than of fear, habit, and timidity. In totalitarian and despotic regimes, on the other hand, authority is absent not because politics is a matter of interest-group compromise but because in such regimes policy serves the ideology and the personal or class interest of the rulers. It has contact neither with reality nor with the common good of the whole society. Another reason to doubt the alleged communal nature of the body politic is the plurality of commitments and communions in most nations. Since authority is rooted in commitment, a plurality of different, often competing, commitments has the potential, at least, of undermining single-minded loyalty to political authority if that authority claims ultimate loyalty.

4. A fourth major bond of communion, love, seems only minimally, if at all, present in nation-states. In communion members exhibit not simply love for the same objects of commitment but also strong affection and concern for one another as persons. Signs of a bare minimum of concern of fellow citizens for each other are undoubtedly present in our times, but such concern is hardly the kind of love which characterizes friendships, families, fraternities, clubs, and religious congregations. Despite minimal affection, nations are riven by ethnic, class, regional, sexual, occupational, and religious prejudices and antagonisms. Sheer size makes any kind of intense affection impossible. In the face of such obstacles, nations are fortunate if citizens tolerate, let alone love, one another. Indeed, civic tolerance "is probably as close as we can come to that 'friendship' which Aristotle thought should characterize relations among members of the same political community."[2]

5. The final critical bond of communion is common work or participation in the life of the group. Once again, the nation-state lacks a vital

element of communion. In modern nations political participation has at best minimal significance as a bond of national communion. Periodic voting, plebiscites, and occasional rallies may have significance as part of a national ritual, but they do not constitute the kind of work with others or the participation in decisions about a common future which characterize genuine communal participation. While the numbers of active political participants, and the forms of participation, vary widely from nation to nation, in no case does the level rise to that necessary to serve as a bond of communion. For the vast majority of citizens, participation is sporadic, illusory, coerced, or meaningless. Or all four at once.

What conclusions should be drawn from these observations? In the first place, the degree of truth in the view of the body politic as a communion should be acknowledged and appreciated. It is a good thing that the nation is to some degree a communion. Political loyalty to a particular national entity provides a concrete, personal setting for the living out of political affection. People need the support of actual political and social structures and contact with particular others as a focus for their political energies. "World society" or "mankind" has a certain inspiring ring, but the words are too abstract to provide much motivation for concrete political action. The nation can be a proper soil for human obligations and duties and for the roots of local loyalties. It can be a "vital medium" of the necessary human devotion to something outside oneself, a medium of sacrifice and obligation.[3] Decline in commitment to common national values and rituals often signals an increase in alienation. Since alienation is untenable for naturally social creatures, the cry for conformity to national values is raised. Thus the decay of free loyalty stimulates the growth of coerced conformity.[4] Finally, in many cases, the national value system is devoted more to justice and the common good than are local values. Thus loyalty to national symbols is often a worthy antidote to narrow local loyalties. In the United States, for example, national political institutions effectively challenged local resistance to justice for racial minorities, labor union members, and the poor.

The second conclusion to be drawn from these observations about the nation as communion is that attempts to unite intensity of commitment and the size and power of the nation are extremely dangerous. Such attempts most often take the form of making the nation and its symbols the highest commitment of all citizens and of coercing participation in commitment-building activities. In these cases attempts are made as well to stress the authority of the nation and, often, the common brotherhood of all citizens. Such efforts often take the form of finding a "common enemy." Once one is found or created, a "threat" is perceived, and common sentiments of resistance are encouraged. The threat then seems more real, and patriotic fervor is even more stimulated. The cycle may continue until the pressure for cohesion explodes or until the instruments of control are firmly in the hands of those attempting to build national unity. In short, because genuine communion is intimately connected with the character of the person and thus with his whole life, the attempt to make the nation such a communion is inevitably totalitarian. Despite the value of a degree of national unity and loyalty, dissatisfaction with its limits and desire for intense levels of national patriotism and community must be shunned. The effort to create such cohesion is, moreover, doomed to failure, for only pseudocommunity can emerge from it. Forced participation is not genuine participation, especially when it involves commitment building rather than decision making. The ability to impose a creed and direct action according to it is power rather than authority. The cohesion of citizens is conformity, not love. Forced commitment is not faith but brainwashing.

The effort to make the nation a communion is doomed to the fate of totalitarianism for an additional reason. The structural obstacles are insurmountable. The most important obstacle is size. Participation is based upon persuasion, the give and take of practical reasons, and persuasion is severely limited by size. Persuasion is effective only where there is familiarity, trust, and the ability to discuss and weigh reasons.[5] Of course, large numbers of people may be swayed by rational, emotional, or psychological means, whether such means are direct or work through the mass media. Yet participation in common work, in policy formation, and in the day-to-day life of a communion depend upon the give and take of discussion. In the same way, though large numbers can share emotional reactions in times of crisis or triumph, such as the assassination of President Kennedy or the end of World War II, ties of affective unity can be jointly experienced by relatively few. Many people cannot share the small emotions on which the daily life of communion depends, nor can they know each other, except as stereotypes.

The industrial/commercial focus of the nation-state system also stymies communion. The political system focuses on producing material goods and insuring an increasing material standard of living. In such a world the dominant theme becomes happiness to be enjoyed in the private realms of psyche or home, not in the public realm of participation and responsibility. Industrial/commercial society presents obstacles to authority. Since authority pursues common goods, it finds little place in a politics devoted to guaranteeing private goods. The conditions of modern society guarantee that citizens have widely different ideas of what the obligations of membership in society are, again making authority, love, and participation of a communal quality impossible.[6]

In summary, an important partial truth behind the idea of political communion emerges. Commitment to common national political values and rituals is a necessary element of political unity in the modern world. Yet the idea of national political communion is flawed and dangerous. Community and politics do have an important and legitimate relationship, but the temptation of seeing it as the idea of national political communion must be resisted.

Politics and
Human Excellence

Theorists throughout the history of political thought have believed that politics should help to develop maturity or excellence in human beings. Maurice Stein has argued that "human communities exist to provide their members with full opportunities for personal development through social experimentation."[7] This is only a less sharply focused expression of Aristotle's dictum that the polis exists for the "good life," that is, for the moral perfection of its citizens. It was, indeed, a fundamental assumption of Greek life that the polis existed to educate men, to shape their characters toward a model of the best life.[8] Closer to our own time, Hawthorne believed that the state was necessary to educate man, to develop the highest excellence of which he is capable. And Simon thought that authority has a "perfective" function when leaders communicate excellence to their followers.[9]

My own previous arguments seem to reinforce the assertions of these thinkers that politics makes a significant contribution to character. Responsibility was seen in the preceding chapter to be a fundamental political concept. Whether we take authority, freedom, interest, representation, or a host of other basic political concepts, we invariably discover that they make no sense unless political actors are capable of intentionality, rationality, and self-restraint; in other words, unless they are capable of responsibility. Since a political system must promote these qualities to be healthy, it must promote responsibility. Moreover, politics has some relation to commitment. To the extent that political objects play an important role in a person's life, to that extent is politics capable of affecting his commitments in a positive or negative way. Since two essential elements of character are thus linked to politics, it seems that politics can take an important part in shaping character.

As with the relation between politics and communion, the argument so far has revealed a critical, but partial, truth. It is clear that political systems affect the character of citizens. Such is the ruling analogy of Plato's Republic. A political system which is corrupt and irresponsibly led will tend to encourage dishonesty, venality, and irresponsibility in citizens. One rooted in twisted principles will tend to encourage perverted commitments. On the other hand, a state with largely honest, responsible, and properly committed leaders will tend to produce citizens with these same qualities. The relationship holds in the other direction as well and holds out a critical truth. But what conclusions are to be drawn from this truth?

A realistic assessment of human tendencies toward greed, power, and self-righteousness suggests that a political order principally charged with developing the character of its citizens would not stop at encouraging responsible action or commitment but would begin to fill in a substantive content for commitment and responsibility. That is, instead of encouraging responsible participation by presenting a choice of candidates, it would limit candidate selection to one, since only one party is "the responsible choice." Instead of encouraging a variety of faiths to present themselves for the allegiance of citizens, it would attempt to insure that each citizen is committed to the "true" faith—Marxism-Leninism, Fascism, Catholicism, Capitalism. Of course, these would be perversions of the ideals of responsibility and commitment, but they are encouraged by the human inclination to pride and the misinterpretation of a genuine truth. They thus have a certain attractiveness.

The qualities of character at the heart of the theory of political order developed in this book are not susceptible to such treatment. Indeed, it would be most difficult to conjure up a way in which a regime could enforce solitude among its citizens. Indeed, a totalitarian state strives in precisely the opposite direction, attempting to form its subjects into an undifferentiated mass. By destroying solitude's space for reflection, it hopes to prevent the genuine thought which could undermine the status quo. Here is a clue to the error of the misinterpretation of politics and character under consideration. Since regimes based on this misinterpretation cannot promote solitude, they cannot promote responsibility or faith either, because both are dependent upon solitude. Responsibility without solitude is also without effective choice, because solitude is a time for reflection on choice. No genuine responsibility is encouraged in such a setting. Similarly, faith requires reflection, and thus solitude, since it is a real movement of the heart in the midst of possibilities for commitment.

The notion that commitment and responsibility are the chief aims of politics must, then, be rejected. But it will not do to make the opposite error and disregard the true connection between politics and character. For just as political realism tells us that politics chiefly concerned with character will be despotic, so it tells us that politics without any concern for character will be corrupt and disordered. Character and community are more fragile than we like to think, and the kernel of truth in the Hobbesian account of the state of nature is revealed when politics collapses. In the reign of disorder character is hard-pressed. Many forget their commitments, follow their worst desires, and give up any claim to responsibility. Distrust and deception rule the day. In times of riot, civil war, or collapse of authority, the critical importance of politics for character is starkly revealed.

We have seen, then, that politics is related to character and community, and we have examined conceptions of this relationship which contain partial truths. When extended beyond the grain of truth, however, they suggest a dangerous conception. We are warned, then, that a full account of how politics should promote character and community will be more complicated than these concepts. A full account should contain within itself not only the principles governing the advancement of community and character but also intrinsic principles of the limits of politics, so that the totalitarian temptations above are avoided.

Politics, Community, and Common Good

The foundation of such an understanding of politics rests on the account earlier in this chapter of the communal aspects of politics and in the account in chapter 5 of political authority. Political society is, in some measure, a communion, and has a role to play in promoting communion among its members. To admit so much is to acknowledge that political society requires authority. I have already shown that political authority is that which directs a political community to its proper ends of justice and the common good. Moreover, authority strengthens communion by protecting the weak and by teaching the norms. The key to understanding politics and communion is political authority, which may be grasped by means of the idea of the common good.

The term "common good" is not much in use of late. "Public interest" has largely replaced it. Yet some of the problems of modern political thought are evident in widespread disagreement about the meaning of "public interest." Many reject the concept altogether; others identify it with an aggregation of particular individual or group interests. The public interest is conceived most commonly as the policy which emerges from the conflict of groups within the democratic process or, occasionally, as the very process of conflict and compromise. The most fundamental flaw of such ideas is their failure to see politics as anything beyond the encounter of interests—that is, as wants, desires, or preferences. In the politics of interest, no public exists to possess an interest, nor are there any criteria according to which an interest's moral or political worth might be assessed.[10] Yves R. Simon's theory best points the way to a coherent account of the common good.

According to Simon, the common good is not a sum of individual goods, yet it demands constant distribution to individuals. Perhaps an example will help. A public highway is a common good, but not because the happinesses of users may be summed in a fashion which increases total individual happiness. Rather, it is a common good because each may use it (it is constantly distributed to individuals) and in so using it enhance the common intercourse (life together) of the community. Of course, private happiness may also be increased by public roads. On the other hand, a thoroughfare may require individuals to sacrifice private goods (e.g., land for the right-of-way). The common good, then, seems capable of both harmony and conflict with individual goods.[11]

In developing Simon's contribution to resolving this dilemma, I shall refer to a distinction developed by Jacques Maritain.[12] Personal goods would include rationality, integrity, freedom, virtue, and relation to God. They are intimately related to the qualities of character I have described in this book. Individual goods include such material goods as health, income, and occupation. Personal goods are of higher value than individual goods, for the latter are essentially means to personal goods. Since, as we have seen above, the common good of a society must be shared by the members of the society and not external to men, it must promote the personal goods of its members. It is essentially related to them. Yet because it is so related, the common good takes precedence over the individual goods of each member.

It is important to state explicitly that Simon considers the pursuit of individual goods which contribute to personal good to be necessary and legitimate.[13] Simon also recognizes that the individual goods of different persons diverge. He denies, however, that the personal goods of citizens could be opposed; they have an objective, transcendent focus. Persons do not come into conflict in their ends, for the goal of full human development and autonomy is the same for each. The full development of one does not detract from that of others. The goods, however, which are possible means to such development very often are mutually incompatible.

Cases of legitimate conflict between the personal and the common good may also occur in which the former is ethically superior to the latter. In such cases the personal good concerns the supernatural order (the order of charity and salvation) and the common good the natural order. Here the order of charity is prior to the order of natural virtue. A person may not deny God to preserve the common good. "Of this common good it should not be said that it is the ultimate absolutely speaking, for it is ultimate within an order which is not itself ultimate."[14]

We may now summarize the ethical principles which Simon employs to resolve the dilemma of legitimate conflict among goods. First, the person pursuing his personal good accepts the precedence of the common good over his individual goods, for he takes into himself the authority which directs the use of these goods. The common good, for Simon, does not stand against the development of personality but contributes to it. Therefore, because the personal takes precedence over the particular, the common good also takes precedence. Though valid goods clash, the common good has priority. Tax laws, for example, where such laws do, in fact, promote the common good, stand not as external commands and sanctions to the mature man but as embodiments of his moral obligation to support the common good. Second, the proper functioning of authority requires that the promotion of individual and personal goods be left to the care of individuals or to the smallest association possible. The common good itself requires autonomy as well as authority. The former asserts that "wherever a task can be satisfactorily achieved by the initiative of the individual or that of smaller social units, the fulfillment of that task must be left to the initiative of the individual or to that of small social units." The latter asserts that "wherever the welfare of the community requires common action, the unity of that common action must be assured by the higher organs of that community."[15] But Simon goes even further to say that the free man should promote his own good wholeheartedly, even in the debate over the requirements of the common good, though he must, of course, defer to authority when the common good is determined. The legitimate conflict between the common and the individual good is always to be resolved in favor of the common. Third, legitimate conflict between personal and common good must be resolved in favor of the common good when the two are of the same order but in favor of the personal good when it pertains to the order of salvation. Such a conclusion does not at all deny the tragedy and sacrifice inherent in political life, but it does give them meaning.

This summary of Simon's theory suggests that a sound theory of the common good must see it as an end or a goal normatively defined and hence not perfectly or wholly attainable, for no society subject to sin and the contingencies of this world can ever actualize fully its moral and social potential. The common good has the character of a form and a final end. The most a political order can do is to pursue (not procure) its goal through policies and actions which are the care of authority and which are means to or requirements of the common good.

Political society possesses features of communion, but that among the members of any society can never be perfect or complete. It can always be deepened and strengthened. Thus the common good must be defined as a communion of love, sharing, and coresponsibility. And the common good of any particular society lies in its pursuit and always imperfect approach to such communion. Understood in this way the common good can be sought, means to it must be devised, and common goods must be shared. But *the* common good can never be procured or attained fully.

I am suggesting, then, that the common good be identified with the life of communion itself, not with any particular policy or goal. Only the common life, experience, and action of a communion are ultimately both common and distributable to each individual. Particular goods or policies—such as public safety, schools, libraries, public roads—may be for the common good, or a requirement of the good, or even *a* common good. But they cannot constitute *the* common good. They promote the common good because they make possible and enhance the common life of the society and thus in turn enhance the personal goods of its members. Therefore, they may take precedence over individual goods. A rich communal life is requisite to the full development of character. These goods or policies also promote the common good when they promote hospitality among the members of a political order.

If the common good refers to the set of communal relationships among the members of a society, a policy will be adjudged "in the common good" if it protects, strengthens, improves, or extends those relationships. Policy in the common good preserves what communion and hospitality already exist, attempts to make them better wherever possible, and strives to extend them to those not yet or only imperfectly included. For example, civil rights legislation is justified not only on the basis of justice but also for its contribution to bringing minority groups more fully into the life of the whole. The idea of reconciliation at the heart of amnesty for draft resisters and evaders also expresses the wish to repair community where it has been ruptured.

The key to understanding how policy can accomplish such an end when communion among the members of a national society is only partial and fragmentary is to view political society and the common good pluralistically. I am suggesting not the bankrupt interest-group pluralism of contemporary political science but a communal pluralism. While the body politic itself cannot be a communion in the full sense, it can contain and support a variety of smaller groups which can be, or can approach being, communions in the full sense—families, churches, neighborhoods, clubs, unions, scientific and artistic associations, communes, and so forth. While the political order itself cannot be fully hospitable, it can provide spaces and occasions for the encounter of hospitality. The common good, then, would be the promotion of the proper, limited unity of the whole body politic. The relation of politics to community, then, would have to be viewed as the relation of politics to communions and to hospitality.

These suggestions are incomplete without the explanation of the idea of communal pluralism that I shall provide in the following section. First, however, I wish to consider the possibility that the present account of the purpose of politics is too narrow. Should politics not also be concerned with justice, equality, freedom, and material prosperity, for example? Of course it should; yet to acknowledge this poses no difficulty for the position just articulated. Certainly the prominence of justice as an ordering concept in the history of political philosophy would strongly suggest that it not be ignored in a discussion of the goals of political life. Justice, however, is closely related to community and common good.

Justice as a concept in political theory has been used in two ways: first, as the most comprehensive ordering concept for political life, and second, as a particular concept of the proper distribution of benefits and burdens within a political society. The ancients favored the first use, and moderns the second, but they are never completely separated. I shall not attempt to sort out all of the issues revolving around justice or to defend a new or old definition of it. Given the recent growth of the Rawls and Nozick industries, that would take another book. I shall suggest only a few basic considerations connecting community and the two senses of justice above.

First, I would submit that community and the first use of justice are equivalent symbols; that is, they refer to the same fundamental experience of an order among persons which best molds individual and collective potential. Clearly Plato's idea of justice and the type which Aristotle designated general righteousness symbolize such an order. A society is just in this sense when it manifests the most perfect unity among its members and when the members themselves manifest human excellence. Person and group, person and person, are harmoniously integrated. This experience of harmony, however, is also indicated by the concept of community as I have developed it. Community symbolizes that relationship among persons which best fulfills their potential for unity while at the same time contributing to their highest personal growth.

The argument, of course, does not imply that Plato defines justice exactly as I define community. He does not. I mean only to propose that each of us is attempting to symbolize a basic human experience, the fullest blending of sociality and individuality.[16] If so, then to argue that the goal of politics is to promote and extend community is equivalent to arguing that it is to promote and extend justice in the richest sense of justice.

Second, I would suggest that justice in the particular sense is a necessary condition of communion. There can be no solidarity among persons who perceive an injustice in their basic relations. Justice must always be one of the shared values to which they commit themselves, though the commitment may be only tacit. Lacking fairness, the bonds among persons seem founded on force. When the relations among persons in a communion are perceived as just, there is an easy flow of talk, mutual exchange of benefits, and a willingness to work together. When perceived as unjust, relations are tense, benefits are exchanged only when return is guaranteed, and work together occurs only on the basis of force or mutual self-interest.[17] It follows, then, that one way of promoting communion is to promote distributive justice. To remedy an injustice is to remove a source of resentment standing in the way of communion and, indeed, of hospitality. Extending justice is, along with maintaining basic order, the most important way in which politics promotes communion. Justice is an end in itself, and politics must have it as a goal for that reason. But it is also a means to and a necessary condition of communion, and politics indirectly advances communion when it furthers justice.

Third, communion is a higher goal than particular justice. Since there are rare situations in which these principles may clash, politics must at times sacrifice part of justice in the interest of communion.[18] Such occasions would occur chiefly when the preservation of the society itself is in question from foreign attack, civil war, riot, or natural disaster. In such times, detention without trial, for example, which is certainly an injustice, may be permitted for brief periods. Such measures will undoubtedly have negative effects on communion (persons detained will be bitter), but such negative effects may have to be accepted in order to have communion at all. It is obvious also that rulers will frequently attempt to justify such measures in situations that are less than emergencies. Such efforts must be firmly resisted, and the extraordinary rarity of the conflict between justice and communion should be repeatedly stressed.

Other possible goals of politics may be treated briefly, since the principles governing them are the same as those governing justice and community. Equality is an important goal, but the proper sort to be pursued is defined by justice, so justice is the controlling principle. Those kinds of equality which are just are proper goals of political action and indirectly promote community. Those which are unjust are not proper goals and are damaging to community. Politics also properly takes a hand in developing the material bases of society, but material goods are, according to the theory of the common good, subordinate to the common good. Indeed, their use and distribution is also governed by the principle of justice. Politics' role in promoting the material welfare of society is clearly subordinate to its task of promoting the common good. It may, then, encourage, restrict, or even forbid the production and distribution of material goods according to their effect on the common good.

I have said enough in previous chapters to indicate the place of freedom in politics and community. Community requires free space for the relations among members to take place and for the development of the particular capacities of each person. Politics has a proper role to play in promoting voluntariness, initial freedom, and terminal freedom. Freedom is both a condition of and subordinate to community in the same way as justice. Because freedom has such a close connection with hospitality, I shall consider other aspects of politics and freedom in the next chapter, when I consider how politics contributes to hospitality.

Pluralism and Political Community

Politics enhances communion by reinforcing and pursuing the basic commitments of the society as a whole. Since society as a whole is only quasicommunal, politics makes its most important contribution to communion in preserving and improving pluralism.

It must be clear at the outset that the idea of pluralism which I shall develop has little in common with the justifiably criticized pluralism of political science. My own perspective on pluralism is closer to, though by no means identical with, that of the English pluralists of the early twentieth century: Figgis, Laski, Cole, and others. It is greatly indebted to Simon, Maritain, and Nisbet.[19]

I view the body politic as an association made up of thousands of different small and large communions and groups. I do not deny that the body politic contains interest groups, nor do I deny their legitimacy, as the idea of the common good does not deny the legitimacy of concern with personal and individual goods. But not all groups are or should be interest groups. Many are and should be communions in the full sense of that term. Such a pluralism places greater value on groups growing toward communion than on other groups, because such groups make a more substantial contribution to the development of character. This pluralism, while not excluding other considerations, focuses on the body politic as a *communitas communitatum,* a community of communities. It views the task of the state as an instrument of the body politic and the goal of the organization of the body politic itself as conservation of existing small communions and as fostering the political and social conditions necessary for the creation and growth of new communions. The body politic itself cannot be a communion in the full sense, but it can nurture communion by preserving pluralism where it does exist and by encouraging pluralism where it does not.

How can such a plural body retain its unity? First, its unity is enhanced by the commitment to common values and rituals present throughout the body politic and by policies which preserve that commitment. Second, unity is preserved by the hospitality which characterizes such a plurality and by policies which strengthen that hospitality. When the political order is viewed as a communitas communitatum, hospitality is automatically called for among the communions which constitute it. I shall consider the first aspect of unity in this section. The next chapter will consider hospitality and politics.

The first aspect of pluralism is that it is an order. A society organized pluralistically is not a jumble of communions with no definite links to one another, nor is it an order of conflict. There will undoubtedly be tensions and prejudices between various groups, but plural societies evolve a set of customs and principles for cooperation and toleration among groups. There is an order in pluralism, but it is more difficult to perceive than the order of centralism.[20] That of centralism proceeds from the arrogant assumption that order cannot emerge unless it is imposed from the top.

> There came a time (Early Modern) when, apparently, life lost the ability to arrange itself. It had to *be* arranged. Intellectuals took this as their job. From, say, Machiavelli's time to our own this arranging has been the one great gorgeous tantalizing misleading disastrous project.[21]

A plural order, on the other hand, is largely arranged by the spontaneous decisions and the division of social functions of the groups which compose it. This is not to say that there is no central coordination. Such coordination is the principal function of the state. Law and justice, national defense, and mediation of major social disharmonies are necessary and important tasks for central institutions in a plural political society. But the primary responsibility for the shape of the society lies with the associations themselves.

The order described above springs from the principle of communal autonomy, which states that tasks within society should be handled by particular persons or the smallest communions or groups capable of handling them. Larger social units should assume responsibility only for functions that cannot be accomplished at a lower level.[22] The principles of pluralism and communal autonomy are intended to limit any part of the body politic from expanding beyond its proper sphere. They are not limits on the authority of the body politic per se in its pursuit of the common good but rather principles which restrict the shape that the body politic may take and the scope of authority which may be exercised by any part of the body politic.

Notice that the principle of communal autonomy has a prudential form. It does not state that particular functions must always and everywhere be performed by particular communions or other groups. Circumstances will influence whether a communion continues to be capable of handling a function or whether it can no longer effectively do so. For example, the principle seems, prima facie, to favor private property and free enterprise. This is indeed the case. Yet, unlike the ideology of capitalism, which makes an absolute principle of property and enterprise, the principle of communal autonomy allows substantial political intervention into economic matters when private property and free enterprise damage the common good or grow so large as to be incapable of local regulation. It prefers that as many economic regulations as possible be enforced at the local level but recognizes that certain industries, such as communications, which inherently transcend local or regional boundaries, can only be regulated at a national or international level.

More positively stated, the principle encourages small units to undertake responsibility for their own welfare before looking to large units. Neighborhood government, forms of which were widely discussed in the 1960s and 1970s, is a logical application of this principle, as is substantial decentralization of national, state, and local administration. There are good reasons for centralization, but communal autonomy can develop strong ties of common work, participation, sharing, and commitment. It can increase personal and communal self-esteem and competency.

The discussion above implies a number of subordinate principles. Each group must have an authority rooted in its own faith, not derived from some larger unity. Churches, unions, families, and universities have distinctive functions and commitments. They should be free to make their own rules for internal governance and to impose obligations on their members. The large society should have the authority to intervene only in cases of substantial injustice which violate its basic commitments, cases, for example, of child abuse, violence, discriminatory admissions procedures, and the like. In the case of churches or other communions of ultimate commitment, political intervention should be extraordinarily rare, given the limits of the political common good.

It may be objected that communal autonomy and authority leave the central authority less able than presently to correct injustices and abuses of authority perpetrated by local governments, economic enterprises, and social groups. I must admit that this is true, though I must also point out that since the principles are prudential rather than absolute, they do admit action in cases of serious abuse. It is true, however, that communal abuse is more possible under the principles articulated. This likelihood is a cost of the theory. I would only point out that I believe the costs of centralism to be greater—bureaucratic impersonality and insensitivity, destruction of communal authority and hence weakening of communion, concentration of power and the severity of the consequences of its abuse, and other costs well documented in recent experience. Moreover, citizens with the qualities of responsibility, competence, and interest made possible by participation in communal life are better able to resist the abuse of authority than the passive, apathetic citizenry of a centralized, nonpluralistic political society could.

Another principle is indirect administration. As far as possible the administration of policy should make use of existing communions and their authorities in order to strengthen communion throughout the entire society. The concept of "mediating structures" developed by Peter Berger and Richard Neuhaus makes use of this principle.[23] Their concept is, however, less communal than my perspective. Education policy should make full use of existing private, parochial, and public schools by instituting the "voucher plan," for example. Industrial safety regulations should be administered largely by unions or by committees of workers and management. Welfare programs should be designed to keep families intact and so should be directed to the needs of the entire family unit. Income maintenance programs should be provided nonpaternalistically, that is, through some form of negative income tax or guaranteed annual income.

Another principle is that public policy in the common good will encourage not only the life of existing communions but also the creation of new types of communions appropriate to contemporary conditions. Just as cooperatives, unions, mutual aid societies, guilds, and communes were created in the past to respond to new economic and social conditions, the contemporary world needs such invention. By adhering to principles discussed in this section and by maintaining an atmosphere in which experimentation is possible, politics will encourage such communions. What they will look like is impossible to say, because the conditions required have not been present. Communitas communitatum is a normative principle whose function in the contemporary world is not so much to describe as to reorient political life. Nevertheless, hints of new directions in communion may be in the air. The most prominent is renewed concern for ethnicity. Ethnic movements and organizations have communal roots and may provide a communal orientation to many parts of social and cultural life. The new ethnicity should not strive to create total communions, but it could give a communal accent to some areas of life. The series of ethnic festivals in Baltimore is already the highlight of the summer for many citizens and not just for those whose week it happens to be.

The new forms of communion, if they come into existence, will be far less spatially defined than in the past.[24] Advances in transportation and communication make it possible that widely dispersed persons who share interests or commitments may meet on a regular basis and develop communal ties. Examples are professional societies of scientists, scholars, and lawyers and occupational groups such as firemen, policemen, safety inspectors, and salesmen. Hobby groups, from old groups such as stamp collectors to new ones such as beer can collectors and recreational vehicle enthusiasts, may also become more communal. Of course, the number of interest groups organized by various shared economic interests is legion, from older business and union groups to the newest insurgency groups, such as the American Agriculture Movement. The trick will be to create ways of making some of these groups less interest oriented and more communion oriented. By "communion oriented" I do not mean that such groups will or should be transformed into groups which always care for the common good over their own. Rather, I mean that their internal life could take on more of the qualities of communion. The technological basis for change is present; the difficult leadership work has hardly begun.

The final principle is social tolerance. Pluralism is founded upon the differences among persons which lead them into different communions. A pluralist society must foster a genuine tolerance; that is, an attentive-ness to and appreciation of differences in belief, language, hobby, occupation, and color. Tolerance is not mutual indifference, but mutual respect and hospitable encounter.

Politics, then, in promoting the common good is to maintain and defend those things necessary for the quasicommunal unity of society. It is also to promote and defend a pluralistic structure for the body politic. It must protect and nurture such pluralism as already exists, and it must enact policies designed to lay the groundwork for further pluralism. Politics cannot create communion out of whole cloth, but it can remove the obstacles which make communion difficult, and it can foster conditions which make communion more likely to emerge from collective efforts. By definition, if pluralism is part of the common good, it must be distributable to individuals; that is, it must be better, ceteris paribus, for persons to live in plural than in nonplural societies. A few words should be said about this claim.

I have already argued at great length that communion is an essential requirement for the development of character. If that is so, then it is not necessary to argue any further that pluralism, to the extent that it builds communions, is a good distributable to persons. But more than this, the very diversity of communions is a good for persons.

Diversity is good, first, because it protects freedom. In a pluralist society a person will have loyalties to a variety of relatively independent communions, none able to claim the whole of his life. An individual may be a member of a religious group, a family, a political party, a commercial enterprise, and a softball club, among others. Unjustifiable claims and pressures from one group can be met by relying on the principles and support of others.[25] From the more positive side, such multiple loyalties also present greater choice opportunities and more perspectives on them. These opportunities increase the likelihood of responsible choice. The person who has access to a variety of symbol worlds is less likely to be trapped in ideology than one who has access to only one.

This argument may seem to contradict the thrust of early chapters, since it seems to play down the importance of fundamental faith. Actually, the argument is simply a reflection on the distance between the reality to which commitment is made and the institutions which symbolize it and unite the faithful. The Christian is to place his faith in Christ, not in the Methodist or Anglican church; the Marxist in dialectical materalism, not the Russian or Chinese Communist Party. The organizations created to reveal truth and organize a communion around it often distort or hide truth. Therefore the deeply committed Christian or Marxist should be loyal members of church and party but had better not rely on church or party for all of their contact with reality. If they do, their symbols become dogma, and faith in the symbols comes to replace faith in reality. The diversity of pluralism helps to prevent such a tragedy. Since a pluralist society offers a variety of communions growing out of the same faiths, it is possible for a person to sever his association with a particular group when it distorts the faith and to join a group which more perfectly embodies this commitment. I am aware that the diversity I support also makes it possible for individuals never to commit themselves fully but to hop from group to group. Once more, however, the advantages of diversity outweigh the costs.

There are other ways in which pluralism benefits individual persons. Ecological systems which contain a diversity of flora and fauna are more stable and more adaptable to changing conditions than systems with limited diversity. The same is true of social systems; plural systems adapt better. Plural systems are also critical in promoting hospitality, an essential contributor to human development. Hospitality by definition requires a diversity of beliefs and ways of life. Pluralism guarantees such diversity and insures a common meeting ground for persons with different commitments.[26] Pluralism also provides occasions for individual display of creativity and excellence. In a plural society the chances that an individual will be recognized and that his talents will be elicited are multiplied.[27] A large number of communions with important purposes requires a large number of leaders, supporters, and activities. Individuals have frequent chances to develop and display their talents and virtues in such a situation. On the other hand, in a highly centralized and homogeneous society, relatively few have opportunities for significant action. In a society, for example, in which most charity and philanthropy is centrally dispensed, individual persons have few chances to develop or act upon the virtue of generosity.

One final, very critical value of pluralism must be considered when discussing the body politic. I have argued that politics and authority are good and necessary parts of human life. But like all good things, they are subject to terrible abuse and corruption. The concept of pluralism constitutes an inherent limitation on politics. A plural body politic is less subject to abuse of political authority than a centralized body politic. It supports multiple centers of resistance to abuse of authority. For this reason totalitarian regimes attempt to destroy all independent centers of authority.

The principles of pluralism and communal autonomy are not imported into the theory of the common good from the outside. They are intrinsic to the theory as natural limitations. Their primary justification is that the common good is best served when particular persons and associations care for particular goods. The principle of pluralism, then, is an intrinsic demand of the proper functioning of the body politic as well as a restraint on the ever-present reality of abuse of authority by particular units of the body politic. Thus social authority should be divided among a plurality of communions, and even functions which seem wholly of one type should be handled by numerous societies of different types. Work, for example, should be not only under the control of associations of workers but also tied as closely as possible to family life. Economic exchange should be controlled not only by private enterprise but also by government and private philanthropic institutions.[28] Pluralism, however, does not impose any specific organization on the body politic. Different structures and divisions of functions will be appropriate at different stages of history and in different circumstances.

The state is that part of the body politic specifically devoted to the pursuit of the common good. This means that *in principle* no areas of life open to intervention by the body politic are closed to state intervention. While the state may legitimately intervene in any sphere of temporal human life to protect or extend the common good, the principles of pluralism and communal autonomy demand that the state not intervene in all areas at once and that it limit its intervention to the minimum necessary for the maintenance of public order and justice and for the smooth coordination of a pluralist society. Because the freedom of particular communions to pursue their own goods is an essential complement to the authority of the state and an essential part of the common good, state activity must remain within narrow bounds and leave the principal tasks of the common good to the plural units of society. If it does otherwise, it has become illegitimate power rather than legitimate authority. It is, then, entirely proper for the body politic, that is to say, the people as a whole whose instrument the state is, to call it back to order.

The principles just developed govern the question of the limits of state intervention in human life. In practice, prudence will indicate the limits, which will be fewer at some times than at others.[29] In periods of widespread disorder or injustice or crisis, or at times when the natural cooperation of plural units in the body politic is sporadic, the state must play a large role in the life of society. Such state action is also called for when local governmental units are facing problems which have outgrown their competence. The international ramifications of economic decision making today make economic life particularly subject to political intervention. On the other hand, when conditions allow the promotion of the common good by a more spontaneous plural economic, political, and social cooperation, the state should shrink and remove itself from as many areas of life as possible.

Pluralism cannot work unless the smaller associations of political society have their own proper authority. Moreover, autonomy in the organization of the state itself—federalism, for example—inhibits the abuse of state power by dividing it. An abuse in one part remains largely restricted to that part and only with difficulty infects the whole. Pluralism and communal autonomy work together, for the autonomy of the various units provides grounds for resisting any attempt by the state to take over a function best pursued by smaller units of society. Pluralism is a training ground for freedom, and free men are best able to resist the designs of potential tyrants. Federalism can hinder not only abuse of central power but also good and effective use of central power. When such obstruction occurs, federalism contributes to its own demise. The costs of federalism are worth its benefits, but a good that is sufficiently abused becomes an evil.

The dialectic of abuse and resistance to abuse is a two-way street. Just as political authority is subject to corruption, so is religious, economic, social, and cultural authority. Pluralism may provide a convenient veil for such abuse and an argument against political intervention when abuse occurs and when smaller units of society will not perform functions they are capable of performing. Indeed, neglect of their responsibilities by local and state government is as much to blame for the growth of national government in the United States as the failures and corruptions of private economic enterprise. Politics, like nature, abhors a vacuum.[30] Moreover, tolerance and harmony among different communions do not always prevail. Such communions will, in fact, often be at odds, fighting each other and fighting for the total allegiance of members of society. Such a result is perhaps more common than examples of harmony in bodies politic with important differences among the population.

These observations leave us with a dilemma. Because all forms of authority are subject to abuse, the state may intervene in any area of temporal life to protect the common good in a plural society. Yet one justification of a plural society is limitation of the state. What principle allows us to say when state intervention is justified and when it must be resisted? Fortunately or unfortunately, there is no principle available. Practical, contingent judgments based upon an internalization of the principles of pluralism and appreciation of the actualities of each situation are all that can guide us in answering such a question. Yet a few points to guide such judgments might be made. First, political authority, particularly that of the nation-state, is perhaps more subject to abuse and more dangerous than other authority because its special relationship to the common good might tempt it to view itself as the whole society instead of as an instrument of the whole for pursuit of the common good. Second, pluralism brings with it the costs of variation from locality to locality, inefficiency, abuse of power, and seeming disorder. But centralization also has costs. Perhaps greater toleration of local inequities and inefficiencies is called for today in the face of the alternative of bureaucratic suppression of initiative, creativity, diversity, and scope for effective participation. The state, in other words, may simply have to bear some abuses as the price of avoiding greater ones in a very imperfect world.

Politics, Hospitality, and Character

Do you know . . . that it is necessary that there also be as many forms of human characters as there are forms of regimes? Or do you suppose that the regimes arise "from an oak or rocks" and not from the dispositions of the men in the cities, which, tipping the scale as it were, draw the rest along with them?
Plato, *The Republic*

Politics and Hospitality

Different as they are, hospitality and communion are similar in being relations which involve the fundamental elements of character. More to the point, hospitality is a communal condition which is distributable, making important contributions to individual development. This suggests that hospitality is related to the common good of a political society. The common good, the protection and furtherance of community throughout the body politic, involves the extension of hospitality as well as of communion. Since hospitality is one of the fundamental communal conditions, it would be entirely arbitrary to exclude it from the definition of the common good.

Hospitality is part of the common good for another reason as well. Since a pluralist political order is not itself a communion in the full sense (for it includes many communions), its goals cannot simply be creating, protecting, and extending communion. Such a political order must also be concerned with the living together of the communions and of the persons who are members of them. If this cohabitation is to be the most fruitful possible, it must be hospitable. Political order, therefore, must have hospitality as a fundamental aim. But how? Since hospitality is a social relationship which depends upon the free choice of particular persons and groups to encounter one another in openness and attentiveness, how can such a condition be directly encouraged? No one can be forced to be hospitable. Coerced encounter is not open or attentive. It is difficult, then, to see how politics can contribute to hospitality. Of course, politics cannot create hospitality directly. What politics can do is to promote hospitality indirectly by advancing the conditions which facilitate it, principally by encouraging freedom and tolerance, both of which are necessary for hospitality.

I have already connected politics and freedom and freedom and hospitality in chapter 6. Here let it be recalled that hospitality requires the freedom of choice necessary to have open spaces for the encounter of different communions or commitments. Freedom of choice is also necessary for the existence of differences that will be encountered. Politics, then, will promote hospitality by promoting freedom. In a good political society, individuals will have the basic freedoms of speech, press, and assembly, the right to travel, to be spared arbitrary arrest and imprisonment, and as well to vote and to hold public office. Groups will also be entitled to these freedoms, with the obvious exceptions occasioned by the differences between real and "artificial" persons. When such rights and freedoms are available to and are used by individuals and groups, they cannot help but encounter one another as they speak about similar issues and act on the same matters, whether on the same or opposite sides of the issues. Such encounters do not guarantee hospitality, but they do provide an opening for it. Without these rights and freedoms, differences of communion and commitment would be either obscured or accentuated, making hospitality among their adherents difficult or impossible.[1]

Yet the freedoms and rights alluded to will not be considered absolute or interpreted in a rigid and dogmatic way. Such rights and freedoms as necessary conditions for hospitality will have to be considered along with other aims and principles of political society in particular policy questions. In any case, such freedoms cannot be simply relegated to second-class status. They are critical for the existence of a fundamental communal development. Political, economic, and social freedoms, then, must take their proper places beside the principles of pluralism, communion building, and communal autonomy. Indeed, these freedoms are inseparable from communal autonomy.

The promotion of hospitality demands not only the freedom to act and so to encounter others but as well the use of that freedom. Politics, then, promotes hospitality by encouraging an active citizenry. Measures such as workers' participation in workplace decision making, community control and urban decentralism, and requirements for citizen participation in policy formation encourage greater participation by ordinary citizens in decision making. It is only through such participation that encounter can happen. Freedom of speech cannot contribute to hospitality unless it is exercised. Policies, political structures, and institutions which make participation easier facilitate hospitality at the same time.

It should be obvious from the foregoing that conflict may be encouraged by greater freedom and participation. Hospitality is not a guaranteed consequence of the encounter of different commitments and communions in the public arena. It is not unusual that persons or ideas seen at a distance are less disturbing than those viewed up close. Often nastiness is not apparent until it spits at you from across the bargaining table or shouts at you from across the meeting room.

This observation suggests that something more than freedom and participation is needed for a hospitable society. Hospitality also requires tolerance.[2] Because of the conflict, anger, and resentment often involved in the encounter of different ideas and communions, tolerance is a difficult and burdensome virtue. Only indifference is easy, but this is not tolerance, nor is it a basis for hospitality. Tolerance, on the other hand, is a basis for hospitality because the tolerant person, while not abandoning his own commitments, is open and attentive to the other, despite the suffering and hurt which may be involved. Mutual indifference is not hospitality, but mutual tolerance is.

A political order promotes tolerance first by being firmly committed itself. The qualities of order, communal unity, authority, and commitment are requisites for tolerance.[3] A political order with no principles of its own is not tolerant, only too weak to object to movements at odds with it. A tolerant society, on the other hand, will have its principles and commitments, but it will not suppress movements, parties, or individuals who dissent from those principles. A liberal democratic society which is also tolerant will allow communist and socialist parties to compete for the allegiance of citizens, but it will not pretend that its own principles are no better than theirs. Similarly, a tolerant socialist society will allow free enterprise to be preached. While tolerance does not require that a society doubt its own principles, it does require that even those persons who speak for them be open to the truth which may be part of opposing principles. Dogmatism and ideology are not found in the company of tolerance.

A political order, then, encourages hospitality when its official representatives display tolerance themselves and encourage it in others. Such a political order may very well exhibit more tension and conflict of ideas, but, difficult as these are to bear, they are worth the cost. Societies with such features are more alive, free, and congenial to individual self-development than are closed, conflict-suppressing societies. The dangers are greater, but if tolerance can be fostered, so are the rewards.

This is not to say that there are no limits to tolerance. Obviously, violence and terrorism in the promotion of a cause cannot be tolerated. Less obviously, circumstances and other principles may limit the toleration of some ideas, movements, and writings. It would, for example, be wrong for the United States to ban Nazi parties, but this action seems appropriate in West Germany.

Finally, hospitality is an important goal for the political order because it, like pluralism, is an intrinsic limitation on the state, and it is needed for the same reasons that those limitations are needed. A political order which is enjoined to encourage a diversity of freedoms and rights, to provide structures and opportunities for its citizens to participate in speaking, writing, and formulating policy, and to tolerate deviant political movements is one which is less likely to get out of line than an order not so enjoined. It is also easier to bring such an order back into line, because it has provided the tools for doing so. Political abuses are easier to spot and remedy in democratic regimes than in totalitarian and dictatorial regimes. The reason, of course, is that the freedom, participation, and toleration present in the former regimes, as imperfect as they undoubtedly are, provide a vantage point and a foothold for detecting and attacking the abuse of power. Aware that such points exist, political leaders are less likely to abuse their power, or at least less likely to do so in fashions as monstrous as in regimes without the conditions necessary for hospitality.

Politics and Character

It offends liberal sensibilities to suggest that politics should be used to improve character. Such a suggestion implies the totally illiberal notion that the state should tell citizens how to live and what to believe. Such a political order would seem to be the antithesis of the pluralistic, hospitable order. Thus the idea that politics should improve character must mean something different from state control over belief and action. The concepts of pluralism and hospitality suggest the parameters of the effect of politics on character. It is clear that pluralism and hospitality require that politics permit and encourage a wide variety of beliefs, actions, and ways of life. It is, on the other hand, clear that many thinkers, from Plato and Aristotle to Arendt, have believed that politics makes an essential contribution to human excellence. How is it possible to believe this and at the same time defend pluralism and hospitality? In this section I shall outline an answer to this question.

First, a little thought reveals that the question contains a false dichotomy. The very defense of pluralism and hospitality is an indirect stimulus to the improvement of character. The dominant thrust of the first part of this book was to show how communion and hospitality make essential contributions to the development of character. If that is true, then politics indirectly contributes to the development of character and to all of its elements when the conditions are created for the building, defense, and extension of communion and hospitality. If politics made this contribution alone, it would still be very important.

The other ways in which politics improves character are also indirect, but less so than the way just indicated. They are indirect in that the political organs, with one exception, do not take particular persons and attempt to mold their commitments and actions in particular ways. Totalitarian regimes do make such attempts, but regimes which follow the principles I am enunciating do not. The exception is the activity of governmental units in promoting the rituals and the education which teach and reinforce commitments to the basic principles of the political order itself. Public schools, Independence Day ceremonies, patriotic speeches, flags, and so forth are evidence of a direct governmental hand in the development of commitments in persons. This is legitimate as long as the political order does not become the ultimate object of commitment. The political order is and should be only quasi-communal; therefore, it may not claim the person's total allegiance. But the political regime may properly claim, so long as it is a just and authoritative regime, part of the person's allegiance.[4] In doing so, it legitimately shapes character.

Granting this exception still leaves the major idea intact: politics improves character in a variety of indirect ways. These improvements are indirect even though government may directly impinge upon the person. That is, they are indirect because they only create conditions favorable to character development; they do not in and of themselves develop character. Some examples may help to make this point. Governments set aside park and wilderness land for a variety of reasons—preservation of resources for the future, aesthetic value, places for retreat for ordinary citizens. The last reason is quite important, because it means such lands are occasions for solitude. People can retreat to mountain or seashore to relax, meditate, and feel in touch with a reality larger than themselves. This policy promotes solitude, but government does not force persons to use park and wilderness for solitude (how could it?), nor does it attempt to construct a "solitude quotient" for each place set aside. Another example: tax systems which depend upon citizens' honesty in filing returns are more conducive to responsibility than those which, because they do not trust citizens, set up elaborate investigative machinery. Nevertheless, the former system does not directly cause people to be responsible. It simply provides an occasion for the exercise of responsibility, an occasion which may be used or misused. But the provision of such occasions is an important contribution to the improvement of character.

These examples indicate that politics makes important contributions to character when it frames substantive policies which elicit or provide occasions for the training or exercise of the essential qualities of character, especially the quality of responsibility. Responsibility is most important in this connection because it is the most public of the elements of character; it involves action. Government can take some steps to promote commitment, but there are many ways to frame law such that it encourages responsibility in citizens. For example, community theory would dictate reduction of paternalism in welfare programs. Paternalism is not always inappropriate; diminished competence in certain areas of life or the necessity of a national program may require some paternalistic measures. Yet the overwhelming paternalism of existing programs seems to stem primarily from distrust of the poor rather than from concern for their well-being. Both the value of encouraging persons to take responsibility for their lives and the demeaning effects of paternalism exercised over normal adults dictate the need for replacement of most in-kind welfare benefits, particularly food stamps and housing subsidies, with their cash equivalents. Nor should services to the poor, such as counseling, budget help, and birth control information, be required for the receipt of welfare benefits. If such services are to be provided, their use should be the responsible choice of the individual recipient. Charging a small fee for such services might even encourage a more responsible exercise of the choice to use them.

Income maintenance programs, from the perspective of community theory, are justified by the requirement that authority protect the weak of a communion, strengthen communion, and extend it to those excluded. Those who suffer poverty are weak in comparison with those who are well off. Weakness is a fact, whether the cause of poverty is sickness, old age, mental or physical handicap, laziness, ignorance, lack of skills, too large a family, or anything else.To be poor is to be subject to the control of those who are not. Moreover, the poor are often despised by the affluent, especially if the former are also largely racially distinct. They are regarded as lazy, stupid, dirty, lustful, and dangerous. There is no possibility of community between the despised and the haughty. Income maintenance programs can encourage responsibility and community; they can help more or less effectively in keeping some from being permanently poor or from being defeated and outcast because of their poverty. Such programs cannot eradicate or prevent poverty, but they can promote justice, community, compassion, and responsibility and are worthy of support for that reason.

In a similar way, responsibility must be the key concept in any discussion of the punishment of crime. Community theory supports the current movement away from deterrence and rehabilitation and toward retribution as the justification of punishment. While mental conditions undoubtedly diminish personal responsibility for action in numerous cases and perhaps totally prevent responsible action in a few cases, a political regime founded on the principles of responsibility, commitment, and community will recognize that the vast majority of lawbreakers are persons capable of responsible action. To treat a person capable of choice as though he were not is to violate the canons of both communion and hospitality, for recognition of personal responsibility is a basic principle of each. Communion requires that each member be regarded as committed to its principles and bound by the rules and organizing structures developed in accordance with these principles. Each member must also be regarded as capable of making his behavior conform to rules; that is, he must be considered to possess the essential human capacity of responsibility.

To view a person primarily as sick or defective, to be reformed or rehabilitated, is to treat him impersonally, unequally. To regard him primarily as a danger to be kept from harming others is to suppose him less than fully human. At the extreme, it is to treat him as a dangerous animal, fit only to be caged. It may be true that the person is immature or irresponsible, but it may also be true that he has broken the law from commitment to principle and that he is, in fact, a mature and responsible person. Such was certainly the case with many civil rights or antiwar lawbreakers. Whatever the case, a fully human relationship with the lawbreaker cannot be established unless he is assumed to be capable of responsible action. It is undoubtedly true that some lawbreakers are extraordinarily dangerous to their fellow human beings and must be kept securely locked in prison. But they are imprisoned as a punishment for a crime committed which carries with it a penalty, not primarily because they are dangerous. Even such persons are to be treated as if they were responsible, and their freedom of action is to be curtailed only if they themselves choose to demonstrate their irresponsibility.

The value of political participation is a much-debated topic today. Just as contentious is the question of whether increased political participation is possible. I shall not review all of the issues raised in debates.[5] I shall merely point out what I believe to be the most important contributions which participation makes to character formation. It goes without saying that the benefits of participation only happen when it is genuine and genuinely encouraged. Devices which seem to promise participation but leave actual decision making in a few hands only produce disillusionment, frustration, and greater resistance to participation once their trickery is discovered, as it inevitably is.

Political participation "arises out of and leads to responsibility."[6] When a person takes part in an action or a decision, he becomes responsible for it and for its consequences. This is a fundamental moral notion. There are legitimate questions concerning types and degrees of responsibility arising out of different kinds of participation, but there is no question that conscious and intentional, uncoerced participation produces responsibility. When a person votes in an election, he becomes in some degree responsible for the qualities of the persons holding positions of authority. When he participates directly in a political decision, he becomes in some degree responsible for the consequences. In a participatory situation, the participants become jointly accountable. Despite complications arising from the degree of responsibility attaching to majorities and minorities in decision making, we can say that the greater the participation, the greater the responsibility attaching to it. Participation, then, becomes a training ground, and politics can make a contribution to responsibility by opening as much decision making and decision implementation to as large a number of persons as possible. It can contribute also by making it as easy as possible for citizens to enjoy the opportunities available. I recognize, however, that it is possible for participation to be too easy, encouraging irresponsible, that is, unconscious or unintentional, participation. Plebiscites, for example, have this danger.

Participation in politics can help develop responsibility for another reason. In participation one necessarily encounters others with different views and experiences from one's own. Here we have an aspect of hospitality. The necessity of dealing with persons whose perspectives are different can be an educative situation. It is, of course, not invariably so, and some encounters are occasions for acrimony and closed-mindedness. Again, the principles I have articulated throughout this chapter are subject to abuse. Nevertheless, only in participation can one learn to consider other views, to modify judgments, and ultimately to form judgments that will be responsible because responsibility demands that action be fitting, not only according to one's own commitments but also according to the situation at hand. Thus responsible political judgments must include awareness of the perspectives of others, because they are part of the total situation. Tocqueville meant something very similar when he spoke of the need to "educate democracy" through participatory institutions, such as juries and committees to petition government for action.[7] Joining with others in political action not simply makes responsibility effective but contributes to responsibility itself and may even be an occasion for the transformation or modification of commitments. Reality is an effective teacher, and participation with others in political activity constantly brings persons into uncomfortable touch with reality.

Political participation also contributes to the sense of mastery which is an aspect of terminal liberty and an important part of maturity. I do not mean mastery in the sense of an individual's being able to dominate events; this would be incompatible with participation by others. Rather, I mean that persons are able to have an impact on future events by having a hand in shaping them. When politics encourages participation, persons who take part feel that they make a difference, that they are able to exert some control over events.[8] Persons with such control are able to develop the qualities of responsibility and commitment necessary to connect the present means available to a political system with its ultimate end, the common good. Put another way, political freedom, in the terminal and the initial senses, requires participation, because it requires responsibility and commitment. Despite its failures, the American Agriculture Movement of 1977–1978 is good example of how ordinary persons can, through participation, develop political knowledge, the ability to work with others, leadership qualities, and an appreciation of the labyrinthine ways of politics. Such qualities can come, not from reading, but only from plunging in. Participation fosters a sense of meaning, dignity, and satisfaction with one's own ability to influence events. These conclusions about political participation again support the contention that politics can and should contribute to character.

Finally, I might point out with respect to participation and character that the sense of being a member of an association, a political order in this case, is strongly tied to commitment to the shared life of the association and to participation in building that life. Since political obligation is tied to a sense of membership, it is critical for the person's development that he be aware of his memberships and obligations in a very concrete way, for only then can he act responsibly.

Though my argument in the preceding paragraphs has been directed toward the contribution that political participation makes to character, it will not be amiss to point out some other benefits from a high level of participation. First, a politics in which rational, intentional, responsible participation is the norm is more likely to be able to cope with abuses. Citizens who are used to this kind of participation will be more inclined to keep politics within its proper bounds and to speak and act effectively should those bounds be exceeded. Second, politics builds communion better when it is participatory than when it is nonparticipatory. Remember that participation is an essential bond of communion. The recent agitation for participatory democracy has been inseparable from a demand for a more communal society. The two were linked, for example, in the "Port Huron statement" of the Students for a Democratic Society. And Barber, describing the meaning of referenda in the Swiss context says, "The point of the referendum was not to count heads or enumerate interests but to discover communality, or in its absence to create it."[9] Michael Walzer has also argued that greater participation can increase the sense of solidarity in a political society.

> In the arena, rival politicians have to speak about the common good, even if they simultaneously advance sectional interests. Citizens learn to ask, in addition to their private questions, what the common good really is. In the course of sustained political activity enemies become familiar antagonists. . . . Men and women who merely tolerated one another's differences recognize that they share a commitment—to *this* arena and the people in it.[10]

The divisiveness of politics can become a ritual of unity, and the political arena can contain generosity, civility, and respect for the rules of the game, even though these will be absent much of the time.

A final point about participation. Participation is clearly most effective in building character in small communions. Political participation will often involve very large units of government, so often it will not be as effective a contributor to character as one might hope.[11] But a pluralist political order should be so organized as to provide a wide variety of types of participation in various types of associations. A body politic should stimulate participation not only in strictly political life, to help develop character, but in many other areas of life as well.

I argued in chapter 7 that government should refrain from action where a plurality of communions is satisfactorily handling a matter of public concern. On the other hand, government action should be designed in such a way that it does not harm existing communions and so that it positively facilitates communal life wherever appropriate. Voluntary associations play a critical role in community theory. In addition to performing valuable functions—educational, social, philanthropic, economic, and spiritual—such associations are also schools of participation. They pass resolutions, elect officers, delegate responsibilities, and call for commitments of time, talent, and money. Therefore, it is appropriate, depending upon circumstances, to grant tax exemptions for the property of such institutions, to grant tax credits or deductions for individual contributions to them, and to use such associations directly or indirectly to accomplish public purposes. They may, for example, take a hand in the administration of health services to the poor. Yet recent tendencies toward centralizing, professionalizing, and bureaucratizing public programs have tended to weaken the independence and the participatory character of voluntary associations in the United States.

Educational vouchers for use at private or religious schools and community control of public schools are two ways of increasing participation and encouraging communion through public policy. Employment of such devices would provide a common good, education, in a fashion responsive to the people of various communities and would facilitate their participation in decisions regarding education in a far more significant fashion than is presently possible. By encouraging the creation of more nonpublic schools, vouchers would provide a multiplicity of opportunities for parent and citizen participation. Vouchers would also reduce the standardization and bureaucratic numbness which so debilitate public education. Such a system might also produce greater social and economic (and perhaps racial) integration than presently exists, since all parents would have the economic resources to select private or religious schools which reflect their basic commitments. The results of the voucher plan would be greater communal autonomy and pluralism, increased freedom of choice for families, greater parental responsibility for school selection and for participation in decisions concerning the schools, and strengthened communion through greater communal influence in education. The advantages of community control in allowing greater diversity, greater parental participation, and reduced professionalism and bureaucracy are precisely parallel.

Worker participation is another example of how participation can be extended to larger numbers of citizens and to a variety of social contexts. Truly effective participation by workers in decisions regarding the workplace and the conditions of work must go beyond collective bargaining and the hierarchical, formal structure of grievance procedures to shared responsibility for decision making. The degree of participation in joint decision making may range from conditions in the work area to those in the plant. The upper reaches may include workers' participation in the management of the entire company, including profits, new products, advertising, and so on or even workers' control of the entire enterprise, in which managers are drawn temporarily from the ranks of workers.

None of these variations on the theme of worker participation should be seen as the only form of genuine democracy or as an answer to political alienation, boredom in the workplace, or economic difficulties. The advantages are far more limited. Opening up avenues for participation does not mean that such avenues will be heavily traveled. Many workers will pass up the opportunity to participate. But there are gains. Some workers who pass up opportunities for political participation avail themselves of the opportunity to take part in decisions regarding their economic lives.

I am arguing, then, not for any ideology of workers' control or for any particular forms of workers' participation. The forms and plans appropriate will vary from company to company and will also depend upon the economic conditions and the sociopolitical traditions of each country. I am only contending that public policy should permit, and in some cases encourage through tax credits or loan guarantees, various forms of workers' participation—from joint consultation to shop floor management to workers' self-management. None of these should be considered the only way to run an economy.

The justification for the position outlined is twofold. First, it promotes pluralism. Whether or not the workplace approaches commmunion, and very few will, different ways of organizing workplaces will allow a greater diversity of employment conditions, a greater variety of work experiences. There will thus be not only greater social and economic pluralism but also greater personal freedom of choice in selecting a career or a job. At present only a few types of careers, such as higher education, offer an opportunity for employee participation in governance. To open more careers to this opportunity would be to give more persons a greater variety of options in selecting a career and an employer. Second, the character-developing features of participation can be extended to more persons if the availability of participation on a small scale and in a familiar setting is brought to more firms. Participation can be learned and enjoyed in family, workplace, school, and club, as well as in directly political settings.

Joint participation of workers and management can also be an occasion for hospitality. Each group will certainly have different interests, experiences, and commitments, though they will share an interest in the prosperity of the firm. Participatory management provides a forum in which these different perspectives may encounter one another and arrive at mutual tolerance and understanding. Such a result is not, of course, guaranteed, but it is possible. Acrimony will often prevail in labor-management relations. But nonparticipation entirely precludes hospitality. Workers' participation cannot guarantee hospitality or even actual use of the opportunities provided. It will often fail. Yet the important benefits of the successes which do occur can justify public facilitation of participatory economic institutions.

Conclusion

I have argued in this and the preceding chapter that politics is essentially related to the central normative principles established in earlier chapters. The body politic and the state are not themselves communities. While they have communal aspects, it is a dangerous illusion to believe that the entire society can be molded into a communion. That is a totalitarian temptation. Similarly, I argued that it is a dangerous error to believe that politics should directly mold the essential elements of character. Only by understanding the concept of the common good as enjoyable by all together and also distributable to each member of the community is a proper understanding of political community possible.

The common good must be seen as the life of a communion itself, but this life must be understood pluralistically. Thus politics contributes to communion by serving, building, defending, and extending communal life in many diverse forms. Politics advances hospitality by promoting tolerance and freedom in this pluralist context. It develops character by furthering communion and hospitality, by framing substantive policies which are likely to elicit commitment, responsibility, solitude, and other critical elements of character, by encouraging and facilitating widespread participation in political, social, and economic life, and by demanding mature character in public officials. I have also argued that a politics which embodies these principles will contain intrinsic limitations on its own scope, thus incorporating protections against the abuse of power.

I have no illusions that any political order will come very close to a full embodiment of these principles or the principles discussed in previous chapters. Failures will be constant and often severe. Many regimes will be corrupt, despotic, and unjust. All regimes will exhibit some corruption, injustice, and failure to pursue the common good. Because of their size and close connection with power and force, political institutions are particularly subject to abuse, mistakes, and failures. Politics must recognize and use human propensities to weakness and sin. The appropriate attitude toward the possibilities of political reality is neither cynicism nor optimism but a "confident pessimism"—or in short, realism.[12] Such a realism teaches that despite constant evil, some degrees of responsibility, commitment, and community are possible. Despite injustice, some justice can be done. Despite power, authority is present in some measure in all genuine communions. Despite force and despotism, freedom somehow manages a foothold in many places. Realism teaches that setbacks in the pursuit of the common good will be frequent but also that the common good can be pursued and to some extent manifested in the body politic. Realism, finally, teaches that the intrinsic limitations on politics will not be enough to keep it in bounds; other measures will also be required to counteract despotic tendencies. Ambition must counter ambition; governmental functions must be separated; judiciaries should be independent, constitutions written, and basic rights protected.

To admit all of this is not to weaken the force of the principles enunciated. Normative principles should be seen as ordering concepts; that is, they should be viewed as goals which, if pursued, will impart a proper order to the society pursuing them. These principles describe a theory of political order because they can be partially embodied and yet still call a body politic toward further progress. Persons and communions can be properly responsible and yet always need to act more responsibly. States can properly be called just and always need to eradicate injustices. The principles articulated in this theory of political order outline the goals and general shape of the good political society. This is their proper function. Public officials and citizens must devise policies designed to pursue these goals and shape a specific order in light of the limitations of the materials at hand. Responsibility, commitment, and community teach us to accept limitation while still pursuing a politics of vision.

Notes

Chapter 1: The Problem of Order

1. The understanding of political theory summarized in this paragraph is inspired by the work of Eric Voegelin. See *The New Science of Politics* (Chicago: University of Chicago Press, Phoenix Books, 1966) and *Order and History*, 4 vols. (Baton Rouge: Louisiana State University Press, 1956–74). It is elaborated in Thomas A. Spragens, Jr., *Understanding Political Theory* (New York: St. Martin's Press, 1976).

2. Readers of earlier drafts of this book have wondered where my concept of community should be placed ideologically. Conservatives, socialists, and radicals have in one way or another all claimed the concept. I have resisted classification, knowing that if I can please or displease all three, I shall have gone at least some distance beyond ideology. I do not pretend to have avoided ideology completely. I have simply attempted to develop a normative framework for discussing political order. Normative theory strives for openness to new evidence and experience; ideology is value-laden, like normative theory, but it is closed to evidence and experience which challenge its premises.

3. For a summary and criticism of "the politics of interest," see Clarke E. Cochran, "The Politics of Interest: Philosophy and the Limitations of the Science of Politics," *American Journal of Political Science* 17 (November 1973),745–66, and Theodore J. Lowi, *The End of Liberalism,* 2d ed. (New York: W. W. Norton & Co., 1979).

4. Alexis de Tocqueville, *Democracy in America*, trans. Henry Reeve, 2 vols. (New Rochelle, N.Y.: Arlington House, n.d.), pt. 2, bk. 2, chap. 2, pp. 104, 106.

5. See Robert Paul Wolff, *The Poverty of Liberalism* (Boston: Beacon Press, 1968), chap. 1; *Encyclopaedia of the Social Sciences*, vol. 8, S.V. "Individualism"; and Steven Lukes, *Individualism* (Oxford: Basil Blackwell, 1973).

6. Buber, *The Way of Response*, ed. N. N. Glatzer (New York: Schocken Books, 1966), p. 56; Wolfe, *Mauve Gloves & Madmen, Clutter & Vine* (New York: Farrar, Straus & Giroux, 1976), p. 143 (emphasis in original). Trilling, *Sincerity and Authenticity* (Cambridge: Harvard University Press, 1972). See also Christopher Lasch, *The Culture of Narcissism* (New York: Warner Books, 1979), who also argues that we are seeing a collapse of the self, rather than its assertion.

7. Philip Rieff, *The Triumph of the Therapeutic* (New York: Harper & Row, Torchbooks, 1968) pp. 56, 13, 24–25.

8. *Leviathan*, ed. Michael Oakeshott (New York: Collier Books, 1962), p. 80.

9. Marvin Zetterbaum, "Self and Political Order," *Interpretation* 1 (Winter 1970): 233–46.

10. Eric Voegelin, "Liberalism and Its History," trans. Mary and Keith Algozin, *Review of Politics* 36 (October 1974): 515–19. See also James L. Wiser, "Michael Polanyi: Personal Knowledge and the Promise of Autonomy," *Political Theory* 2 (February 1974): 77–87. The following paragraphs owe much to John H. Hallowell. See his *Main Currents in Modern Political Thought* (New York: Holt, Rinehart & Winston, 1950), esp. pp. 84–92, and *The Decline of Liberalism as an Ideology* (Berkeley: University of California Press, 1943), esp. chap. 1.

11. It is, of course, a familiar paradox that liberal measures designed to guarantee such freedoms often end in bureaucratic webs which create their own freedom issues. Also paradoxical is liberal unwillingness to trust individual autonomy in economic activity. Here libertarians are more consistent, though not necessarily more correct. A complete discussion of liberalism would have to account for liberal reliance on law and government to deal with social and economic problems.

12. See Michael Oakeshott, "Rationalism in Politics," and "Political Education," in Oakeshott, *Rationalism in Politics* (New York: Basic Books, 1962). Yves R. Simon argues persuasively that moral practice also depends upon a supportive communal context in "Beyond the Crisis in Liberalism," in *Essays in Thomism,* ed. Robert E. Brennan (New York: Sheed & Ward, 1942), pp. 272–74.

13. See Brian Barry, "Liberalism and Want-Satisfaction: A Critique of John Rawls," *Political Theory* 1 (May 1973): 134–53, and Stephen G. Salkever, "Virtue, Obligation and Politics," *American Political Science Review* 68 (March 1974): 78–92.

14. Some of the leading works are: Lowi, *End of Liberalism;* Charles A. McCoy and John Playford, eds., *Apolitical Politics* (New York: Thomas Y. Crowell Co., 1967); Darryl Baskin, *American Pluralist Democracy* (New York: Van Nostrand Reinhold Co., 1971); Peter Bachrach, *The Theory of Democratic Elitism* (Boston: Little, Brown & Co., 1967); and William E. Connolly, ed., *The Bias of Pluralism* (New York: Atherton Press, 1969). See Cochran, "Politics of Interest."

15. Clarke E. Cochran, "Political Science and 'The Public Interest,' " *Journal of Politics* 36 (May 1974): 327–55.

16. Wolff, *Poverty*, p. 159.

17. I owe this suggestion to my colleague, William Oden.

18. "Terminal Cases," *Political Science Reviewer* 1 (Fall 1971): 85.

19. *The Promise of Politics* (Englewood Cliffs, N.J.: Prentice-Hall, 1966), p. 10; see also "Expanding the Political Present," *American Political Science Review* 63 (September 1969): 768–76, and *Open Systems* (Itasca, Ill.: F. E. Peacock Publishers, 1969).

20. "Needs, Wants, and Political Legitimacy," *Canadian Journal of Political Science* 1 (September 1968): 241–60, and "Foundations of the Liberal Make-Believe," *Inquiry* 14 (Autumn 1971): 213–37.

21. "Needs," pp. 251, 255–58; "Foundation," pp. 225–29, 233–35. See also

The Structure of Freedom (Stanford: Stanford University Press, 1958), esp. pp. 83–103.

22. *Anarchy, State, and Utopia* (New York: Basic Books, 1974); *A Theory of Justice* (Cambridge: Harvard University Press, 1971).

23. See Benjamin R. Barber, "Deconstituting Politics: Robert Nozick and Philosophical Reductionism," *Journal of Politics* 39 (February 1977): 2–23.

24. Barry, "Liberalism and Want-Satisfaction."

25. Glenn Tinder, *Community* (Baton Rouge: Louisiana State University Press, 1980), p. 33.

26. Clyde Holbrook, *Faith and Community* (New York: Harper & Bros., 1959), esp. pp. 111–36; see also Egbert de Vries, ed., *Man in Community* (New York: Association Press, 1966); Waldo Beach, *Christian Community and American Society* (Philadelphia: Westminster Press, 1969); "Dogmatic Constitution on the Church" and "Pastoral Constitution on the Church in the Modern World," *The Documents of Vatican II*, Walter M. Abbott, general ed., and Joseph Gallagher, translation ed. (New York: Guild Press, 1966); and H. Richard Niebuhr, *The Responsible Self* (New York: Harper & Row, 1963).

27. *Community and Society*, trans. and ed. Charles P. Loomis (New York: Harper & Row, Torchbooks, 1963), p. 69. See also Robert A. Nisbet, *The Sociological Tradition* (New York: Basic Books, 1966), chap. 3; George A. Hillery, Jr., "Definitions of Community: Areas of Agreement," *Rural Sociology* 20 (June 1955): 111–23; and David W. Minar and Scott Greer, eds., *The Concept of Community* (Chicago: Aldine Publishing Co., 1969).

28. *The Quest for Community* (New York: Oxford University Press, paperback edition, 1969; first published 1953). For a discussion of some of these phenomena in the context of a search for community, see Peter L. Berger, Brigitte Berger, and Hansfried Kellner, *The Homeless Mind* (New York: Vintage Books, 1974), pp. 196–214, and Ralph Keyes, *We, the Lonely People* (New York: Harper & Row, 1973).

29. Keyes, *Lonely People*, pp. 18–19, 141, and David French, "After the Fall—What This Country Needs Is a Good *Counter* Counterculture Culture," *New York Times Magazine*, October 3, 1971, pp. 20–36.

30. *The Idea of Fraternity in America* (Berkeley: University of California Press, 1974), pp. 395, 89.

31. See Carl J. Friedrich, *An Introduction to Political Theory* (New York: Harper & Row, 1967), lectures 7–8; "The Concept of Community in the History of Political and Legal Philosophy," in Friedrich, ed., *Nomos II: Community* (New York: Liberal Arts Press, 1959), pp. 3–24, and *Man and His Government* (New York: McGraw-Hill Book Co., 1963), chap. 8 and pp. 41–50, 532–45, 614–15. Also see Bertrand de Jouvenel, *Sovereignty*, trans. J. F. Huntington (Chicago: University of Chicago Press, 1957); Yves R. Simon, *Freedom and Community*, ed. Charles P. O'Donnell (New York: Fordham University Press, 1968), *A General Theory of Authority* (Notre Dame: University of Notre Dame Press, 1962), and *Philosophy of Democratic Government* (Chicago: University of Chicago Press, Phoenix Books, 1961); Benjamin R. Barber, *The Death of Communal Liberty* (Princeton: Princeton University Press, 1974); Glenn Tinder, *Community,* and *Tolerance* (Amherst: University of Massachusetts Press, 1976); and McWilliams, *Idea of Fraternity.*

32. For elaboration see Cochran, "Politics of Interest."
33. *Death of Communal Liberty*, p. 7.

Chapter 2: Human Character

1. See Lukes, *Individualism*, esp. chaps. 1, 3, 5, 8–13, 19.
2. See the *Oxford English Dictionary*, meanings 8–12. The word is derived from the Greek *charakter*, an instrument for marking or engraving; hence, a distinctive mark or distinctive nature.
3. See the *Oxford English Dictionary*, meanings 15–17.
4. Niebuhr, *Responsible Self*, pp. 137–45; see also Paul Tournier, *The Meaning of Persons*, trans. Edwin Hudson (New York: Harper & Row, 1957), chaps. 2–3.
5. Peter L. Berger, " 'Sincerity' and 'Authenticity' in Modern Society," *The Public Interest*, no. 31 (Spring 1973): 81–90. Trilling, *Sincerity and Authenticity*.
6. *Nichomachean Ethics* 3. 2–4.
7. Tinder, *Tolerance*, p. 16.
8. Tournier, *Meaning*, p. 70.
9. See Robert A. Nisbet, *The Social Bond* (New York: Alfred A. Knopf, 1970), pp. 148–49, 154–55, and chap. 8.
10. Tournier, *Meaning*, p. 183.
11. For this concept I am indebted to George W. Morgan, for his presence to his students and for his book, *The Human Predicament* (Providence, R. I.: Brown University Press, 1968), esp. chaps. 5 and 14.
12. Hannah Arendt, "Thinking and Moral Considerations: A Lecture," *Social Research* 38 (Autumn 1971): 417–46.
13. Jacques Maritain, in *The Social and Political Philosophy of Jacques Maritain*, ed. Joseph W. Evans and Leo R. Ward (London: Geoffrey Bles, 1956), p. 123.
14. For the distinctions which follow, see Rubin Gotesky, "Aloneness, Loneliness, Isolation, Solitude," in *An Invitation to Phenomenology*, ed. James M. Edie (Chicago: Quadrangle Books, 1965), pp. 211–39. For similar distinctions, see Marie Chin, "Lived Privacy and Personal Space," *Humanitas* 11 (February 1975), 45–54, esp. n. 7.
15. Henri J. M. Nouwen, *Reaching Out* (Garden City, N.Y.: Doubleday & Co., 1975), p. 22.
16. Ibid., p. 25.
17. Gustave Thibon, quoted by Gabriel Marcel, *Homo Viator*, trans. Emma Craufurd (New York: Harper & Row, 1962), p. 28; see also Nouwen, *Reaching Out*, p. 30.
18. *Zen and the Art of Motorcycle Maintenance* (New York: Bantam Books, 1975), p. 158.
19. *The Simone Weil Reader*, ed. George A. Panichas (New York: David McKay Co., 1977), pp. 44–52 and passim.
20. See Abraham Maslow, *Motivation and Personality*, 2d ed. (New York: Harper & Row, 1970), pp. 158, 160–62, 165–66; McWilliams, *Idea of Fraternity*, p. 79; and Lasch, *Narcissism*, p. 116.

21. Michael Polanyi, *Personal Knowledge* (New York: Harper & Row, Torchbooks, 1964), p. 266; see also pp. 59–62.

22. Ibid., pp. 64–65, 299–324, and Marcel, *Homo Viator*, pp. 129–34.

23. *Radical Monotheism and Western Culture* (New York: Harper & Row, 1970), p. 16.

24. Ibid., p. 122. Niebuhr argues that all men have a faith, even if it is distrust of Being. Yet, he argues, such a distrust forces the center of valuation into myself, my church, my nation, my race, or some other object less than Being itself. This is the essence of sin. See appendix 3, chaps. 1 and 4, and pp. 114–26.

25. Ibid., p. 41.

26. Marcel, *Homo Viator*, pp. 29–67, esp. pp. 39–41, 46–47.

27. See *Personal Knowledge*; also *The Study of Man* (Chicago: University of Chicago Press, Phoenix Books, 1963) and *The Tacit Dimension* (Garden City, N.Y.: Doubleday & Co., Anchor Books, 1967). For accounts of this epistemology, see James L. Wiser, "Michael Polanyi," and "Political Theory, Personal Kowledge, and Public Truth," *Journal of Politics* 36 (August 1974): 661–74; also Harry Prosch, "Polanyi's Ethics," *Ethics* 82 (January 1972): 91–113. Niebuhr also argues that faith is central to science, *Radical Monotheism*, chap. 6 and appendix 4. Eric Voegelin's concept of the "Between" of existence; that is, of life lived in the tension between the divine Beyond and the demonic depth, expresses a meaning very similar to Polanyi's "indwelling." See *Order and History*, esp. vols. 3 and 4, and Dante Germino, "Eric Voegelin's Framework for Political Evaluation in His Recently Published Work," *American Political Science Review* 72 (March 1978): 110–21.

28. See Polanyi, *Personal Knowledge*, esp. pp. 17, 195–202, 300–302, and *Tacit Dimension*, chap. 1. See also Morgan, *Human Predicament*, pp. 259–65.

29. *Personal Knowledge*, p. 65. For elaboration of Polanyi's concept of calling and commitment, see pp. 308, 312, 322–24, 379; also *Tacit Dimension*, pp. 77ff, and *Study of Man*, p. 36 and chap. 2.

30. Amos 7:14–15; see also the dramatic account of Samuel's call in 1 Sam. 3:1–21.

31. See Charles Donald Combs, "An Inquiry into Political Loyalty," (master's thesis, Texas Tech University, 1974), chap. 1, and John H. Schaar, *Loyalty in America* (Berkeley: University of California Press, 1957), chap. 1. This power of loyalty makes it especially important that faith's object be worthy. Loyalty to evil objects has tremendous potential for harm.

32. José Ortega y Gasset, *Man and Crisis*, trans. Mildred Adams (New York: W. W. Norton & Co., 1958), p. 116.

33. James M. Gustafson and James T. Laney, eds., *On Being Responsible* (New York: Harper & Row, 1968), pp. 12–13.

34. Tinder, *Tolerance*, pp. 64–73.

35. For the idea of the "fitting" as the criterion of responsible action, see Niebuhr, *Responsible Self*, esp. pp. 55–65.

36. Lasch, *Narcissism*, p. 103.

37. *Personal Knowledge*, p. 309 (emphasis in original).

38. *Meaning*, pp. 201–08; Ivan Turgenev, "Spring Torrents," in *Five Short Novels*, trans. Franklin Reeve (New York: Bantam Books, 1961), pp. 401, 407.

39. T. S. Eliot, "The Love Song of J. Alfred Prufrock," *Collected Poems, 1909–1962* (New York: Harcourt, Brace & World, 1963), pp. 3–7.

40. *The Brothers Karamazov*, trans. Constance Garnett (New York: Modern Library, 1950), bk. 5, chap. 5.

41. *Notes from Underground*, trans. Andrew R. McAndrew (New York: New American Library, 1961), p. 103.

42. Stanley Milgram, "Behavioral Study of Obedience," in Aronson, ed., *Readings about the Social Animal* (San Francisco: W. H. Freeman & Co., 1973), pp. 19–33.

43. *Meaning*, p. 205.

44. *Wind, Sand, and Stars*, trans. Lewis Galantière (New York: Harcourt, Brace & World, 1967), pp. 43, 44.

45. On responsibility and Christ, see Niebuhr, *Responsible Self*, pp. 65–68, 143–45, 161–78.

46. *Bread and Wine*, trans. Harvey Ferguson II (New York: New American Library, 1963).

47. See Morgan, *Human Predicament*, pp. 250, 293–97, and Niebuhr, *Responsible Self*, pp. 61–68. Conscience seems intimately related to this second moment. See James F. Childress, "Appeals to Conscience," *Ethics* 89 (July 1979): 315–35.

48. *Ethics* 2. 1.; 6. 5, 8.

49. For discussions of attention, openness, and self, see Morgan, *Human Predicament*, pp. 212–14, 251–55, 306–16; Tinder, *Tolerance*, pp. 72, 83, 103–4, 114–15, 182–83; Niebuhr, *Responsible Self*, chap. 3; and Weil, *Simone Weil Reader*, pp. 44–52.

50. Rainer Maria Rilke, *Letters to a Young Poet*, trans. M. D. Herter Norton (New York: W. W. Norton & Co., 1934), p. 28 (emphasis in original).

51. Nouwen, *Reaching Out*, pp. 69–70.

52. See Morgan, *Human Predicament*, p. 310; and Tinder, *Tolerance*, pp. 81–82.

53. *Wind*, p. 27.

Chapter 3: Communion and Hospitality

1. See René König, *The Community*, trans. Edward Fitzgerald (New York: Schocken Books, 1968), chap. 2. For a discussion of the large variety of uses of "community" in sociology, see Jessie Bernard, *The Sociology of Community* (Glenview, Ill.: Scott, Foresman & Co., 1973); Joseph R. Gusfield, *Community* (New York: Harper & Row, 1975); Marcia Pelly Effrat, "Approaches to Community: Conflicts and Complementarities," *Sociological Inquiry* 43, no. 3–4 (1973): pp. 1–32; Nisbet, *Sociological Tradition*, chap. 3; and Minar and Greer, *Concept of Community*. No purpose would be served by an attempt to locate my own understanding and use of the concept in the morass of sociological usages, not to mention usages in other disciplines and in "ordinary language." My definition grows out of the Gemeinschaft tradition begun by Tönnies, but goes considerably beyond it. See Tönnies, *Community and Society*, and the discussions by Bernard, *Sociology*, chap. 6, and König, *Community*, passim.

2. "Definitions of Community." Divergent uses of the concept are displayed in the works cited in note 1 above.

3. *Concept of Community*, p. ix.

4. *Sociological Tradition*, pp. 47–48.

5. "The Concept of Community: A Re-examination," *Sociological Review*, n.s. 21 (August 1973): 397–416.

6. Julio R. Sabanes, "Biblical Understanding of Community," in de Vries, *Man in Community*, p. 172.

7. Clark, "Concept," pp. 404–5.

8. Alvin W. Gouldner, "The Norm of Reciprocity: A Preliminary Statement," *American Sociological Review* 25 (April 1960): 161–78, esp. p. 176, n. 46.

9. For the former term, see *Personal Knowledge*, chap. 7; for the latter, *Tacit Dimension*, chap. 3.

10. Nisbet, *Social Bond*, pp. 46–49.

11. The literature is voluminous; see, for example, Nisbet, *Quest*; Sebastian de Grazia, *The Political Community* (Chicago: University of Chicago Press, 1963); and Beach, *Christian Community*, pp. 122–24. Philip Abbott criticizes Wilson Carey McWilliams's idea of fraternity partly on this count in "The Tyranny of Fraternity in McWilliams' America," *Political Theory* 2 (August 1974): 304–20.

12. *The Four Loves* (London: Fontana Books, 1963), chaps. 1–3.

13. Ibid.

14. See Aristotle's criticism of Plato in *Politics* 2. 1–5.

15. See McWilliams, *Idea of Fraternity*, esp. pp. 39–40. His distinction between Gemeinschaft and community corresponds to mine between uniformity and communion.

16. Rosabeth Moss Kanter, *Commitment and Community* (Cambridge: Harvard University Press, 1972), pp. 98–99, 110–11, 132–34. Even groups with the same fundamental orientation may diverge widely, some toward communion, others toward pseudocommunity. For two examples, see Sanford Pinsker, "Piety as Community: The Hasidic View," *Social Research* 42 (Summer 1975): 230–46.

17. *The Ways of Friendship*, trans. Bernard Murchland, (New York: Macmillan Co., 1968), pp. 54–55.

18. Schaar, *Loyalty in America*, pp. 178–79; see also pp. 120–22.

19. See the Karamazov family in Dostoyevsky's *The Brothers Karamazov*. Tom, in Tennessee Williams's *The Glass Menagerie*, cannot escape the memory of his mother or of his sister, Laura. The theme also appears in Barry Beckham, *My Main Mother* (New York: New American Library, 1969).

20. *Commitment and Community*, p. 75; see pp. 64–69.

21. Ibid., pp. 67–76, 98–99, 110–11, 132–33. The mechanisms and some examples are conveniently summarized on pp. 126–27. Kanter is not alone in stressing the importance of such mechanisms, though hers is the most complete and systematic account of which I am aware. The importance of sacrifice, investment, renunciation, and mortification is supported by Harold B. Gerald and Grover C. Mathewson, "The Effects of Severity of Initiation on Liking for a Group: A Replication," in Aronson, *Readings*, pp. 114–24. William F. Stone, *The Psychology of Politics* (New York: Free Press, 1974), chap. 1, finds elements very similar to Kanter's at the heart of the success of the Oneida community. König's four major

types of local community integration parallel Kanter's major commitment mechanisms. *Community*, pp. 150–53.

22. This and the next three paragraphs summarize *Commitment and Community*, chaps. 4–5.

23. Ibid., p. 82.

24. Aristotle, *Politics* 1. 2; Cicero, *On the Commonwealth*, trans. George Holland Sabine and Stanley Barney Smith (Indianapolis, Ind.: Bobbs-Merrill Co., n.d.), pp. 51–53, 129–30, 136, 194, 219. The passages quoted are on p. 129.

25. *Human Predicament*, pp. 47–48.

26. McWilliams, *Idea of Fraternity*, pp. 9–32, 43–47, 123–26. See also Alan Wolfe, "Conditions of Community: The Case of Old Westbury College," in *Power and Community*, ed. Philip Green and Sanford Levinson (New York: Vintage Books, 1970), p. 206.

27. McWilliams, *Idea of Fraternity*, pp. 522–24.

28. Wilson Carey McWilliams, "On Equality as the Moral Foundation for Community," in *The Moral Foundations of the American Republic*, ed. Robert H. Horwitz (Charlottesville: University Press of Virginia, 1977), pp. 183–213.

29. Kanter, *Commitment and Community*, pp. 47–49.

30. See Morgan, *Human Predicament*, pp. 18–24, 36–37, 273–83, and McWilliams, *Idea of Fraternity*, p. 90.

31. Beach, *Christian Community*, p. 42.

32. Peter L. Berger and Thomas Luckmann, *The Social Construction of Reality* (New York: Doubleday & Co., 1967), pp. 41–42.

33. Kanter, *Commitment and Community*, pp. 91–103. On participation and communal integration, see Carole Pateman, *Participation and Democratic Theory* (Cambridge: Cambridge University Press, 1970).

34. *Four Loves*, p. 63.

35. Lepp, *Ways*, p. 108; see also pp. 116–17.

36. Muzafer Sherif, "Experiments in Group Conflict," in Aronson, *Readings*, pp. 292–302.

37. The phrase is Kanter's, *Commitment and Community*, pp. 41–42.

38. For portrayals and criticisms of these romanticizations, see McWilliams, *Idea of Fraternity*, passim., esp. pp. 39–40, 99–111, 182, 185, 285–86; König, *Community*, passim., esp. chap. 9; and Tinder, *Tolerance*, pp. 83–86.

39. Nouwen, *Reaching Out*, pp. 83–84; Tinder, *Tolerance*, pp. 83–85.

40. "In Praise of Thrasymachus," in *Essays in the Theory of Society* (Stanford: Stanford University Press, 1968), pp. 129–50; see also Desmond P. Ellis, "The Hobbesian Problem of Order: A Critical Appraisal of the Normative Solution," *American Sociological Review* 36 (August 1971): 692–703. I have argued against this view in "Politics of Interest."

41. Schaar, *Loyalty*, p. 17; see also McWilliams, *Idea of Fraternity*, pp. 50–51, and Lewis, *Four Loves*, chap. 4.

42. Kanter, *Commitment and Community*, p. 174.

43. Gen. 18:1–15; Ovid, *Metamorphoses*, trans. Rolfe Humphries (Bloomington: Indiana University Press, 1955), pp. 200–204.

44. Nouwen, *Reaching Out*, chaps. 4–6; Tinder, *Tolerance* and *Community*.

45. Nouwen, *Reaching Out*, pp. 46–48, 50–58; Tinder, *Tolerance*, pp. 59, 70.

46. Nouwen, *Reaching Out*, p. 70; see also Tinder, *Tolerance*, pp. 60–70.

47. Nouwen, *Reaching Out*, pp. 51–52.

48. Nouwen, *Reaching Out*, pp. 55–68, makes this point forcefully.

49. *Tolerance*, esp. pp. 70–83; see also Tinder, *Community*, esp. chaps. 5 and 9.

50. Tinder, *Tolerance*, pp. 75–76. Nouwen, *Reaching Out*, chap. 2.

51. Nouwen, *Reaching Out*, pp. 50–51, 73–77.

52. Michael Polanyi, *Science, Faith, and Society* (Chicago: University of Chicago Press, Phoenix Books, 1964), p. 70.

53. Tinder, *Tolerance*, pp. 142–48.

54. Ibid., chap. 3.

Chapter 4: Character and Community

1. *Idea of Fraternity*, pp. 58, 59.

2. See Maslow, *Motivation*, pp. 43–45.

3. McWilliams, *Idea of Fraternity*, p. 270. On the psychic rewards of total commitment, see Kanter, *Commitment and Community*, chaps. 3–4 and pp. 129, 167.

4. Clark, "Concept of Community," pp. 404–5.

5. Elliot Aronson and Darwyn Linder, "Gain and Loss of Esteem as Determinants of Interpersonal Attractiveness," in Aronson, *Readings*, pp. 342–58.

6. *Man and Crisis*, p. 22.

7. Buber, *Way of Response*, p. 179.

8. "Synergy: Some Notes of Ruth Benedict," selected by Abraham Maslow and John J. Honigmann, *American Anthropologist* 72 (April 1970): 332.

9. See Monroe Lefkowitz, et al., "Status Factors in Pedestrian Violation of Traffic Signals"; Bibb Latane and Judith Rodin, "A Lady in Distress: Inhibiting Effects of Friends and Strangers on Bystander Intervention"; and Albert Bandura, et al., "Transformation of Aggression through Imitation of Aggressive Models," all in Aronson, *Readings*, pp. 13–18, 34–47, 210–25. On the importance of "significant others," see Berger and Luckmann, *Social Construction*, pp. 50–67.

10. *Social Bond*, p. 59.

11. *Politics*. 1253a. Contrast Hobbes's discussion of bees and men. See *De Corpore Politico*, chap. 6, section 5, in J. Charles King and James A. McGilvray, eds., *Political and Social Philosophy* (New York: McGraw-Hill Book Co., 1973), pp. 96–97.

12. *Philosophy in a New Key* (Cambridge: Harvard University Press, 1942), p. 28.

13. See Berger and Luckmann, *Social Construction*, passim, and Polanyi, *Personal Knowledge*, chap. 5, esp. pp. 104–17.

14. Lewis Mumford, *The Conduct of Life* (New York: Harcourt, Brace & Co., 1951), p. 43.

15. *Simone Weil Reader*, pp. 270–71.

16. *The Magic Years* (New York: Charles Scribner's Sons, 1959), esp. chaps. 2, 4, and 5 and passim; also "The Origins of Human Bonds," *Commentary* 44 (December 1967): 47–57.

17. *Reaching Out*, p. 109.

18. *Simone Weil Reader*, p. 19; see pp. 113, 313–20, and passim.

19. See Maslow, *Motivation*, pp. 158, 160–62, 165–66, and McWilliams, *Idea of Fraternity*, p. 79 and passim. Plato's *Republic* also teaches this lesson.

20. This idea is suggested by Berger and Luckmann, *Social Construction*, pp. 142–43, and by Nisbet, *Social Bond*, p. 61.

21. *Loyalty in America*, p. 21.

22. *Wind*, pp. 32, 229. See Lepp, *Ways*, pp. 32, 48, 111–17, and McWilliams, *Idea of Fraternity*, pp. 62, 354-58.

23. *Personal Knowledge*, p. 203.

24. *Social Construction*, p. 95. The discussion draws primarily on pp. 95–104.

25. *Souls on Fire*, p. 111.

26. See McWilliams, *Idea of Fraternity*, pp. 316–17 on Hawthorne's concept of fraternity.

27. Nisbet, *Social Bond*, pp. 152–53.

28. McWilliams, *Idea of Fraternity*, p. 18.

29. Ibid., p. 309.

30. *Reaching Out*, p. 20; see also pp. 32–33.

31. McWilliams, *Idea of Fraternity*, pp. 11, 37; Kanter, *Commitment and Community*, pp. 1–2; George E. G. Catlin, "The Meaning of Community," in Friedrich, *Nomos II*, p. 133; and Weil, *Simone Weil Reader*, pp. 366–72.

32. See Nouwen, *Reaching Out*, pp. 28–30, and Maurice Stein, *The Eclipse of Community* (New York: Harper & Row, Torchbooks, 1964), pp. 268–69.

33. Tinder, *Tolerance*, esp. pp. 54–116, has dealt brilliantly with this subject. What I say in this and the next section owes much to him.

34. *Between Man and Man*, trans. Ronald Gregor Smith (New York: Macmillan Co., 1965), p. 21.

35. See Paul Goodman, "On Not Speaking," *New York Review of Books*, May 20, 1971, pp. 40–43. Something similar is the subject of J. G. A. Pocock's "Verbalizing a Political Act: Toward a Politics of Speech," *Political Theory* 1 (February 1973): 27–45.

36. See the contrasting accounts of Michael Kahn, "The Return of the Repressed," in Aronson, *Readings*, pp. 389–405, and Sigmund Koch, "The Image of Man in Encounter Groups," *American Scholar* 42 (Autumn 1973): 636–52. See also John H. Marx and David L. Ellison, "Sensitivity Training and Communes: Contemporary Quests for Community," *Pacific Sociological Review* 18 (October 1975): 442–62, and Irwin Rubin, "The Reduction of Prejudice through Laboratory Training," in Aronson, *Readings*, pp. 412–30.

37. Tournier, *Meaning*, p. 70; see Tinder, *Tolerance,* esp. pp. 90–91.

38. See Arendt, "Thinking and Moral Considerations."

39. Tournier, *Meaning*, chap. 9; Nouwen, *Reaching Out*, chaps. 8–9; Buber, *Between Man and Man*, pp. 14–15, 24–25.

40. Tinder, *Tolerance*, pp. 69–83.

41. Ibid., esp. pp. 83, 181–82.

42. Tournier, *Meaning*, chap. 8, describes a large number of such disguises; see also Lepp, *Ways*, pp. 28–29.

43. Tinder, *Tolerance*, p. 69.

44. Nouwen, *Reaching Out*, p. 80.

45. Tinder, *Tolerance*, pp. 133–37.

46. *Simone Weil Reader*, pp. 438, 164.

Chapter 5: Authority

1. "Legitimacy in the Modern State," in *Power and Community*, ed. Philip Green and Sanford Levinson (New York: Vintage Books, 1970), p. 279.

2. Ibid., esp. pp. 285–88, 297–301, 311–15. See also Lowi, *End of Liberalism*, for discussion and examples of the crisis of public authority.

3. Simon, "Beyond the Crisis of Liberalism," p. 273.

4. Salkever, "Virtue, Obligation, and Politics." See also Barry, "Liberalism and Want-Satisfaction."

5. I use "community" in the discussion of Friedrich and of Simon below because it is their term. It is close to "communion" in my terminology.

6. See *Man and His Government*, chap. 9; *Tradition and Authority* (New York: Praeger Publishers, 1972), chap. 9; and *Introduction to Political Theory*, pp. 122–24. Similar criticisms of the idea of authority as a particular form of power may be found in Sebastian de Grazia, "What Authority Is *Not*," *American Political Science Review* 53 (June 1959): 321–31; Robert A. Nisbet, "The Twilight of Authority," *The Public Interest*, no. 15 (Spring 1969), pp. 3–9, and "The Nemesis of Authority," *The Intercollegiate Review* 8 (Winter-Spring 1972): 3–13; and Hannah Arendt, "What Is Authority?" in Arendt, *Between Past and Future* (Cleveland: Meridian Books, 1963), pp. 97–106. See also D. D. Raphael, *Problems of Political Philosophy* (New York: Praeger Publishers, 1970), chap. 3, and Richard B. Friedman, "On the Concept of Authority in Political Philosophy," in *Concepts in Social and Political Philosophy,* ed. Richard E. Flathman (New York: Macmillan Publishing Co., 1973), pp. 126–27.

7. *Man and His Government*, pp. 224–26; *Tradition and Authority*, pp. 46–48; "Authority, Reason, and Discretion," in Carl J. Friedrich, ed., *Nomos I : Authority* (Cambridge: Harvard University Press, 1958), p. 34; and *The Philisophy of Law in Historical Perspective*, 2d. ed. (Chicago: University of Chicago Press, Phoenix Books, 1963), p. 203.

8. *Man and His Government*, p. 222.

9. Ibid., p. 224; see *Tradition and Authority*, chap. 5. For Friedrich's concept of community see "The Concept of Community in the History of Political and Legal Philosophy," in Friedrich, *Nomos II*, pp. 3–24; also *Man and His Government*, pp. 38–44, 136–54; and *Introduction to Political Theory*, pp. 90–104. For a similar view of authority, see Peter Winch, "Authority," in *Political Philosophy*, ed. Anthony Quinton (New York: Oxford University Press, 1967), pp. 97–111.

10. *Tradition and Authority*, chaps. 1–2. An even stronger emphasis on the necessity for tradition grounding authority is made by Arendt, "What Is Authority?" See also Michael Oakeshott's conception of politics as attending to the traditional arrangements of a community, *Rationalism in Politics*, esp. pp. 111–36. See also Winch, "Authority," pp. 107–9.

11. *Man and His Government*, pp. 228–29, 230; see also pp. 260–61; *Philoso-*

phy of Law, pp. 188–91; and *Transcendent Justice* (Durham, N.C.: Duke University Press, 1964).

12. *Man and His Government*, p. 227, and *Tradition and Authority*, pp. 49, 94–97.

13. *Introduction to Political Theory*, p. 129. For a more general criticism of Friedrich's theory of politics, see Richard W. Crosby, "Carl Friedrich's Empirical Theory of Politics," /*Political Science Reviewer* 3 (Fall 1973): 183–200. Peter G. Stillman has attempted to improve Friedrich's definition of legitimacy by making it more value-neutral, objective, and operational. "The Concept of Legitimacy," *Polity* 7 (Fall 1974): 32–56. This, of course, is exactly the wrong way to proceed.

14. See his *Nature and Functions of Authority* (Milwaukee, Wis.: Marquette University Press, 1940) and *General Theory of Authority*; also *Philosophy of Democratic Government*, chap. 1.

15. *Nature and Functions*, pp. 5–6.

16. *Philosophy of Democratic Government*, pp. 21–22; *Freedom and Community*, pp. 49–51.

17. *Philosophy of Democratic Government*, pp. 7–19.

18. Ibid., pp. 29–30.

19. Ibid., p. 33; see also "Common Good and Common Action," *Review of Politics* 22 (April 1960): pp. 210–23, for a slightly different statement of the argument just presented. Simon considered the question of deficiency, perfection, and choice at greater length in *Freedom and Community*, esp. chaps. 1–2, and in *Freedom of Choice*, ed. Peter Wolff (New York: Fordham University Press, 1969), chap. 3.

20. "Common Good and Common Action," p. 227; also *Philosophy of Democratic Government*, pp. 41–42.

21. Simon systematically considered community and common good in: *Philosophy of Democratic Government*, pp. 48–50, 62–66; *The Tradition of Natural Law*, ed. Vukan Kuic (New York: Fordham University Press, 1965), pp. 86–109; "Common Good and Common Action"; *General Theory of Authority*, chap. 2; and *Freedom and Community*, pp. 103–8, 130–44.

22. *Freedom and Community*, pp. 103–9, esp. 107–8. See Vukan Kuic, "The Contribution of Yves R. Simon to Political Science," *Political Science Reviewer* 4 (Fall 1974): 55–104.

23. *General Theory of Authority*, pp. 84, 92.

24. This exposition follows *Personal Knowledge*, pp. 55–131, 255–98; *Tacit Dimension*, pp. 3–25; and *Study of Man*, pp. 11–70. My analysis in the following pages owes much to discussions over a number of years with James L. Wiser. See his "Michael Polanyi"; "Political Theory"; and "Knowledge and Order," *Political Science Reviewer* 7 (Fall 1977): 90–110.

25. *Personal Knowledge*, p. 305 (emphasis in original).

26. Polanyi defends himself against the charge of subjectivity in *Personal Knowledge*, pp. 299–324; see also pp. 104, 132–50.

27. *Tacit Dimension*, p. 61.

28. *Personal Knowledge*, pp. 53–55, 374–80; see also Wiser, "Michael Polanyi," pp. 82–84.

29. *Personal Knowledge*, p. 203; see also chaps. 7 and 13, and *Tacit Dimension*, chaps. 2–3.

30. Wiser, "Michael Polanyi," p. 84 (emphasis in original).

31. *Science, Faith, and Society*, p. 16.

32. On truth, see Polanyi, *Personal Knowledge*, pp. 304–6, 308.

33. Socrates' claim is evident in the *Apology; Gorgias;* and *Republic*, see Voegelin, *Order and History*, vol. 3: *Plato and Aristotle*, esp. pp. 7–10, 36–45, 48–70. See also Wiser, "Political Theory," pp. 664–68, for the two aspects of authority.

34. For Socrates, see n. 33; for Christ, Luke 20:2–8 and Mark 1:21–28.

35. Various aspects of these ideas may be found in Charles W. Hendel, "An Exploration of the Nature of Authority," in Friedrich, *Nomos I*, pp. 3–27; Winch, "Authority," pp. 101–9; Schaar, "Legitimacy," pp. 287–88; and Arendt, "What Is Authority?"

36. See David L. Paletz and William F. Harris, "Four-Letter Threats to Authority," *Journal of Politics* 37 (November 1975): 955–79. Alasdair MacIntyre discusses the phenomenon from a longer perspective in "Secularization and Moral Change," in *Concepts in Social and Political Philosophy*, pp. 163–67. See also McWilliams, *Idea of Fraternity*, pp. 12–18, and Nisbet, *Social Bond*, p. 117.

37. Jaroslav Pelikan, *The Christian Tradition*, vol I: *The Emergence of the Catholic Tradition (100–600)* (Chicago: University of Chicago Press, 1971), p. 9.

38. "Wellsprings of Political Leadership," *American Political Science Review* 71 (March 1977): 266–75. Similarly, Kanter argues the necessity of authority and leadership for transcendence as a commitment mechanism, *Commitment and Community*, pp. 111–25.

39. Rieff, *Triumph of the Therapeutic*, p. 18.

40. See Simon, *Philosophy of Democratic Government*, esp. pp. 37–38, 149–54.

41. Matt. 20:25–28. See Bernard J. Cooke, *Christian Community* (Garden City, N.Y.: Doubleday & Co., 1973), pp. 30–39.

42. Cooke, *Christian Community*, pp. 25–30.

43. See Sebastian de Grazia, "Authority and Rationality," *Philosophy* 27 (April 1952): 99–109.

44. This consideration was suggested to me by my student Carolyn Chandler. Compare McWilliams, *Idea of Fraternity*, pp. 13–24.

45. See Simon, *Philosophy of Democratic Government*, chap. 3.

46. Compare Elizabeth Anscombe, "Authority in Morals," in *Concepts in Social and Political Philosophy*, ed. Flathman, pp. 157–63.

Chapter 6: Freedom

1. For a discussion of freedom and individualism, see Lukes, *Individualism*.

2. See K. J. Scott, "Liberty, License, and Not Being Free," in *Contemporary Political Theory*, ed. Anthony de Crespigny and Alan Wertheimer (New York: Atherton Press, 1970), pp. 96–106.

3. See William E. Connolly, *The Terms of Political Discourse* (Lexington, Mass.: D. C. Heath & Co., 1974), pp. 147–51, and Robert F. Sasseen, "Freedom as an End of Politics," *Interpretation* 2 (Winter 1971): 105–25.

4. *Terms*, pp. 139–78. Gerald C. MacCallum, Jr., "Negative and Positive Free-

dom," in *Contemporary Political Theory,* ed. de Crespigny and Wertheimer, pp. 107–26.

5. *Terms,* p. 154.

6. Ibid., p. 157 (emphasis in original).

7. *Superman and Common Men* (New York: Praeger Publishers, 1971), pp. 37–80.

8. See Hannah Arendt, "What Is Freedom?" in Arendt, *Between Past and Future* (Cleveland: World Publishing Co., Meridian Books, 1963), pp. 143–71.

9. Sasseen, "Freedom as an End of Politics," p. 115. Compare Stephen G. Salkever, "Freedom, Participation, and Happiness," *Political Theory* 5 (August 1977): 391–413.

10. Connolly, *Terms,* esp. pp. 93–101, 160–70.

11. John Ladd's distinction between "descriptive" and "normative" responsibility may be helpful here. The former refers to the actual relation between a person and a state of affairs. For example, "Ann is responsible for the mess in her room." The latter refers to a relation which ought to exist. For example, "Ann is responsible for cleaning up the mess." "The Ethics of Participation," in *Nomos XVI: Participation in Politics,* ed. J. Roland Pennock and John W. Chapman (New York: Lieber-Atherton, 1975), pp. 112–16. The responsible person fulfills her normative responsibilities.

12. *Problems of Political Philosophy,* pp. 119–22.

13. Such is the substance of Isaiah Berlin's famous attack on "positive liberty." "Two Concepts of Liberty," in Berlin, *Four Essays on Liberty* (London: Oxford University Press, 1969), pp. 118–72. For a criticism of Berlin in terms similar to those developed in this book, see Gary Frank Reed, "Berlin and the Division of Liberty," *Political Theory* 8 (August 1980): 365–80.

14. *Simone Weil Reader,* p. 447.

15. *Christian Community,* p. 24.

16. See Simon, *Freedom and Community,* p. 16. Simon's most extensive treatment is found in *Freedom of Choice,* esp. pp. 77–79, 97–127, 152–58. For Maritain, see *Scholasticism and Politics* (London: Geoffrey Bles, 1954), chap. 5, and *Social and Political Philosophy,* pp. 28–36, 41–46.

17. *Freedom and Community,* p. 4.

18. Ibid., p. 41.

19. See Tournier, *Meaning,* chap. 12.

20. "Being Free to Act and Being a Free Man," in *Concepts in Social and Political Philosophy,* pp. 309–21.

21. Both Connolly, *Terms,* pp. 158–59, 167, and Benn and Weinstein, "Being Free," pp. 311, 319–21, consider such situations, linking them to responsibility.

22. See Robert Paul Wolff, *In Defense of Anarchism* (New York: Harper & Row, Torchbooks, 1970). Wolff's argument has been effectively challenged by, inter alios, Harry G. Frankfurt, "The Anarchism of Robert Paul Wolff," *Political Theory* 1 (November 1973): 405–14; Jeffrey H. Reiman, *In Defense of Political Philosophy* (New York: Harper & Row, Torchbooks, 1972); and Lisa H. Perkins, "On Reconciling Autonomy and Authority," *Ethics* 82 (January 1972): 114–23.

23. See Friedman, "On the Concept of Authority."

24. See Schaar, *Loyalty in America,* pp. 101–3, and "Legitimacy in the Modern State," pp. 291–92, 309–10.

25. "Authority," pp. 102–5. For a sociological account of the importance of habit in providing an ordered background for choice, see Berger and Luckmann, *Social Construction of Reality*, pp. 53–57.

26. Cooke, *Christian Community*, pp. 14–25.

27. Arendt, "What Is Authority?" p. 106; see Simon, *Freedom and Community*, pp. 103–9; and Ignas Skrupskelis, "Royce and the Justification of Authority," *Southern Journal of Philosophy* 8 (Summer & Fall 1970): 165–70.

28. *Ethics.* 2. 1.

29. *Death of Communal Liberty*, p. 137.

30. See Barber, *Superman*, pp. 73–80.

31. *Freedom and Community*, pp. 96–97.

32. *Death of Communal Liberty*, p.11.

33. *Superman*, pp. 94–95. Tinder, *Tolerance*, criticizes most effectively the liberal idea of tolerance and substitutes for it a communal idea. See esp. chaps. 1–2.

34. See, for example, Walter Berns, "Free Speech and Free Government," and David Lowenthal, "Obscenity and the Law," both in *Political Science Reviewer* 2 (Fall 1972): 217–41, 242–90.

35. See, for example, *Quest*, pp. xii–xiii.

36. Berlin, "Two Concepts of Liberty," pp. 129–30.

37. Hannah Arendt sees such institutions in the spontaneous councils generated in every modern revolutionary movement. *On Revolution* (New York: Viking Press, Compass Books, 1965). Barber sees them in the Swiss communes, *Death of Communal Liberty*. Others see the institutions of workers' control or industrial democracy in this light.

Chapter 7: Pluralism and the Common Good

1. See *Political Community*.

2. Michael Walzer, "Civility and Civic Virtue in Contemporary America," *Social Research* 41 (Winter 1974): 601.

3. Weil, *Simone Weil Reader*, pp. 235–39. A number of the points above draw on Glenn Tinder, "Against Fate," manuscript, chap. 6.

4. Schaar, *Loyalty in America*, chap. 4.

5. James L. Wiser, "Reason and the Role of Persuasion," *Journal of Politics* 39 (May 1977): 427–45.

6. See Karen Johnson, "Political Obligation and the Voluntary Association Model of the State," *Ethics* 86 (October 1975): 17–29; McWilliams, *Idea of Fraternity*, pp. 64–94, 618–24.

7. *Eclipse of Community*, p. 335.

8. See Werner Jaeger, *Paideia*, vol. I, 2d ed., trans. Gilbert Highet (New York: Oxford University Press, 1965), passim., esp. pp. xvii–xxix.

9. McWilliams, *Idea of Fraternity*, p. 314; Simon, *General Theory of Authority*, chap. 4. Maritain believed that the person who serves the common good of the body politic develops virtues of charity and justice which promote his eternal salvation. *The Person and the Common Good*, trans. John J. Fitzgerald (New York: Charles Scribner's Sons, 1947), pp. 49, 53–66.

10. See my article, "Political Science and 'The Public Interest.' " See also Bruce Douglass, "The Common Good and the Public Interest," *Political Theory* 8 (February 1980): 103–17; also William E. Connolly, "The Public Interest and the Common Good," paper presented at the 1979 Meeting of the American Political Science Association, Washington, D.C., August 31–September 3. The alternate theory developed below is elaborated in my article, "Yves R. Simon and 'The Common Good': A Note on the Concept," *Ethics* 88 (April 1978): 229–39, upon which the following pages draw.

11. The reduction of the common good to some form of private advantage, preference, or happiness is the flaw which characterizes a number of recent discussions of "the public interest." See Theodore M. Benditt, "The Concept of Interest in Political Theory," Felix E. Oppenheim, "Self-Interest and Public Interest," and Richard E. Flathman, "Some Familiar but False Dichotomies Concerning 'Interests,' " all in *Political Theory* 3 (August 1975): 245–87. See also J. W. Roxbee Cox, "The Appeal to the Public Interest," *British Journal of Political Science* 3 (April 1973): 229–42. Even B. J. Diggs, despite his insistence on the notion of a common morality, defines the common good basically as a fair procedure for cooperative interest accommodation. See "The Common Good as Reason for Political Action," *Ethics* 83 (July 1973): 283–93.

12. *Person and Common Good.*

13. *Philosophy of Democratic Government*, pp. 39–57.

14. Simon, *Tradition of Natural Law*, p. 105.

15. *Nature and Functions of Authority*, p. 47; see also *Philosophy of Democratic Government*, p. 140.

16. The idea of symbols of experience is taken from the work of Eric Voegelin. See particularly, "Equivalences of Experience and Symbolization in History," in *Eternita' e storia* (Florence: a cura dell 'Istituto Accademico de Roma, 1970), pp. 215–34.

17. This connection between communion and justice has been recognized throughout history by the most diverse set of thinkers. It is possibly a universal social axiom. See, for example, Aristotle, *Ethics*, 5. 5–7; Jacques Maritain, *The Rights of Man and Natural Law* (London: Geoffrey Bles, 1958), pp. 23–24; Tinder, *Tolerance*, pp. 125–27; Emile Durkheim, *The Division of Labor in Society*, trans. George Simpson (Glencoe, Ill.: Free Press, 1933), pp. 374–88, 407; and Rawls, *Theory of Justice*, pp. 5, 105–6.

18. On the clash, see Brian Barry, "Justice and the Common Good," in *Political Philosophy*, ed. Anthony Quinton (London: Oxford University Press, 1967), pp. 189–93.

19. Among the many incisive criticisms of interest-group pluralism, the ones which come closest to my own perspective are Lowi, *End of Liberalism*, and Baskin, *American Pluralist Democracy*. See my "Politics of Interest" for a critique of this pluralism. On the English Pluralists, see David Nicholls, *Three Varieties of Pluralism* (London: Macmillan Press, 1974), and *The Pluralist State* (New York: St. Martin's Press, 1975). Substantial criticisms of such pluralist theories are found in: Paul H. Conn, "Social Pluralism and Democracy," *American Journal of Political Science* 17 (May 1973): 237–54, and F. M. Barnard and R. A. Vernon, "Pluralism, Participation, and Politics," *Political Theory* 3 (May 1975): 180–97.

20. Simon, *Freedom and Community*, pp. 88–92.

21. Bellow, *Humboldt's Gift* (New York: Viking Press, 1975), p. 29 (emphasis in original).

22. This principle is central to Simon's theory; see, for example, *Freedom and Community*, pp. 135–40. See also Robert A. Nisbet, *The Social Philosophers* (New York: Thomas Y. Crowell Co., 1973), chaps. 5–6. See also Durkheim, *Division of Labor*, pp. 1–31.

23. *To Empower People* (Washington: American Enterprise Institute for Public Policy Research, 1977). Berger and Neuhaus rightly point out that liberalism, conservatism, and socialism have all been relatively blind to the importance of such structures, often dismissing them as anachronistic or oppressive (pp. 4–6).

24. See Melvin M. Webber, "Order in Diversity: Community without Propinquity," in *Neighborhood, City and Metropolis*, ed. Robert Gutman and David Popenoe (New York: Random House, 1970), pp. 791–811.

25. See Schaar, *Loyalty in America*, pp. 27–30, 68–71, 177.

26. Tinder, *Tolerance*, pp. 166–73.

27. Simon, *Philosophy of Democratic Government*, pp. 311–13; Nisbet, *Social Bond*, pp. 90–91.

28. Yves R. Simon, *Work, Society, and Culture*, ed. Vukan Kuic (New York: Fordham University Press, 1971), pp. 70–83, 139–42.

29. R. L. Nichols and D. M. White have pointed out the value of reviving the ancient virtue of prudence. "Politics Proper," *Ethics* 89 (July 1979): 372–84.

30. I am indebted to Carolyn Chandler for reminding me of this.

Chapter 8: Politics, Hospitality, and Character

1. It should be clear, then, that a strong commitment to the practice of rights is not as problematic for a communitarian theory of political order as some suggest; see Richard E. Flathman, *The Practice of Rights* (New York: Cambridge University Press, 1977), chap. 9.

2. For fuller development of the relationship between politics and tolerance, the reader is encouraged to consult Tinder, *Tolerance*, esp. pp. 132–84; also *Community;* "Transcending Tragedy, *American Political Science Review* 68 (June 1974): 547–60; and "In Defense of Pure Tolerance," *Polity* 6 (Summer 1974): 446–68.

3. These are similar, but not identical, to the requirements listed by Tinder, *Tolerance*, pp. 152–58.

4. On the proper understanding of patriotism, see John H. Schaar, "The Case for Patriotism," in *American Review #17* (New York: New American Library, 1973), pp. 59–99.

5. Pateman's *Participation and Democratic Theory* contains an excellent summary of the arguments for and against a more participatory democracy. Two good collections of essays on the question are Geraint Parry, ed., *Participation in Politics* (Manchester, England: Manchester University Press, 1972), and Pennock and Chapman, eds., *Participation in Politics*.

6. Ladd, "The Ethics of Participation," in Pennock and Chapman, eds., *Participation in Politics*, p. 103.

7. *Democracy in America*; see, for example, vol. 1, "Author's Introduction" and chaps. 2, 3, 5, 14, 17; vol. 2, bk. 2, chap. 4.

8. See Pateman, *Participation and Democratic Theory*, chap. 3, and McWilliams, *Idea of Fraternity*, p. 67.

9. *Death of Communal Liberty*, p. 182. See also pp. 182–86.

10. "Civility and Civic Virtue," p. 610 (emphasis in original).

11. Jane Mansbridge, "The Limits of Friendship," in Pennock and Chapman, eds., *Participation in Politics*, pp. 246–75.

12. "Confident pessimism" is Simon's description of the appropriate attitude toward the possibility of human progress. *Freedom and Community*, chap. 6. "Realism" is the term favored by Reinhold Niebuhr; see "Augustine's Political Realism," in Niebuhr, *Christian Realism and Political Problems* (New York: Charles Scribner's Sons, 1953), pp. 119–46.

Bibliography

Abbott, Philip. "The Tyranny of Fraternity in McWilliams' America." *Political Theory* 2 (August 1974): 304–20.

Abbott, Walter M., general ed., and Gallagher, Joseph, translation ed. *The Documents of Vatican II.* New York: Guild Press, 1966.

Anscombe, Elizabeth. "Authority in Morals." In *Concepts in Social and Political Philosophy*, edited by Richard E. Flathman, pp. 157–63. New York: Macmillan Publishing Co., 1973.

Arendt, Hannah. *Between Past and Future.* Cleveland: World Publishing Co., Meridian Books, 1963.

———. *On Revolution.* New York: The Viking Press, Compass Books, 1965.

———. "Thinking and Moral Considerations: A Lecture." *Social Research* 38 (Autumn 1971): 417–46.

Aristotle. *The Nicomachean Ethics.* Translated by J. A. K. Thomson. Rev. ed. by Hugh Tredennick. New York: Penguin Books, 1976.

———. *The Politics of Aristotle.* Edited and translated by Ernest Barker. New York: Oxford University Press, 1962.

Aronson, Elliot, ed. *Readings about the Social Animal.* San Francisco: W. H. Freeman & Co., 1973.

Bachrach, Peter. *The Theory of Democratic Elitism: A Critique.* Boston: Little, Brown & Co., 1967.

Barber, Benjamin R. *The Death of Communal Liberty: A History of Freedom in a Swiss Mountain Canton.* Princeton: Princeton University Press, 1974.

———. "Deconstituting Politics: Robert Nozick and Philosophical Reductionism." *Journal of Politics* 39 (February 1977): 2–23.

———. *Superman and Common Men: Freedom, Anarchy, and the Revolution.* New York: Praeger Publishers, 1971.

Barnard, F. M., and Vernon, R. A. "Pluralism, Participation, and Politics: Reflections on the Intermediate Group." *Political Theory* 3 (May 1975): 180–97.

Barry, Brian M. "Justice and the Common Good." In *Political Philosophy*, edited by Anthony Quinton, pp. 189–93. London: Oxford University Press, 1967.

———. "Liberalism and Want-Satisfaction: A Critique of John Rawls." *Political Theory* 1 (May 1973): 134–53.

Baskin, Darryl. *American Pluralist Democracy: A Critique.* New York: Van Nostrand Reinhold Co., 1971.

Bay, Christian. "Foundations of the Liberal Make-Believe." *Inquiry* 14 (Autumn 1971): 213–37.

———. "Needs, Wants, and Political Legitimacy." *Canadian Journal of Political Science* 1 (September 1968): 241–60.

———. *The Structure of Freedom.* Stanford: Stanford University Press, 1958.

Beach, Waldo. *Christian Community and American Society.* Philadelphia: Westminster Press, 1969.

Bellow, Saul. *Humboldt's Gift.* New York: Viking Press, 1975.

Benditt, Theodore M. "The Concept of Interest in Political Theory." *Political Theory* 3 (August 1975): 245–58.

Benedict, Ruth. "Synergy: Some Notes of Ruth Benedict." Selected by Abraham Maslow and John J. Honigmann. *American Anthropologist* 72 (April 1970): 320–33.

Benn, S. I., and Weinstein, W. L. "Being Free to Act and Being a Free Man." In *Concepts in Social and Political Philosophy*, edited by Richard E. Flathman, pp. 309–21. New York: Macmillan Publishing Co., 1973.

Berger, Peter L. " 'Sincerity' and 'Authenticity' in Modern Society." *The Public Interest*, no. 31 (Spring 1973), pp. 81–90.

Berger, Peter L., Berger, Brigitte, and Kellner, Hansfried. *The Homeless Mind.* New York: Vintage Books, 1974.

Berger, Peter L., and Luckmann, Thomas. *The Social Construction of Reality: A Treatise in the Sociology of Knowledge.* New York: Doubleday & Co., 1967.

Berger, Peter L., and Neuhaus, Richard John. *To Empower People: The Role of Mediating Structures in Public Policy.* Washington: American Enterprise Institute for Public Policy Research, 1977.

Berlin, Isaiah. *Four Essays on Liberty.* London: Oxford University Press, 1969.

Bernard, Jessie. *The Sociology of Community.* Glenview, Ill.: Scott, Foresman & Co., 1973.

Berns, Walter. "Free Speech and Free Government." *Political Science Reviewer* 2 (Fall 1972): 217–41.

Buber, Martin. *Between Man and Man.* Translated by Ronald Gregor Smith. New York: Macmillan Co., 1965.

———. *The Way of Response.* Edited by N. N. Glatzer. New York: Schocken Books, 1966.

Burns, James MacGregor. "Wellsprings of Political Leadership." *American Political Science Review* 71 (March 1977): 266–75.

Childress, James F. "Appeals to Conscience." *Ethics* 89 (July 1979): 315–35.

Chin, Marie. "Lived Privacy and Personal Space." *Humanitas* 11 (February 1975): 45–54.

Cicero. *On the Commonwealth.* Translated by George Holland Sabine and Stanley Barney Smith. Indianapolis, Ind.: Bobbs-Merrill Co., n.d.

Clarke, D. B. "The Concept of Community: A Re-examination." *Sociological Review*, n.s. 21 (August 1973): 397–416.

Cochran, Clarke E. "Political Science and 'The Public Interest.' " *Journal of Politics* 36 (May 1974): 327–55.

————. "The Politics of Interest: Philosophy and the Limitations of the Science of Politics." *American Journal of Political Science* 17 (November 1973): 745–66.

————. "Yves R. Simon and 'The Common Good': A Note on the Concept." *Ethics* 88 (April 1978): 229–39.

Combs, Charles Donald. "An Inquiry into Political Loyalty." Master's thesis, Texas Tech University, 1974.

Conn, Paul H. "Social Pluralism and Democracy." *American Journal of Political Science* 17 (May 1973): 237–54.

Connolly, William E., ed. *The Bias of Pluralism.* New York: Atherton Press, 1969.

————. "A Note on Freedom under Socialism." *Political Theory* 5 (November 1977): 461–72.

————. "The Public Interest and the Common Good." Paper presented at the 1979 Meeting of the American Political Science Association, Washington, D.C., August 31-September 3.

————. *The Terms of Political Discourse.* Lexington, Mass.: D. C. Heath & Co., 1974.

Cooke, Bernard J. *Christian Community: Response to Reality.* Garden City, N. Y.: Doubleday & Co., 1973.

Cox, J. W. Roxbee. "The Appeal to the Public Interest." *British Journal of Political Science* 3 (April 1973): 229–42.

Crosby, Richard W. "Carl Friedrich's Empirical Theory of Politics." *Political Science Reviewer* 3 (Fall 1973): 183–200.

Dahrendorf, Ralf. *Essays in the Theory of Society.* Stanford: Stanford University Press, 1968.

De Vries, Egbert, ed. *Man in Community.* New York: Association Press, 1966.

Diggs, B. J. "The Common Good as Reason for Political Action." *Ethics* 83 (July 1973): 283–93.

Dostoyevsky, Fyodor M. *The Brothers Karamazov.* Translated by Constance Garnett. New York: Modern Library, 1950.

————. *Notes from Underground.* Translated by Andrew R. McAndrew. New York: New American Library, 1961.

Douglass, Bruce. "The Common Good and the Public Interest." *Political Theory* 8 (February 1980): 103–17.

Durkheim, Emile. *The Division of Labor in Society.* Translated by George Simpson. Glencoe, Ill.: Free Press, 1933.

Effrat, Marcia Pelly. "Approaches to Community: Conflicts and Complementarities." *Sociological Inquiry* 43, no. 3–4 (1973): 1–32.

Eliot, T. S. *Collected Poems, 1909–1962.* New York: Harcourt, Brace & World, 1963.

Ellis, Desmond P. "The Hobbesian Problem of Order: A Critical Appraisal of the Normative Solution." *American Sociological Review* 36 (August 1971): 692–703.

Encyclopaedia of the Social Sciences. Vol. 8. S.v. "Individualism."

Flathman, Richard E. *The Practice of Rights.* New York: Cambridge University Press, 1977.

————. "Some Familiar but False Dichotomies Concerning 'Interests': A Comment on Benditt and Oppenheim." *Political Theory* 3 (August 1975): 277–87.

Fraiberg, Selma H. *The Magic Years: Understanding and Handling the Problems of Early Childhood.* New York: Charles Scribner's Sons, 1959.

————. "The Origins of Human Bonds." *Commentary*, December 1967, pp. 47–57.

Frankfurt, Harry G. "The Anarchism of Robert Paul Wolff." *Political Theory* 1 (November 1973): 405–14.

French, David. "After the Fall—What This Country Needs Is a Good *Counter* Counterculture Culture." *New York Times Magazine*, October 3, 1971, pp. 20–36.

Friedman, Richard B. "On the Concept of Authority in Political Philosophy." In *Concepts in Social and Political Philosophy*, edited by Richard E. Flathman, pp. 121–46. New York: Macmillan Publishing Co., 1973.

Friedrich, Carl J. *An Introduction to Political Theory.* New York: Harper & Row, 1967.

————. *Man and His Government: An Empirical Theory of Politics.* New York: McGraw-Hill Book Co., 1963.

————. *The Philosophy of Law in Historical Perspective.* 2d ed. Chicago: University of Chicago Press, Phoenix Books, 1963.

————. *Tradition and Authority.* New York: Praeger Publishers, 1972.

————. *Transcendent Justice.* Durham, N.C.: Duke University Press, 1964.

Friedrich, Carl J., ed. *Nomos I: Authority.* Cambridge: Harvard University Press, 1958.

————. *Nomos II: Community.* New York: Liberal Arts Press, 1959.

Germino, Dante. "Eric Voegelin's Framework for Political Evaluation in His Recently Published Work." *American Political Science Review* 72 (March 1978): 110–21.

Goodman, Paul. "On Not Speaking." *New York Review of Books*, May 20, 1971, pp. 40–43.

Gotesky, Rubin. "Aloneness, Loneliness, Isolation, Solitude." In *An Invitation to Phenomenology*, edited by James M. Edie, pp. 211–39. Chicago: Quadrangle Books, 1965.

Gouldner, Alvin W. "The Norm of Reciprocity: A Preliminary Statement." *American Sociological Review* 25 (April 1960): 161–78.

Grazia, Sebastian de. "Authority and Rationality." *Philosophy* 27 (April 1952): 99–109.

————. *The Political Community: A Study of Anomie.* Chicago: University of Chicago Press, 1948.

————. "What Authority Is *Not*." *American Political Science Review* 53 (June 1959): 321–31.

Gusfield, Joseph R. *Community: A Critical Response.* New York: Harper & Row, 1975.

Gustafson, James M., and Laney, James T., eds. *On Being Responsible.* New York: Harper & Row, 1968.

Hallowell, John H. *The Decline of Liberalism as an Ideology.* Berkeley: University of California Press, 1943.

————. *Main Currents in Modern Political Thought.* New York: Holt, Rinehart, & Winston, 1950.

Hillery, George A., Jr. "Definitions of Community: Areas of Agreement." *Rural Sociology* 20 (June 1955): 111–23.

Hobbes, Thomas. *Leviathan*. Edited by Michael Oakeshott. New York: Collier Books, 1962.

Holbrook, Clyde A. *Faith and Community: A Christian Existential Approach*. New York: Harper & Bro., 1959.

Jaeger, Werner. *Paideia: The Ideals of Greek Culture*. 2d ed. Vol. 1. Translated from the 2d German ed. by Gilbert Highet. New York: Oxford University Press, 1965.

Johnson, Karen. "Political Obligation and the Voluntary Association Model of the State." *Ethics* 86 (October 1975): 17–29.

Jouvenel, Bertrand de. *Sovereignty*. Translated by J. F. Huntington. Chicago: University of Chicago Press, 1957.

Kanter, Rosabeth Moss. *Commitment and Community: Communes and Utopias in Sociological Perspective*. Cambridge: Harvard University Press, 1972.

Kariel, Henry S. "Expanding the Political Present." *American Political Science Review* 63 (September 1969): 768–76.

———. *Open Systems: Arenas for Political Action*. Itasca, Ill.: F. E. Peacock Publishers, 1969.

———. *The Promise of Politics*. Englewood Cliffs, N.J.: Prentice-Hall, 1966.

———. "Terminal Cases." *Political Science Reviewer* 1 (Fall 1971): 74–92.

Keyes, Ralph. *We, the Lonely People: Searching for Community*. New York: Harper & Row, 1973.

King, J. Charles, and McGilvray, James A., eds. *Political and Social Philosophy*. New York: McGraw-Hill Book Co., 1973.

Koch, Sigmund. "The Image of Man in Encounter Groups." *American Scholar* 42 (Autumn 1973): 636–52.

König, René. *The Community*. Translated by Edward Fitzgerald. New York: Schocken Books, 1968.

Kuic, Vukan. "The Contribution of Yves R. Simon to Political Science." *Political Science Reviewer* 4 (Fall 1974): 55–104.

Langer, Susanne K. *Philosophy in a New Key*. Cambridge: Harvard University Press, 1942.

Lasch, Christopher. *The Culture of Narcissism*. New York: Warner Books, 1979.

Lepp, Ignace. *The Ways of Friendship*. Translated by Bernard Murchland. New York: Macmillan Co., 1968.

Lewis, C. S. *The Four Loves*. London: Fontana Books, 1963.

Lowenthal, David. "Obscenity and the Law." *Political Science Reviewer* 2 (Fall 1972): 242–90.

Lowi, Theodore J. *The End of Liberalism*. 2d ed. New York: W. W. Norton & Co., 1979.

Lukes, Steven. *Individualism*. Oxford: Basil Blackwell, 1973.

MacCallum, Gerald C., Jr. "Negative and Positive Freedom." In *Contemporary Political Theory*, edited by Anthony de Crespigny and Alan Wertheimer, pp. 107–26. New York: Atherton Press, 1970.

McCoy, Charles A., and Playford, John, eds. *Apolitical Politics: A Critique of Behavioralism*. New York: Thomas Y. Crowell Co., 1967.

MacIntyre, Alasdair. "Secularization and Moral Change." In *Concepts in Social and Political Philosophy*, edited by Richard E. Flathman, pp. 163–67. New York: Macmillan Publishing Co., 1973.

McWilliams, Wilson Carey. "On Equality as the Moral Foundation for Community." In *The Moral Foundations of the American Republic*, edited by Robert H. Horwitz, pp. 183–213. Charlottesville: University Press of Virginia, 1977.

———. *The Idea of Fraternity in America*. Berkeley: University of California Press, 1974.

Marcel, Gabriel. *Homo Viator*. Translated by Emma Craufurd. New York: Harper & Row, 1962.

Maritain, Jacques. *The Person and the Common Good*. Translated by John J. Fitzgerald. New York: Charles Scribner's Sons, 1947.

———. *The Rights of Man and Natural Law*. London: Geoffrey Bles, 1958.

———. *Scholasticism and Politics*. London: Geoffrey Bles, 1954.

———. *The Social and Political Philosophy of Jacques Maritain*. Edited by Joseph W. Evans and Leo R. Ward. London: Geoffrey Bles, 1956.

Marx, John H., and Ellison, David L. "Sensitivity Training and Communes: Contemporary Quests for Community." *Pacific Sociological Review* 18 (October 1975): 442–62.

Maslow, Abraham H. *Motivation and Personality*. 2d ed. New York: Harper & Row, 1970.

Minar, David W., and Greer, Scott, eds. *The Concept of Community*. Chicago: Aldine Publishing Co., 1969.

Morgan, George W. *The Human Predicament: Dissolution and Wholeness*. Providence, R.I.: Brown University Press, 1968.

Mumford, Lewis. *The Conduct of Life*. New York: Harcourt, Brace & Co., 1951.

Nicholls, David. *The Pluralist State*. New York: St. Martin's Press, 1975.

———. *Three Varieties of Pluralism*. London: Macmillan Press, 1974.

Nichols, R. L., and White, D. M. "Politics Proper: On Action and Prudence." *Ethics* 89 (July 1979): 372–84.

Niebuhr, H. Richard. *Radical Monotheism and Western Culture*. New York: Harper & Row, Torchbooks, 1970.

———. *The Responsible Self*. New York: Harper & Row, 1963.

Niebuhr, Reinhold. *Christian Realism and Political Problems*. New York: Charles Scribner's Sons, 1953.

Nisbet, Robert A. "The Nemesis of Authority." *The Intercollegiate Review* 8 (Winter-Spring 1972): 3–13.

———. *The Quest for Community*. New York: Oxford University Press, 1969.

———. *The Social Bond*. New York: Alfred A. Knopf, 1970.

———. *The Sociological Tradition*. New York: Basic Books, 1966.

———. *The Social Philosophers*. New York: Thomas Y. Crowell Co., 1973.

———. "The Twilight of Authority." *The Public Interest*, no. 15 (Spring 1969), pp. 3–9.

Nouwen, Henri J. M. *Reaching Out: The Three Movements of the Spiritual Life*. Garden City, N.Y.: Doubleday & Co., 1975.

Nozick, Robert. *Anarchy, State, and Utopia*. New York: Basic Books, 1974.

Oakeshott, Michael. *Rationalism in Politics*. New York: Basic Books, 1962.

Oppenheim, Felix E. "Self-Interest and Public Interest." *Political Theory* 3 (August 1975): 259–76.

Ortega y Gasset, José. *Man and Crisis*. Translated by Mildred Adams. New York: W. W. Norton & Co., 1958.

Ovid. *Metamorphoses*. Translated by Rolfe Humphries. Bloomington: Indiana University Press, 1955.

Paletz, David L., and Harris, William F. "Four-Letter Threats to Authority." *Journal of Politics* 37 (November 1975): 955–79.

Parry, Geraint, ed. *Participation in Politics*. Manchester, England: Manchester University Press, 1972.

Pateman, Carole. *Participation and Democratic Theory*. Cambridge: Cambridge University Press, 1970.

Pelikan, Jaroslav. *The Christian Tradition*. Vol.1: *The Emergence of the Catholic Tradition (100–600)*. Chicago: University of Chicago Press, 1971.

Pennock, J. Roland, and Chapman, John W., eds. *Nomos XVI: Participation in Politics*. New York: Lieber-Atherton, 1975.

Perkins, Lisa H. "On Reconciling Autonomy and Authority." *Ethics* 82 (January 1972): 114–23.

Pinsker, Sanford. "Piety as Community: The Hasidic View." *Social Research* 42 (Summer 1975): 230–46.

Pirsig, Robert M. *Zen and the Art of Motorcycle Maintenance*. New York: Bantam Books, 1975.

Plato. *The Republic of Plato*. Translated by Allan Bloom. New York: Basic Books, 1968.

Pocock, J. G. A. "Verbalizing a Political Act: Toward a Politics of Speech." *Political Theory* 1 (February 1973): 27–45.

Polanyi, Michael. *Personal Knowledge: Towards a Post-Critical Philosophy*. New York: Harper & Row, Torchbooks, 1964.

———. *Science, Faith, and Society*. Chicago: University of Chicago Press, Phoenix Books, 1964.

———. *The Study of Man*. Chicago: University of Chicago Press, Phoenix Books, 1963.

———. *The Tacit Dimension*. Garden City, N.Y.: Doubleday & Co., Anchor Books, 1967.

Prosch, Harry. "Polanyi's Ethics." *Ethics* 82 (January 1972): 91–113.

Raphael, D. D. *Problems of Political Philosophy*. New York: Praeger Publishers, 1970.

Rawls, John. *A Theory of Justice*. Cambridge: Harvard University Press, 1971.

Reed, Gary Frank. "Berlin and the Division of Liberty." *Political Theory* 8 (August 1980): 365–80.

Reiman, Jeffrey H. *In Defense of Political Philosophy*. New York: Harper & Row, Torchbooks, 1972.

Rieff, Philip. *The Triumph of the Therapeutic: Uses of Faith after Freud*. New York: Harper & Row, Torchbooks, 1968.

Rilke, Rainer Maria. *Letters to a Young Poet*. Translated by M. D. Herter Norton. New York: W. W. Norton & Co., 1934.

Saint-Exupéry, Antoine de. *Wind, Sand, and Stars.* Translated by Lewis Galantière. New York: Harcourt, Brace & World, 1967.

Salkever, Stephen G. "Freedom, Participation, and Happiness." *Political Theory* 5 (August 1977): 391–413.

———. "Virtue, Obligation, and Politics." *American Political Science Review* 68 (March 1974): 78–92.

Sasseen, Robert F. "Freedom as an End of Politics." *Interpretation* 2 (Winter 1971): 105–25.

Schaar, John H. "The Case for Patriotism." In *American Review #17,* pp. 59–99. New York: New American Library, 1973.

———. "Legitimacy in the Modern State." In *Power and Community,* edited by Philip Green and Sanford Levinson, pp. 276–327. New York: Vintage Books, 1970.

———. *Loyalty in America.* Berkeley: University of California Press, 1957.

Scott, K. J. "Liberty, License, and Not Being Free." In *Contemporary Political Theory,* edited by Anthony de Crespigny and Alan Wertheimer, pp. 96–106. New York: Atherton Press, 1970.

Silone, Ignazio. *Bread and Wine.* Translated by Harvey Ferguson II. New York: New American Library, 1963.

Simon, Yves R. "Beyond the Crisis in Liberalism." In *Essays in Thomism,* edited by Robert E. Brennan, pp. 263–86. New York: Sheed & Ward, 1942.

———. "A Comment on Censorship." *International Philosophical Quarterly* 17 (March 1977): 33–42.

———. "Common Good and Common Action." *Review of Politics* 22 (April 1960): 202–44.

———. *Freedom and Community.* Edited by Charles P. O'Donnell. New York: Fordham University Press, 1968.

———. *Freedom of Choice.* Edited by Peter Wolff. New York: Fordham University Press, 1969.

———. *A General Theory of Authority.* Introduction by A. Robert Caponigri. Notre Dame: University of Notre Dame Press, 1962.

———. *Nature and Functions of Authority.* Milwaukee, Wis.: Marquette University Press, 1940.

———. *Philosophy of Democratic Government.* Chicago: University of Chicago Press, Phoenix Books, 1961.

———. *The Tradition of Natural Law: A Philosopher's Reflections.* Edited by Vukan Kuic. New York: Fordham University Press, 1965.

———. *Work, Society, and Culture.* Edited by Vukan Kuic. New York: Fordham University Press, 1971.

Skrupskelis, Ignas. "Royce and the Justification of Authority." *Southern Journal of Philosophy* 8 (Summer and Fall 1970): 165–70.

Spragens, Thomas A., Jr. *Understanding Political Theory.* New York: St. Martin's Press, 1976.

Stein, Maurice R. *The Eclipse of Community: An Interpretation of American Studies.* New York: Harper & Row, Torchbooks, 1964.

Stillman, Peter G. "The Concept of Legitimacy." *Polity* 7 (Fall 1974): 32–56.

Stone, William F. *The Psychology of Politics.* New York: Free Press, 1974.

Tinder, Glenn. "Against Fate." Manuscript. Boston, 1979.

————. *Community.* Baton Rouge: Louisiana State University Press, 1980.

————. "In Defense of Pure Tolerance." *Polity* 6 (Summer 1974): 446–68.

————. *Tolerance: Toward a New Civility.* Amherst: University of Massachusetts Press, 1976.

————. "Transcending Tragedy: The Idea of Civility." *American Political Science Review* 68 (June 1974): 547–60.

Tocqueville, Alexis de. *Democracy in America.* Translated by Henry Reeve. 2 vols. New Rochelle, N.Y.: Arlington House, n.d.

Tönnies, Ferdinand. *Community and Society.* Translated and edited by Charles P. Loomis. New York: Harper & Row, Torchbooks, 1963.

Tournier, Paul. *The Meaning of Persons.* Translated by Edwin Hudson. New York: Harper & Row, 1957.

Trilling, Lionel. *Sincerity and Authenticity.* Cambridge: Harvard University Press, 1972.

Turgenev, Ivan. *Five Short Novels.* Translated by Franklin Reeve. New York: Bantam Books, 1961.

Voegelin, Eric. "Equivalences of Experience and Symbolization in History." In *Externita' e storia*, pp. 215–34. Florence: a cura dell 'Istituto Accademico de Roma, 1970.

————. "Liberalism and Its History." Translated by Mary and Keith Algozin. *Review of Politics* 36 (October 1974): 515–19.

————. *The New Science of Politics.* Chicago: University of Chicago Press, Phoenix Books, 1966.

————. *Order and History.* 4 vols. Baton Rouge: Louisiana State University Press, 1956–74.

Walzer, Michael. "Civility and Civic Virtue in Contemporary America." *Social Research* 41 (Winter 1974): 593–611.

Webber, Melvin M. "Order in Diversity: Community Without Propinquity." In *Neighborhood, City and Metropolis*, edited by Robert Gutman and David Popenoe, pp. 791–811. New York: Random House, 1970.

Weil, Simone. *The Simone Weil Reader.* Edited by George A. Panichas. New York: David McKay Co., 1977.

Wiesel, Elie. *Souls on Fire.* Translated by Marion Wiesel. New York: Random House, 1973.

Winch, Peter. "Authority." In *Political Philosophy*, edited by Anthony Quinton, pp. 97–111. New York: Oxford University Press, 1967.

Wiser, James L. "Knowledge and Order." *Political Science Reviewer* 7 (Fall 1977): 90–110.

————. "Michael Polanyi: Personal Knowledge and the Promise of Autonomy." *Political Theory* 2 (February 1974): 77–87.

————. "Political Theory, Personal Knowledge, and Public Truth." *Journal of Politics* 36 (August 1974): 661–74.

————. "Reason and the Role of Persuasion." *Journal of Politics* 39 (May 1977): 427–45.

Wolfe, Alan. "Conditions of Community: The Case of Old Westbury College." In *Power and Community*, edited by Philip Green and Sanford Levinson, pp. 195–222. New York: Vintage Books, 1970.

Wolfe, Tom. *Mauve Gloves & Madmen, Clutter & Vine.* New York: Farrar, Straus & Giroux, 1976.

Wolff, Robert Paul. *In Defense of Anarchism.* New York: Harper & Row, Torchbooks, 1970.

———. *The Poverty of Liberalism.* Boston: Beacon Press, 1968.

Zetterbaum, Marvin. "Self and Political Order." *Interpretation* 1 (Winter 1970): 233–46.

Index